THE IRISH LANDSCAPE

THE
IRISH LANDSCAPE

FRANK MITCHELL

COLLINS
St James's Place, London

TO THE MEMORY
OF
ARTHUR WILSON STELFOX
AND OF
KNUD JESSEN

First published 1976
© G. F. Mitchell 1976

ISBN 0 00219262 4

Made and Printed in Great Britain by
William Collins Sons & Co. Ltd Glasgow

Contents

6 *Contents*

Plates

7

Text Figures

9

Preface

THROUGHOUT the forty years I have spent wandering around Ireland, one thing has impressed itself on me with ever increasing force, and that is the extent to which the landscape that we see to-day is essentially the product of human hands. Admittedly great geological forces had moulded the rocks, and the Ice Age had plastered them with glacial deposits, long before man appeared in Ireland. But from about five thousand years ago when the first felling-axes made woodland clearance possible, man's hands have borne down ever more heavily on the Irish landscape. To-day no matter where we stand and look around us, we cannot see any area, large or small, high or low, that has not been altered, and is still being altered, by man's activities.

It has been my aim in writing this book to visualise the Irish landscape not as a static picture-postcard, but as a dynamic structure in a process of continuous evolution. I am therefore presenting the record of the Irish landscape as an uninterrupted story, even though there are some very considerable blanks. For parts of the record the amount of information available is large, and here my story may be sound, in other parts information is scanty, and my story may be correspondingly shaky. But there must have been *a* story, and so I have risked presenting a continuous narrative, rather than a string of ifs and ans and buts.

I have also decided to begin at the geological beginning, and go straight through to the speculative end. I know that for most of my readers the part that man played in moulding the landscape will have the greater interest, and such readers can begin at Chapter 3 (p. 80). Those interested in the fluctuations of heat and cold that set the scene for man's arrival in Ireland – and are probably still continuing – can start at Chapter 2 (p. 35), while those interested in the whole story will begin at the beginning.

Text-figures are not individually numbered: they are referred to in the text by the page on which they occur. References to plates are placed at the ends of relevant paragraphs, and not at the particular point in the paragraph where their relevance arises.

The book is dedicated to Arthur Wilson Stelfox and Knud Jessen. Though his primary training was as an architect, Arthur Stelfox's deep interest in natural history led him to work in that division of the National Museum in Dublin. His ever deepening knowledge of arctic-alpine plants, freshwater molluscs and ichneumon flies, and his unorthodox but important breeding of snails in his garage, brought visitors and letters from all over the world to his room in the museum and his garden at home. Unfortunately he never received in the museum service the promotion that he so richly deserved. This embittered him against 'Establishments', but his heart remained open to people, and his never failing encouragement of budding naturalists, of whom I was one, placed a large number of workers permanently in his debt. Stelfox first spoke to me when, as a boy of twelve, I was looking at a case of birds in the museum; he was over eighty when we went on our last field trip together.

Knud Jessen was trained in the Geological Survey of Denmark, where examination of glacial and later deposits placed special importance on the study of the seeds, leaves and woods that they contained. Jessen added the study of pollen-grains to the repertoire, and he was soon able to trace out the development of the Danish woodlands not only in postglacial but also in inter-glacial times. The Royal Irish Academy invited him to extend his studies to Irish deposits, and so he came to Ireland with his research assistant, Hagbard Jonassen. An Irish student was sought to accompany Jessen in the dual capacity of courier and brain-picker, and I was fortunate enough to be selected. In both 1934 and 1935 we visited every county in Ireland, and I had the privilege of learning to see through his eyes the foundations of the landscape. His intelligence and his capacity for sustained hard work, coupled with great humanity and complete lack of self-importance, made him the most agreeable of mentors, and to him also I shall always be indebted. If Arthur Stelfox was my godfather in science, then Knud Jessen was my father.

I wish to thank all those colleagues and friends who have been bothered by my enquiries in recent years, many of whom have allowed me to use photographs and figures from their publications, and also to draw on their still unpublished work. For the figures and photographs that have been used, acknowledgement is gratefully made. I wish especially to thank Edward Culleton, Elizabeth FitzPatrick and Basil and Eleanor Megaw, who read the first drafts of the various sections, and suggested numerous amendments and improvements. Last, I thank Michael Walter of Collins Publishers for his enthusiastic support and his penetrating criticism.

April 30, 1975   *Frank Mitchell*
                                                                    Trinity College
                                                                    Dublin

Acknowledgements

THE author and publishers wish to thank the photographers whose names appear in the list of Plates for permission to reproduce their pictures, and the following for permission to reproduce figures: Dr R. H. Buchanan and the Cambridge University Press; Dr R. Common, Dr R. E. Glasscock and Thomas Nelson and Sons; Dr D. Gillmor and Gill and Macmillan Ltd; Professor P. D. Moore, Dr D. J. Bellamy and the Elek Science Press; Professor A. R. Orme and the Longman Group.

The author wishes to acknowledge the inspiration he drew from many of the illustrations in the splendid twelve volumes on the natural history of Denmark – *Danmarks Natur* – edited by Bocher, Schou and Volsøe, and published by Politikens Verlag. A drawing in *Sveriges geologi* by Magnusson, Granlund and Lundqvist, and a table in *Physical Geology* by Longwell, Flint and Sanders, both provided a basis for a figure. To mention only a few, the work of J. Bromage, G. R. Coope, G. F. Eogan, R. F. Hammond, Elizabeth Huckerby, E. M. Jope, H. H. Lamb, Eileen McCracken, Sylvia Peglar, V. B. Proudfoot, G. Singh, A. G. Smith, C. Thomas and W. H. Zagwijn was also drawn on. The soil map was specially drawn by J. Lynch, Soil Survey Division, An Foras Talúntais. The author offers his sincere thanks to all.

1

The Rock Skeleton

THE rocky skeleton around which the Irish landscape is built has not only an extent in space, but also a history in time. Of the latter, as Hutton said so long ago, we have 'no vestige of a beginning, no prospect of an end'. In Ireland we find our oldest rocks at Rosslare and Kilmorequay in Wexford, and these have been given an age of 2000 million years; elsewhere in the world still older rocks are known. With the passage of so much time, the primary structures of these ancient rocks have been deformed by later upheavals, and the record of their origin has become very blurred.

When a geologist attempts to decipher the sequence of rock deposition, he depends heavily on being able to find remains of former animals and plants, or *fossils*, in them. If he can then place the fossils in an evolutionary sequence, his task will be very much easier. But if there are no fossils, he is in a quandary. Fossils made their first appearance in abundance about 600 million years ago, and fossiliferous deposits of this age occur in Wales. These rocks have been named Cambrian, and the archaic forms of life represented by the fossils are called Palaeozoic. The vast majority of still older rocks have either no fossils, or only a very limited range of them, and have so far largely defeated all attempts to sort them out. In despair geologists have lumped them together under the single name of Pre-Cambrian (p. 16), even though the period of time they represent is immensely long.

Because of the presence of fossils it has been possible to divide the later part of geological time into units, and the names of these units, together with an indication of their estimated durations is shown in a table. It will be seen that geological time is very long, and is measured in millions of years.

THE LOWER PALAEOZOIC SEA

Our first view of the area where Ireland lies today is not of a land-mass, but of a great sea stretching south-westwards from Scandinavia across northern Britain, across Ireland, and out into the Atlantic Ocean (p.17). The waters of the sea rested on a floor of still older Pre-Cambrian rocks, but of these we can only get tantalizing glimpses. One shore lay to the south-east, perhaps across central Wales, and the second to the north-west, where the Outer Hebrides give some indication of older lands. From these lands sediments, chiefly of sand and clay, were washed out on to the sagging floor of the sea, where they accumulated to thicknesses of thousands of metres.

15

SCALE OF GEOLOGICAL TIME

Subdivisions of Geological Time			Apparent Ages (millions of years before the present)	Relative Lengths of Major Time Divisions to True Scale
Eras	Periods	Epochs		

The sea had come into existence about 700 million years ago, and it perhaps lasted until 400 million years ago. Marine plants and animals lived in its waters, and about 600 million years ago many of the animals started to protect themselves with external skeletons, usually of calcium carbonate, which stood a good chance of being preserved in the sediments, and abundant fossils appear. Because of their fossil content, the rocks can now be identified and defined precisely. They are called Cambrian and the sea belongs to the Lower Palaeozoic Era. Before the sea came to an end, fish with internal vertebrate skeletons of bone or cartilage had appeared in its waters, and simple land plants were appearing on its shores.

The earth is constantly radiating away some of its internal heat into space,

PLATE 1 *Above*, Errigal, Co. Donegal, a residual cone of quartzite, 750m, mantled by frost-shattered scree; the low land in the foreground is at about 60m. *Below*, Ben Bulbin, Co. Sligo, a cliffed block of Carboniferous limestone, 525m, rises above lower ground at about 60m; relatively recent earth-movements may have caused the contrasting relief. The block emerged as a nunatak during the most recent glaciation, and arctic-alpine plants still cling to the cliff-ledges: the flat top is buried by blanket-bog.

PLATE 2 *Right*, a quarry at Magheramorne, Co. Antrim, with chalk capped by basalt. A chalk-fissure, up which molten rock moved, is filled with a *dyke* of basalt. Later earth-movement has moved the upper part of the dyke sideways: here we have a minor *wrench-fault*. *Below*, near the Giant's Causeway, Co. Antrim, lower basalt forms the base of the cliff (below the lower line). In Palaeogene times its surface was tropically weathered to a soil of clayey oxides of iron and aluminium with plant fossils (between the lines). Further outflows of basalt (above the upper line) first buried the soil, and then developed columnar structure as they cooled.

and if an insulating layer of sediment blankets part of its surface and prevents this heat loss, the temperature below the sediments will rise, and melting of rock may take place. At times, as sediments accumulated during the life of the sea, this did happen, and volcanic activity took place chiefly near the shores, with molten material either injecting itself into the sediments, or pushing up through them to flow out on the sea floor.

As the sediments grew thicker, the lower layers were not only heated, but came under increasing pressure as the overlying weight got heavier and heavier. The fine clay particles were squeezed together to become the sedimentary rock, *shale*, and the sand grains were cemented together into *sandstone*. The molten material solidified into various igneous rocks; these were of more varied chemical composition than the shale and sandstone, and thus were in a position to make a contribution to the fertility of the soils that were

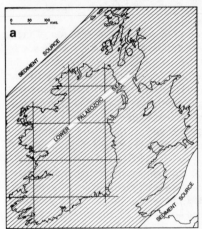

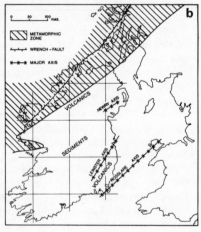

In **a** the area of Ireland is submerged below the waters of the Lower Palaeozoic sea, on whose floor sediments are accumulating. In **b** we see the area convulsed and uplifted by the earth pressures of the Caledonian upheaval, which produced land-masses in Scotland and Ireland. In **c** the high ground is being attacked by erosion, and sandy debris (which will consolidate to Old Red Sandstone) is being deposited in the intervening Devonian basins.

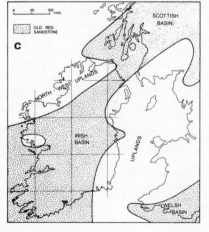

to be derived from them many millions of years later. The barley farmer of Wexford still derives benefit from this early vulcanicity.

The ultimate origin of the forces that operate in the crust of the earth is still a matter of controversy, but of the power of these forces to produce convulsive changes in the distribution of land and sea there can be no doubt. Whatever the real complexities may be, it is sufficient for us to picture the crustal masses that lay to the north-west and to the south-east of Ireland as coming together like the jaws of a vice, and folding and uplifting the sediments that lay between them. The former sea was thus replaced by a land-mass with a structural grain running from north-east to south-west; this grain is very strongly developed in the Highlands of Scotland, which were similarly crushed, and so we speak of a Caledonian upheaval (p. 17).

Rock-folding on this scale is often accompanied by the injection of great masses of molten rock into the axes of the folds, and this happened in south-east Leinster, where the *granite* core was subsequently partly exposed by later erosion, and today stands up as the Wicklow Mountains; a similar injection took place near Newry. The marine sediments had been deposited on a floor of Pre-Cambrian rocks, and another fold, parallel with that in which the Wicklow granite lies, brought them high enough for them to be exposed at the modern surface at Rosslare and in the island of Anglesey. Radiometric determinations of the age of these rocks assess them at not less than 2000 million years old.

In the north-west of Ireland pressures and temperatures were more severe, and the properties of the original sediments were drastically *metamorphosed*. The clays were not merely consolidated into shale, but were recrystallized into tiny flakes of mica regularly aligned by the prevailing pressures so that resulting rock splits easily as *slate* or *schist*. The vast majority of the sand grains were composed of *quartz*, a mineral resistant to chemical and physical change; the quartz grains were welded together into *quartzite*, a tough and durable rock that resists erosion. When the other rocks weather away, the quartzite survives, and tends to be left behind in isolated peaks, mantled by a scree of its own debris, broken off it by frost action, but unaltered chemically or physically. Errigal in Donegal is a splendid example. In some cases the heat and pressure of metamorphism produced entirely new minerals, and 'Connemara Marble', a handsome rock streaked green and white, was formed in this way. There were also injections of granite and other igneous rocks. (Pl. 1).

The earth forces were often capable of thrusting great masses of rock forwards, or wrenching them sideways, for distances of tens of miles, and in north-west Ireland we have a sector of such a lateral thrust or *wrench-fault*. The wrench-fault also cuts across Scotland, where the Great Glen has been hollowed out along its course, and it is called the Great Glen wrench-fault.

THE DEVONIAN BASINS AND THE OLD RED SANDSTONE

The Caledonian upheaval left Ireland high and dry, with the nearest sea in south-west England. This state of affairs lasted about 50 million years, and for this period we have very few Irish fossils; on the other hand the marine deposits of Devonshire have many fossils which can be used to date and correlate the geological events, and so geologists speak of the Devonian Period, which lasted from 400 million years ago till 350 million years ago.

In Ireland there was higher ground in the east and in the north-west, with a lower-lying basin in between. The climate was relatively dry and continental, with considerable changes in temperature between day and night. The hills were splintered by alternate heat and cold, and the rivers carried the debris down on to the lower ground in wide spreads of sand and gravel. Under these conditions the iron in the debris became fully oxidized and reddened in colour, and the sandstone that formed as the debris became cemented together has long been known as *'Old Red Sandstone'* (p. 17). Slow earth movements allowed the hills to continue to rise and the floor of the basin to sag, with the result that the basin sediments grew to very great thickness. Quartz, the main component of the sandstones, is, as we have seen, an inert substance incapable of offering any nutrient material to plant life. When modern weathering breaks down the sandstones, it is difficult to bring the sandy soils they produce to any reasonable level of fertility, and today they are often planted with trees, rather than farmed.

Fossils from other parts of the world tell us that this was a time of considerable development both for plants and animals, and thus Upper Palaeozoic time begins. Air-breathing vertebrates appeared, and some of these began to struggle out of the water and to develop limbs to move about on the land. Land plants developed woody tissue, and could now grow to tree size. In Ireland shifting sands in ever-changing river channels made conditions for fossilization difficult, but here and there freshwater ponds collected fossiliferous clays, and at one of these we can get our first glimpse of an Irish landscape. At Kiltorcan, Co. Kilkenny, the pond was surrounded by tree-ferns, with leaves up to five feet in length. In the water there were freshwater mussels, not far removed from the mussels of our modern lakes and streams, and also archaic fishes, heavily armoured with bony plates, and capable of taking in oxygen, both from the water by means of gills and from the air by means of lungs.

THE CARBONIFEROUS SEAS

About 350 million years ago a warm tropical sea came flooding in over Ireland, leaving only the higher ground unsubmerged. There was one large island formed by a union of the granite of Leinster with the high ground of Wales – often called 'St George's Land'. The northern shore ran across north Mayo and north Donegal (p. 20).

Except near the northern shore and also in the extreme south of Ireland, not much debris was carried from the land into the sea, and the bulk of the

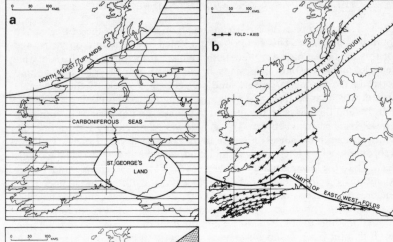

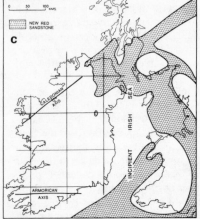

The Upper Palaeozoic sea has flooded Ireland, and in **a** we see the extent of the Carboniferous seas. Again convulsion takes place, and in **b** we see the land-masses produced by the Armorican upheaval. Erosion sweeps debris down to lower ground, and in **c** we see the basins in which New Red Sandstone is accumulated. The birth of the Irish Sea basin is also suggested.

sediment came from the calcareous skeletons of the invertebrate animals that flourished in the warm seawater. That the water was warm is certified by the abundant presence of fossil corals, often in the form of coral reefs. Today these animals only flourish where the water temperature in winter does not fall below $18^{\circ}C$; the winter temperature around Ireland is less than $10^{\circ}C$. As a result the sediment was rich in calcium carbonate, and has been transformed into a *calcite*-rich *limestone*, which today makes an important contribution to the fertility of Irish soils.

At first the sea-floor sagged beneath the weight of the sediments, but the rate of sagging then became slower and slower, and as the limy sediment continued to accumulate the water grew shallower and shallower. As this happened, the rivers that were draining the land were able to build up sandy deltas farther out into the sea, and layers of sand (now transformed into sandstones) were deposited on the limy sediments.

Eventually the sediments became so thick that the entering streams had to meander across the deltas, whose surfaces became clothed with tropical swamp-forests, analogous to the mangrove-swamps of today. Great layers of rotting plant debris accumulated, and if further downward movement did take place, layers of sand and clay were deposited on the vegetable debris, which slowly consolidated into *coal*. Such sequences of seams of coal interspersed with layers of sandstone and shale form the valuable 'Carboniferous' deposits which are the basis of the coal-mining industry of the British Isles. Under today's weathering conditions the shales break down into soils very rich in clay; such soils are difficult to drain, and are among the poorest we have in Ireland.

In the fluctuating conditions of the coal-swamp, river channels were constantly changing, and plant and animal debris could accumulate in an abandoned channel. Such channel-fills can be seen in the Castlecomer coal deposits, and their contained fossils reveal a very unfamiliar Ireland. We would see trees, one hundred feet and more in height densely crowded together, but on looking more closely we would see that they had long strap-like leaves springing directly from the stem, and not delicately-built multi-veined leaves supported on stalks, and that while some did reproduce themselves by seeds, the majority still depended on the more primitive spore. There would be fish and shell-fish in the river, and in addition, poised on its banks, we would see large clumsy amphibians, capable of breathing air, but still moving slowly on awkward limbs, not yet far removed from their ancestral fins.

THE ARMORICAN UPHEAVAL AND THE NEW RED SANDSTONE

About 270 million years ago major earth forces began to influence Ireland once more. A major pulse came from the south, and this raised and folded the sediments of south-west Ireland along axes that ran east and west. The same movements can be seen in south Wales and in Brittany, as well as still farther east in Europe, and the old name for Brittany, Armorica, is often used for these movements. The pulse from the south met resistance from the block to the north – if indeed this block itself did not move southwards – and when the rocks in the rest of Ireland yielded to the crumpling forces, they did not follow the new fold direction, but repeated the north-east/south-west grain that had been earlier impressed by the Caledonian upheaval, and would appear again at still later dates. Stretching as well as compression seems to have been involved, and from Co. Sligo right across the North Channel and on across Scotland a great strip of sediments, bounded by massive fractures or faults, was dropped down to lower levels in a *fault-trough*, something like the Great Rift Valley in East Africa today (p. 20).

In many ways the Armorican upheaval was very similar to the earlier Caledonian upheaval, and it is important to note that in each case Great Britain and Ireland reacted to the forces in the same way as a single unit. It was the same in the periods of sedimentation also, as essentially the same type of material was deposited in the two areas.

But now the picture was to change. The end of the Armorican upheaval appears to have left Great Britain and Ireland relatively higher than the Caledonian episode had done. It is as though this part of the rim of continental Europe had been tilted up, leaving Ireland – and to a lesser extent western Britain – raised above the general level of the flooding seas, which had little difficulty in overrunning eastern England.

When upheaval ended, about 260 million years ago, Ireland was high and dry. Continental conditions seem to have prevailed once more, and there must have been vigorous erosional attack on the land surface. Unfortunately the upheaval followed almost immediately after the deposition of the coal-bearing rocks, with the result that the latter were left exposed to the elements. Long-continued erosion has stripped away all the coal, except in two small areas, one near Arigna, and the second near Castlecomer. Great Britain was much more fortunate in this respect, as there are still vast deposits of coal in England, Wales and Scotland. Ireland's poverty, and Britain's prosperity, in the nineteenth century reflect the coal stocks of the two areas.

In the earlier Post-Caledonian phase, great masses of eroded debris were trapped in basins within Ireland where they formed thick deposits of Old Red Sandstone. By analogy the red desert sandstones formed after the Armorican upheaval are the *New Red Sandstone*, but relative to their predecessors their remaining volume in Ireland is remarkably small. We can, of course, say that they formerly did exist, but have subsequently been removed by still further erosion, because Ireland in its higher position was again only rarely protected by an invading sea.

Also it is not impossible that this time saw the first appearance of a north–south trough down what is now the basin of the Irish Sea, and that the bulk of the sediment was deposited here, as this is the area where New Red Sandstone is most common today (p. 20). Desert sandstone was not the only material deposited, because at Larne, Carrickfergus and Kingscourt, there are intercalated deposits of *rock salt* and *gypsum*, and these indicate at least inter-mittent flooding of the area by seawater. The main body of ocean was now in south-central Europe, with shallower water in eastern England. At times an arm of this sea extended north-westwards across the English Midlands (where it has left vast deposits of salt on the Cheshire plain) and into the north end of the developing Irish Sea Trough, where – if its connection with the sea was interrupted – it evaporated away, leaving salt and gypsum behind.

It was in New Red Sandstone times that the reptiles were beginning to establish themselves as the dominant land animals. Conditions in Ireland were not conducive to the preservation of fossils, but at Scrabo Hill, near Belfast, a reptile obligingly walked across some soft muds, and from the casts of his footprints which have survived, we can deduce that Ireland had some reptilian population at this time.

THE MESOZOIC SEAS

The stretch of geological time that extends from 225 million years ago to 70 million years ago is usually known as the Mesozoic Era; this was the time when the reptiles were the dominant form of land animal, and the era came to an end when they were displaced by the mammals. The era opens while New Red Sandstone was still being deposited, as it was then that the reptiles began their upward surge.

About 180 million years ago the European sea flooded into south-east England, and marine deposits began to accumulate there on a substantial scale. Though these deposits, chiefly limestones and clays, are well exposed in England, and have long been studied there in detail, the lower parts of the deposits take their name, not from an English locality, but from the Jura Mountains which are largely built up of rocks of this age, and are therefore known as Jurassic. But once we get west of a line from Newcastle-upon-Tyne to Torquay, deposits of this age are very rare indeed, and it is difficult to decide for how long, and to what extent, the Jurassic sea pushed farther to the west where it flooded the Irish Sea Trough for the first time.

In mainland Ireland Jurassic deposits of calcareous marine clays only occur in the north-east, where they have been protected from erosion by being buried beneath later volcanic rocks; it is impossible to say what their former extent may have been. Such deposits do survive in numerous basins in the floor of the Irish Sea Trough: to the west of Ireland there is a further basin, and this also probably contains Jurassic rocks. As Neville George has said, from Jurassic time on we appear to have in Great Britain and Ireland, and on a smaller scale in the Isle of Man, positive blocks of land which have maintained their positions despite the fact that they are surrounded and separated by deep basins of long continued subsidence.

The fauna of the Jurassic sea included corals, and so its waters must have been warm, like those of the earlier Carboniferous stage. Just as the mammals in the form of whales have taken to a marine life, the Mesozoic reptiles did the same thing, and fossils of fish-like pelagic reptiles with limbs transformed into paddles have been found in Ireland.

It seems very probable that at this time both the sea and the land were oscillating in level, and that periods of erosion alternated with periods of deposition. The known Irish Jurassic deposits lie at the base of the sequence; a little farther north higher Jurassic beds are found in the western isles of Scotland. Almost certainly similar ones were deposited in Ireland, but were removed by erosion, and then deposition set in again.

This renewal of deposition set in about 135 million years ago, when a sandy material was laid down. Again it is only known in north-east Ireland, where it has been protected from later erosion. Dramatic developments then followed. The sea expanded into regions that had been undergoing vigorous erosion; the supply of land-derived debris fell off sharply, and a white calcareous ooze with traces of silica – now transformed into *chalk* containing nodules of siliceous *flint* – was deposited on the sea floor. Recent underwater investigations have shown that a great mass of chalk lies off the south Irish coast, a tiny patch survives in a subsidence hollow near Killarney, and there are extensive deposits of chalk in north-east Ireland (p. 24).

It is not easy to say to what extent the main body of Ireland was submerged below the Cretaceous seas, and thus received a mantle of chalk. The long-established area of high ground in north-west Ireland almost certainly

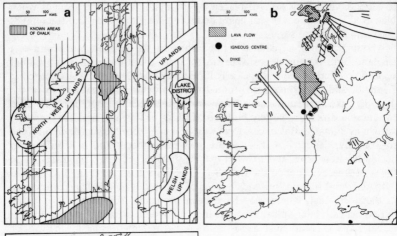

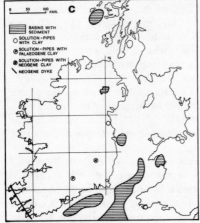

In **a** the Cretaceous sea engulfs Ireland, and on its floor a fine-grained white sediment accumulates, later to appear as chalk. **b** shows the subsequent Palaeogene volcanic activity. Basins again form, **c**, though on a relatively small scale, and sediments of Palaeogene and Neogene age are deposited in them.

emerged as an island, and some authorities suggest that the Midlands also remained unsubmerged. In any case the thickness of the chalk probably varied greatly from place to place, depending on the topography of the ground surface it had buried.

Positive evidence of chalk in and around Ireland is a new discovery, but for long many geomorphologists have been demanding the former existence of such a cover in order to explain the courses of the rivers of the south of Ireland. The pre-Cretaceous rocks were not only very varied in nature, but they had been subjected several times to intense folding and faulting, which had given rise to complicated structures; in addition, the countryside they composed had long been etched and dissected by weathering and erosion. The modern courses of the rivers completely ignore the geological structures, and they can only do this because *either* the structures were buried beneath a layer of younger rock on whose slopes the rivers initiated their courses, and that as the land-surface was lowered and the younger rocks disappeared through weathering, the rivers were able to maintain their courses by trenching through the old structures as they gradually protruded, *or* slow tectonic movements raised the old structures with river erosion keeping pace with the elevation, so that the rivers were able to maintain their courses across the rising structures. Most geomorphologists have favoured the first explanation, but it seems most unlikely that slopes that came into existence some 70 million years ago on a surface of chalk, which itself has long since vanished, could still be maintaining a dominating influence on the topography. Much younger tectonic movements must also be involved.

It was during the Cretaceous that plant reproduction by the seed rather than by the spore became the rule rather than the exception, and our modern forms of vegetation became established. Before the period ended modern forms of trees, both coniferous and deciduous, grasses and herbs were all present in force, but their distribution was very different to that which obtains today.

PALAEOGENE VULCANICITY AND WEATHERING

As Cretaceous time was coming to an end, dramatic events were taking place to the west of Ireland, where the modern Atlantic Ocean was beginning to take shape, as Greenland drifted away from Europe. About 60 million years ago another split appeared, and the rocky platform on which the minute and controversial islet of Rockall later formed was left behind, as Greenland moved still farther off. We can picture the west side of Ireland as deprived of support by these movements, and sagging oceanwards, causing great tensional fissures to open up. These fissures were most numerous in the vicinity of the North Channel, and here quantities of molten material welled up from below and flowed out over the surrounding countryside, in Scotland as well as in Ireland, burying it beneath great sheets of dark-coloured *basalt*. The Irish Sea Trough continued to sag, and it is probably due to this sagging that the basalt flows have survived in this area, preserving chalk and other rocks below them. If the molten material should solidify in the fissure before it reaches the surface of the ground it becomes a *dyke*, and dykes trending north-west/south-east are known throughout the northern half of Ireland. Lava flows may formerly have covered much more of Ireland than they do today. (p. 24, Pl. 2).

In Ireland, as well as regional lava flows, we had igneous centres, both on a large and on a small scale. Large-scale centres created the Mourne Mountains and Carlingford Mountain; on a small scale we have Doon Hill in Connemara; eruptions like both those of Hawaii and those of Vesuvius must have been common at this time. Similar igneous activity took place in Scotland, Wales and south-west England.

By the time the lavas of the north of Ireland were being poured out, the dominance of the reptiles was over, and we have moved on into the so-called

Age of Mammals, or Cenozoic Era. The era can be sub-divided in detail, but for our purposes fewer units will suffice. At first climate remained warm, plant distribution was very different from that of today, and the mammals were still relatively undifferentiated, and here we have the Palaeogene, which lasted from about 70 million years ago till 25 million years ago, when the Neogene, with a cooling of climate, and more specialized plants and animals, began.

The basalts lie at the beginning of the Palaeogene, and we are fortunate that they have preserved a record both of the climate and of the vegetation, though not of the animals, and through the record we can see a warm Irish landscape covered with dense tropical forest. After a first outpouring of lava there was a lull, during which the surface of the lava weathered into soil which became covered by vegetation, and then a second series of flows buried and preserved the soil and the plant fossils. (Pl. 2)

Molten rock is rich in silicon, oxygen, aluminium and other metals, and when the rock solidifies the metals combine with the silicon and oxygen to form complex *silicate* molecules. When weathered under cool temperate climates such as we have in Ireland today, the silicates tend to take up water while retaining the silicon and the aluminium, and turn into tiny plate-like particles of *hydrated aluminium silicate*, or *silicate clay*; the other metals tend to be removed in solution. But under moist tropical conditions very different changes take place; it is the silicon that is now carried away in solution, while the aluminium and the iron are left behind to take up water and become *hydrous oxide clays*, again in tiny particles; the other metals are removed in solution. If developed in sufficient quantity the hydrous aluminium oxide clay forms the ore of aluminium, *bauxite*, and its iron equivalent forms *limonite*, and in the past both of these ores were mined in the weathered inter-basaltic layer in north-east Ireland.

The evidence of warm conditions thus given by the inter-basaltic soils is confirmed by the plant remains that they contain, chiefly in the form of *lignites* formed by the alteration of lake-muds or peats in which tree-stumps and logs were embedded. Among the conifers pine (*Pinus*), cypress (*Cupressus*) and monkey-puzzle (*Araucaria*) are present, and there is a wealth of deciduous leaf debris, including leaves of alder (*Alnus*). Ferns are also present, but herbs are only poorly represented. Throughout the Palaeogene there were extensive and broadly homogeneous forests in quite high northern latitudes, and the tropical woodlands of Ireland drop into place among these Palaeogene forests.

Minor earth movements had accompanied the outpouring of the basalts, and these continued in north-east Ireland after the volcanic activity had ceased. The downward dropping of a large block created a depression in which a lake formed, and we can regard Lough Neagh as the modern descendant of that lake (p. 24). Palaeogene rivers carried clay, sand and plant debris out into it, where they accumulated to a thickness of 350 m. Again the surrounding country must have been densely wooded. Trees now confined to North America, such as redwood (*Sequoia*), swamp-cypress (*Taxodium*) and black gum (*Nyssa*) are present, together with more familiar forms, such as alder, holly (*Ilex*), lime (*Tilia*) and oak (*Quercus*). There were other similar basins west of Mull, off the Dublin coast, in Tremadoc Bay, in St George's Channel, in the Bristol Channel, and off the Cork/Waterford coast. Today these basins are sites for oil-drilling activities, as it is not impossible that quantities of oil and gas are trapped in their structures.

The prevailing tropical weathering had powerful effects on nearly all types of rock, and not only on those composed of silicates; quartzite alone had perhaps some chance of survival. The calcite of limestone and chalk can be directly dissolved by percolating water, and as solution proceeds the small amounts of clay that were also present in the rock will be left behind as a superficial mantle. In the case of chalk the embedded flints will disappear more slowly than the calcite, and a capping of 'clay with flints' develops. In some places we can see such material on the old chalk surface underneath the basalt, and this shows that the stripping away of the chalk by the weather had started even before the basalt was poured out.

Once the chalk had been removed, Carboniferous limestone appeared over a large part of central Ireland. Earth movements had produced cracks in the limestone, and percolating water widened these by its solvent action as it descended into the rock, and drilled out underground watercourses. If the roofs of these channels collapsed, then hollows and sink-holes were created, and a *karstic* landscape developed. But as the calcite of the limestone was carried away in solution, the clay was left behind and gradually accumulated as a superficial mantle. As the protective layer developed, the rate at which the calcite could be removed was slowed down, and perhaps halted altogether. If there were metallic ores in the limestone, then these were also attacked by weathering, and complex hydrated compounds were left behind to form part of the protective mantle; this seems to have been the history of the valuable ore deposit at Tynagh, where altered ores are lying in karstic hollows; the finding of a log of cypress wood in the ore supports a Palaeogene age for the deposit.

Over considerable areas of Ireland and of western Britain (see figure on p. 24), the limestone is perforated by vertical pipes which contain weathered material, and in one such pipe at Ballymacadam near Cahir the fill contains pollen, which indicates woodland of the same general type as that of the Lough Neagh clays, and is presumably also of Palaeogene age. The fill must have been lowered into the pipe from a land surface at a now disappeared higher level, and questions immediately arise – How much higher? – Is the fill the last remnant of the sediment that formerly occupied a now vanished basin? – questions which are obviously of the greatest significance for the origin of the modern Irish landscape.

In Co. Clare today the limestone which has been scoured by later ice-sheets lies naked at the surface without any protective mantle of clay, and it is being dissolved away at a rapid rate. Estimates suggest that the limestone surface is currently being lowered at a rate of 0·53 mm *per annum*; if this rate is projected backwards, it means that the surface would be lowered by 53 m in one million years, and that a layer of limestone more than one kilometre thick would have vanished since the end of Palaeogene time about 25 million years ago.

Such a rapid erosion would obviously long since have destroyed not only the Ballymacadam pipe fill but also the ore deposit at Tynagh. We are therefore driven to the position that the karstic limestone surface of the Irish midlands, ranging between 60 and 120 m in height, must be a very old one, and that it has only been enabled to survive by the former possession of a protective mantle of clay. The modern rapid rate of solution has only set in after that protective mantle had been torn away by later frost and ice.

At the end of the Palaeogene there were probably very few exposures of solid rock to be seen in Ireland. The soil mantle would have been very thick and relatively uniform, because original differences due to the character of the underlying rocks would have been very largely eliminated by the vigour of the chemical weathering processes. The surface layer would probably have been brown or grey in colour, due to the presence of small quantities of decayed vegetable debris or *humus* and the absence of iron; the colour of the underlying weathered hydrous oxide clays would have been red or yellow due to the presence of fully oxidized iron; gradually this weathered clay would merge into unaltered rock below, probably at a depth to be measured at least in tens of metres. On low-lying ground, where soil drainage was poorer, there would have been a greater accumulation of humus, and a black clayey soil would have formed. The whole country would have been densely wooded by trees, many of which would have been unfamiliar to our modern eyes, and if we wish to see them growing today, we must seek them out in the mountains of eastern North America or of China.

NEOGENE COOLING

About 25 million years ago temperatures all over the world started to fall in an irregular way, periods of falling temperature being followed by periods of recovery, but always with an overall downward trend. At the same time, possibly by the elimination of some archaic forms, the flora and fauna took on a more modern aspect, and we move from the Palaeogene into the Neogene. By about 13 million years ago cooling had reached the point at which ice-caps could begin to form in polar regions; though the amount of ice at the poles has fluctuated since then, it seems that at all times there has been some ice present.

The Neogene was thus a period of falling temperature, and a period of diminishing vigour on the part of the soil-forming agencies. But the changed conditions could not give anything back to the already heavily depleted soils, and they probably altered but little. Rainfall may have increased, and there may have been some erosion of the soil mantle, with increased deposition of clays, sands and gravels on lower ground. There are extensive deposits of plant remains of this age in northern Europe, and they indicate a warm temperate woodland, again similar to that of eastern North America today. There were also raised-bogs, perhaps not very different from those we know. Some of the conifers appear to be identical with modern species, and many of the genera are broadly similar to modern forms. We can see magnolias, sweet gums (*Liquidambar*), black gums, swamp cypress and other forms. The hemlock (*Tsuga*) makes its first appearance.

What was the relief of the land surface? What was sea-level doing? Was Ireland emergent or submerged at this time? Neville George would see Ireland as largely submerged, and being subjected to wave erosion which produced relatively flat surfaces; when Ireland later emerged above the sea, it was on these surfaces that the modern river system developed. But at least two of the basins now submerged below the Irish Sea, that off the Cork/Waterford coast and that off the Dublin coast (p. 24), continued to receive shallow-water sediment in Neogene time, and were perhaps lacustrine rather than marine; were these sediments at their present level when they were deposited, with the sea still lower in level, or were they at a higher level, with the corollary that the basin must have subsided since they were formed?

On shore we have only one deposit, and again a problematic one in a solution-pipe. At Hollymount, north of Carlow, where the ground is at a height of about 70 m, a well which was expected to hit Carboniferous limestone at about 10 m, went instead to a depth of over 60 m, i.e. almost down to modern sea-level, before it was abandoned without hitting solid rock. The fill sediment was very finely divided powdery quartz, with lignite and pollen at some levels. As well as leaves of heather (*Erica*), pollens of the heather family (including *Rhododendron*) were very common; there were some spores of *Sphagnum* moss; coniferous trees were represented by pollen of pine, red-wood, hemlock and umbrella pine (*Sciadopitys*), and among the broad-leaved trees were alder, birch (*Betula*), hazel (*Corylus*), holly, hornbeam (*Carpinus*) and willow (*Salix*). The plant evidence suggests a forest, rich in variety of tree, growing when temperatures were slightly higher and seasonally more uniform than at present. *Sphagnum* and heathers will have been growing in wet hollows; as these plants require acid conditions, here we have evidence that the underlying calcareous limestone rock must have been mantled by a layer of clayey soil, out of which all lime had been leached by deep weathering.

Some geomorphologists have recognized in the south of Ireland a planation-surface lying between 200 and 250 m which they regard as of Neogene age, and of considerable importance for the evolution of the Irish river system. But it is difficult to believe that the Hollymount plants could have grown on a surface more than 100 m above the level at which we now find them, as their fossil remains could not have descended through that distance without becoming widely scattered if not completely destroyed. In south-west Britain there is a prominent planation-surface at about 130 m, and this also has been regarded as of late Neogene age.

On the other hand there are French geomorphologists who consider that by the late Neogene the relief of the modern landscape was already established, its river valleys were in existence, and the level of the sea was essentially of the order of that of today. In southern Brittany the youngest Neogene sediments were deposited within already existing river valleys when these were flooded by the sea, either by a rising in sea-level, or by a sinking of the land. The landscape of south-east Ireland has much in common with that of south Brittany, and the rivers, such as the Barrow in Ireland, and the Vilaine in

France, exhibit the same paradox – their valleys are on the one hand incised into the landscape, and on the other are drowned by the sea in their lower reaches, with the result that the tide runs up them for many kilometres inland.

There is no doubt that vulcanicity and earth movements continued in the area of the British Isles well on into the Neogene. In the south-west tip of Ireland an extensive volcanic dyke has been given a radiometric age of 17 million years. In some areas abrupt changes in relief suggest that there may have been differential movement of adjoining blocks of terrain.

In north-west Ireland some blocks of Carboniferous limestone with karstic surfaces stand surrounded by steep slopes above more low-lying similar limestone, again with a karstic surface. An originally single surface may have been split into two by earth movements. (Pl. 1)

Gordon Davies has drawn attention to the problem of the granite-built Wicklow Mountains. To have achieved its coarsely crystalline texture the molten granite, which was intruded during the Caledonian upheaval, must have cooled slowly below a thick insulating layer of older rock; despite such burial granitic debris appears in the nearby Old Red Sandstone, showing that already by that early date erosion had cut down to expose at least part of the granite at the surface. If erosion had continued without interruption, one would think that at least all of the protecting cover would have been removed. But the highest point on the range today, the summit of Lugnaquilla at about 1000 m, is not of granite, but is part of the not yet completely removed roof. It seems impossible not to conclude that for much of its long geological history this part of the Wicklow granite lay at a lower level, protected by younger sediments. At a late date it was uplifted as a block, and erosion is now attacking it once more.

The same problem presents itself in western Ireland where to the west of Lough Mask patches of basal Carboniferous rock lie on the relatively flat top of Maumtrasna at elevations between 600 and 700 m, while to the east of the lough the same rocks are buried beneath Carboniferous limestone, whose karstic surface lies at an elevation of less than 70 m. That there were young earth movements in this area is certified by the fact that at Benchoona, south of Killary Harbour, a dyke of Palaeogene basalt has been broken by later faulting.

Lough Hyne, Co. Cork, suggests relatively recent subsidence. Here a small basin, which is surrounded by rock and is connected to the sea by a tidal channel, lies in terrain with some suggestion of a planation-surface at about 80 m. North-west of the lough there is a hill which rises almost to 200 m, while the present floor of the basin has in places the surprising depth of 45 m. The basin must hold a considerable quantity of recent unconsolidated debris, and the rock floor will lie at a substantially lower level. It has been suggested that the rock-basin is a corrie excavated by ice when sea-level was lower than it is at present; I can see no corrie-like features. Nor does it seem possible that it was gouged out by a flow of glacier-ice. It cannot have been created by wave erosion, nor by river erosion for no rivers flow into or through it. The surrounding rock is of Old Red Sandstone, so it cannot be a solution hollow. When all these agencies have been eliminated, differential movement of the order of at least 300 m, which has created a hill on one side, and a hollow below sea-level on the other, becomes a possibility. (Pl. 3)

As we have already seen, the rivers of the south of Ireland are spectacularly indifferent to the geological structures across which they pick their way. In the south-east three of them, the Nore, the Barrow and the Slaney, all have cut narrow gorges through the granite ridge which seems to bar their courses. If we reject the view that they have been lowered to their present level by the gradual wasting away of a higher land surface, we can picture that, as the granite block was slowly raised, they trenched across it as fast as it rose, and thus by maintaining their original courses, they now find themselves leaving open country, passing through a steep-sided gorge, and emerging to open country once more. The present steepness of the gorges may be partly due to the fact that during the melting-away of the later ice-sheets of the midlands, great quantities of meltwater were discharged through them into a sea much lower in level than that of today, but meltwater overflow is unlikely to have initiated the gorges.

On the other hand if we look at the rivers of Co. Cork, the Blackwater, the Lee and the Bandon, set in a planation-surface, and with their trellis-patterns of long eastward-flowing stretches truncated by short southward-flowing discharge channels, it is difficult not to think that the original streamflow was from north to south down a surface which had been cut on to complex east–west geological structures produced by the Armorican upheaval, and that the later developments have been due to erosional etching of those structures.

I think we must agree with Neville George that, granted what we know of rates of erosion and of later earth movements, we cannot see in the Irish river systems any legacy from a chalk surface formed 70 million years ago, and that the whole relief of the modern landscape must be very much younger. But there can be no precision for our dating of the evolution of that relief, in which both planation and earth movement probably played a part, until we get more evidence either from further discoveries of fossiliferous deposits, or of rocks to which radiometric methods of dating can be applied.

Across the channel at St Erth in Cornwall we perhaps get a picture – and an Irish picture would not be very different – of the final stages of the Neogene. Here on sandy terrain we had coniferous woodland, with pine, fir (*Abies*) and hemlock, and a ground vegetation dominated by heathers. The marine clay which contained the plant fossils also had molluscs and foraminifera which suggested a final Neogene age. The clay was at a height of 40 m, but again the usual ambiguity presented itself as to whether the sea was 40 m above its present level when the deposit was being formed, or whether we are dealing with a basin which was formerly at a lower level, and has since been raised to its present height.

As the Neogene was drawing to an end the rate of climatic deterioration steepened sharply. Grasslands and open vegetation replaced the forests, and as the woodlands broke up many Tertiary plants disappeared for ever from the European landscape. At a date probably about 2 million years ago severe conditions of cold established themselves in north-west Europe, and we pass from the Neogene into the Pleistocene.

THE APPEARANCE OF COLD AND ICE

It was about one hundred years ago that geologists realized that the ice-polished rock-bosses and the striated boulders that could be seen in many parts of north-west Europe were identical with those currently produced by modern ice in the Alps, and that the areas in which these features occurred must once have been buried below great masses of ice. It was from this realization that the concept of a 'Great Ice Age' sprang, and it was only gradually and much later that it came to be realized that the ice-masses of Europe represented only part of a much longer story in which periods of cold – in some of which ice-masses formed – alternated with periods of warmth.

As we have seen, signs of developing cold can be traced back for some 25 million years, and it is a matter of some difficulty to decide exactly where to draw the boundary line that will separate the Neogene from the very cold Pleistocene. How do geologists attempt to demarcate such a boundary? It is the aim of stratigraphical geologists – who deal with a time-scale measured in millions of years – to arrange the sedimentary rocks of the world into a sequence of units, each containing a characteristic group of fossils derived from a corresponding environment, or *biozone*. As time proceeds species evolve and disappear, and the boundary between a particular biozone and its successor is often placed at the horizon in a rock sequence at which a new fossil type appears, presumably by evolution from an earlier type. Thus it is possible to picture ourselves as driving in an imaginary 'golden spike' at the horizon that separates one unit from another.

Where are we to drive in the golden spike that will separate the Pleistocene from the Neogene? Older British textbooks contrast the warm forests of the Neogene with the 'Great Ice Age' of the Pleistocene, and in general the contrast between warmth and severe cold is a valid one. But the period of time we are dealing with is relatively short – measured in thousands rather than in millions of years – and the rate at which evolution proceeds is slow, with the result that not enough new types have appeared to make a clear definition of biozones possible. The problem is further complicated by the fact that there was not one single change from warm to cold, but many oscillations from relatively warm to relatively cold were superimposed on an overall drift from warm to cold. These oscillations or climatic cycles offer a basis for the sub-division of time, and if we can trace them out, we can hope to bring some order into this latest part of the geological record.

This part of the record was first studied in north-west Europe, and it was inevitable that thinking in this area should have greatly influenced the concepts of this sub-division. Here we have the latitudinal contrast between the forests of the south and the tundras of the north, and if we can find in our geological column a vertical contrast between a biozone with woodland fossils below, and a biozone with tundra fossils above, we have a potential horizon for our golden spike. On this basis the boundary will lie at the level where the final phase of the Neogene woodlands gives way to the first spreading of the Pleistocene tundra, about two million years ago. Deposits which

PLATE 3 Lough Hyne, Co. Cork, is connected to the sea by the channel on the right (the picture shows high tide). We look north, and, as soil cover is thin, the east-west rock structure imposed by Armorican folding can be seen. The heavily shadowed scarp may be due to Neogene earth-movements, which raised a block of rock, and lowered the floor of the lough. In the blind arm on the left there is 'submerged' peat. In the rocky foreground there are small fields made at a time of greater population.

PLATE 4 *Above left*, modern ice-wedge in frozen silt, nr. Fairbanks, Alaska (rule is 50 cm). *Right*, fossil ice-wedge-cast in Late Midlandian outwash gravels, Gorticross, Co. Londonderry (match-box gives scale). *Below*, fossil ice-wedge-polygons, probably of Midlandian age, Broomhill Point, Co. Wexford.

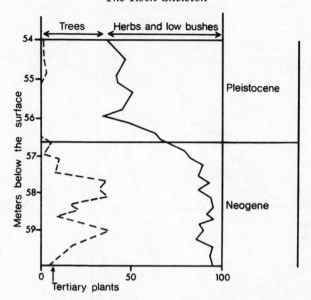

A schematic pollen-diagram from the Netherlands, showing the transition from the Neogene to the Pleistocene. The broken line traces the disappearance of the Tertiary plants, and the full line shows the changeover from the Neogene woodlands to the open countryside of the early Pleistocene. (After W. H. Zagwijn).

straddle such a boundary can be found in the Netherlands, where they have been energetically studied by Waldo Zagwijn and others.

In a schematic pollen-diagram both the extinction of the Tertiary plants and the replacement of archaic woodland by Pleistocene herbs and bushes can be clearly seen. In England, at about the same time, the Neogene Coralline Crag, an estuarine deposit with warmth-loving molluscs, is succeeded by the Pleistocene Red Crag, a similar deposit but with cold-loving forms represented in its fauna – though these forms have probably appeared as a result of migration rather than evolution. This horizon can also be traced in the south of Italy in Calabria, where cold-loving foraminifera and molluscs enter the Mediterranean Sea for the first time.

We have seen that earlier workers in Europe thought of the onset of a 'Great Ice Age', but it now seems that cold must have come and gone many times before large masses of ice did form in Europe, as it is now thought that this ice first formed about 600,000 years ago.

What can the Irish record tell us? If we accept a late Neogene age for the flora at Hollymount, then perhaps about eight million years ago we still had warmth-loving woodlands with an archaic quality growing in Ireland. Our first record of Pleistocene cold is unsatisfactory, because for it we have to depend on fossils in a secondary position. About forty years ago a gravel-pit

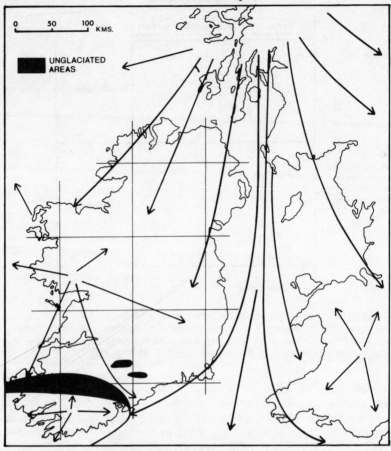

A map to indicate greatest extent to which Ireland was ever covered by ice at one time; black areas were ice-free.

in outwash gravels from a late advance of ice down the basin of the Irish Sea at Killincarrig in Wicklow produced a considerable number of large mollusc shells of cold-loving Red Crag type, and thus of early Pleistocene age. Derived 'Crag' shells are also found in other glacial deposits around the Irish Sea basin, and are particularly common in Wexford and in the Isle of Man. This molluscan evidence, slight as it is, thus suggests that about 1·75 million years ago a cold-water sea with Pleistocene molluscs of northern aspect lay between Britain and Ireland. The first occasion on which great masses of ice actually formed in Ireland probably took place about 200,000 years ago, and at some times almost the whole country must have been buried by ice.

2

Alternating Heat and Cold

FROST AND ICE IN COLD STAGES

MODERN studies of sea-floor deposits suggest that there may have been more than twenty climatic oscillations in the not too distant geological past. In Britain at least seven cold stages are documented, but in Ireland so far there is only evidence for the last three of these, as well as for the very much earlier episode recorded at Killincarrig. In Britain great masses of ice formed in each of the last three cold stages, but there is no record of ice before that, and opinion is now beginning to swing away from the concept that great masses of ice were the chief features of the Pleistocene.

The picture is now becoming one of a period of cold, which had its origin far back in the Neogene. In the Pleistocene the cold intensified, but in the main it seems to have been a period of dry cold when frost processes – often described as periglacial processes – were dominant. This dry cold was interrupted by shorter periods of two other types, in one of which meteorological conditions favoured the formation of ice, while in the other temperature ameliorated sufficiently to allow woodland to re-establish itself in north-west Europe. And so we have the new concept of 'cold stages' with frost action, in some of which ice-masses may have formed, alternating with 'warm stages', defined as having sufficient duration and a temperature adequately high for the establishment of closed deciduous woodlands in north-west Europe.

As there is no reason to think that the relatively genial climate of today is any more firmly established than that of previous transient 'warm stages', here the view will be taken that the so-called 'postglacial' or 'Holocene' in which we live is merely another 'warm stage', now named in Ireland the Littletonian Warm Stage (see p. 84), which will in all probability be succeeded in due course by yet another 'cold stage'.

In Ireland the deposits laid down by ice have been studied for more than one hundred years, but the study of the effect of cold, unaccompanied by masses of ice, is still in its infancy. Familiarity with our moist oceanic climate makes it difficult for us to picture Ireland in the dry grip of perennial frost, with a landscape typical of cold polar deserts.

Round the margins of modern ice-sheets climatic conditions are severe, and frost processes are active; such a region and the processes can both be described as 'periglacial'. But these processes are largely brought about by the energy produced by water as it expands and contracts in volume on freezing and thawing, and this freeze-thaw activity is not confined to regions

35

in the vicinity of ice-sheets. We might more correctly speak of 'cryokinetic processes', but, as Richard West has pointed out, this is a field of study that has been beset with synthetic jargon, and here the term 'periglacial' will continue to be used.

Periglacial processes flourish best where summer thaws do not entirely melt away the frosts of previous winters, and where at some times of the year there is repeated oscillation of temperature backwards and forwards through the freezing-point of water.

If winter freezing consistently exceeds summer thaw, then an ever-thickening layer of permanently frozen subsoil – *permafrost* – will develop. Heat flow from the earth's interior will inhibit freezing below a limiting depth, but in Siberia today the permafrost may extend to a depth of 500 m. It is not known to what depth it formed in Ireland, but structures characteristic of it were formed in more than one cold stage. Marked contraction of the surface layer of the ground during the cold of winter caused tapering shrinkage-cracks to develop, and these became filled with wedge-shaped tongues of ice; if when the ice later melted foreign material took its place, an ice-wedge-cast was formed, and such structures are widely known in Ireland. Sometimes the shrinkage-cracks were arranged in a polygonal pattern, and ice-wedge-polygons, whose patterns can still be traced today, were formed. (Pl. 4)

If in summer the surface thaws while a still frozen layer remains below, then water cannot drain away downwards, with the result that the surface layers become supersaturated with water and highly mobile, forming the so-called 'active layer'. If the surface has a slope of even as much as 1°, the active layer will move downslope in a generally unsorted condition – though there may be a tendency for any elongated stones which it contains to align themselves parallel with the slope – and when it eventually comes to rest it will form a deposit of *head*. Deposits of head are common in Ireland. If the slope is less than 1°, gravity may not be able to draw the material away, and the super-saturated material will stand in a stagnant condition. Water near its freezing-point varies in density with slight changes in temperature, and these variations will produce movements analogous to convection-currents in the super-saturated layer; under the influence of these movements, the materials of the active layer become sorted into coarser and finer units. In plan a net-like pattern may appear, with finer material in the interstices of the net, and coarser material along the strands; in section irregular columns of stones arranged with their long axes vertical underlie the strands, while below the interstices irregular material has the appearance of a basin-fill. Polygonally patterned ground – not to be confused with ice-wedge-polygons – is formed, and such patterned ground can be seen from Donegal to Kerry. Less regular currents churn the active layer in a tumultuous manner, and strings of stones are drawn out into irregular bands or involutions. Where the ground does slope very slightly, the sorted stones may be drawn out into stripes running downhill. Both involutions and stone-stripes are common in Ireland.

As summer gives way to autumn, the surface of the active layer will refreeze, trapping a layer of as yet unfrozen water between the frozen ground below and the thickening rind of refreezing material above. Sooner or later

PLATE 5 *Above*, modern pingo, nr. Yakutsk, Siberia. *Centre*, collapsing pingo, in permafrost with ice-wedge-polygons, nr. Tuktoyaktuk, NWT, Canada. *Below*, fossil pingos, Camaross, Co. Wexford.

PLATE 6 *Above*, Midlandian end-moraine with kettle-holes, nr. Blackwater, Co. Wexford, showing very irregular topography in a 'young' landscape. *Below*, Drumlins, The Temple, Co. Down.

this trapped pocket of water will itself freeze, and as it does so it must create space in which it can expand on changing from the liquid to the solid state. Under certain special circumstances, not yet clearly understood, the expanding water forces its way upwards, elevates the frozen surface layer with its contained soil, and so creates a dome-like space within which it can turn into ice. An ice-cored mound is thus created; such mounds are well known in arctic Canada today, and are called by the Eskimo name of *pingo*. When such a structure starts to thaw, the outer layer with its contained soil melts first and starts to slump down, surrounding the still unmelted central ice with a ring of earth and soil. When melting is complete, the former pingo is represented by a residual central hollow, surrounded by a raised rim. Fossil structures of this type are very common in south-east Ireland. (Pl. 5)

We have thus in Ireland ample evidence that in certain stages of the Pleistocene the general aspect of the landscape must have been essentially identical with what we can see in arctic Canada and arctic Siberia today. By contrast Greenland today is buried by ice, and we have also evidence to show that Ireland too once carried an extensive ice-cover, with large areas at all levels completely buried by a very great thickness of ice (see figure on p. 34).

In order that such large masses of ice may form, the amount of snow that falls in the winter must exceed the amount that can be melted away in the summer. The excess snow increases in thickness, and gradually consolidates into ice; a dome of ice builds up, and as the centre rises the margins move outwards under the influence of gravity, and creep slowly across the surrounding countryside.

As the ice advances it picks up the superficial weathered material that lies in its path, and thus comes in contact with the underlying rock. It is now armed with incorporated sand and pebbles and can abrade the rock, producing a surface which is in general rounded but shows on closer examination scratches or striae produced as stones embedded in the base of the ice were dragged across the rock. The ice carries along not only the pebbles and clay it picked up as it advanced, but also the new material detached from the underlying rock; such material can range in size from blocks of rock several cubic metres in volume to the finest of rock-flour. When the ice deposits its load, there is usually little possibility of sorting, and rocks, pebbles, sand and clay are disgorged in an indiscriminate mixture to form what used to be called boulder clay, but is now generally named *till*. The ice sometimes moulds the till into ovoid masses aligned with the direction of its flow, and when the ice has disappeared a field of *drumlins* is revealed. This land-form was first described in Ireland, and the name is a blundered form of the Irish word for a small hill. (Pl. 6)

Ice *ablates* or disappears from the ice-mass in two ways, either by direct evaporation into the air from the entire surface, or by melting into water which drains away from the margins. As the meltwater flows away it carries with it some of the ice-enclosed debris released by the melting. If through a decrease in snowfall the rate at which the ice was ablating came to equal the rate at which the ice was advancing, the front of the ice would appear to stand still, and the debris that had been dispersed through a great volume of ice would all be released along the line of the apparently stationary front. Great quantities of sand and gravel would be built up into an *end-moraine*, while the escaping meltwater would carry the clay fraction away in suspension. If the meltwater stream flowed into a lake, the clay would be deposited on the lake floor. If the rate of disappearance overtook the rate of advance, then the ice-mass became almost stationary or 'dead', and ablated away *in situ*, often producing a very confused topography of sand and gravel. Detached lumps of ice would become embedded in gravel, and when they later melted out, small lake-basins or *kettle-holes* would form. (Pl. 6)

Meltwater on the ice surface would sink down through fissures in the ice to its base where major discharge tunnels would gradually be established. The water in the tunnels often flowed vigorously under hydrostatic pressure, and was capable of cutting the floor of the tunnel down into the ground below the ice and creating a sub-glacial chute, with the result that on the final disappearance of the ice a segment of incised valley, usually bearing no relation to the modern surface drainage, would be exposed. Similarly changes in discharge routes might lead to a section of tunnel being abandoned by the main stream flow, and it would then silt up with sand and gravel. When the ice ultimately disappeared, the tunnel fill would emerge as an *esker*, a ridge running across country often for several kilometres, and bearing no relation to the local topography. In boggy country such ridges provided natural causeways, or *eiscirs* in Irish, and this Irish word has also passed into international geological usage. (Pl. 7)

Where the ice-fronts abutted against hilly ground, ice-dams would hold up lakes in valleys, and great deltas would form where meltwaters discharged sand and gravel into the lake. Such deltas form important sources for concrete aggregate. Standing-water might spill from one valley across a ridge into the next valley, and a deep overflow channel might be cut in this way. There are splendid examples of such deltas and channels in many parts of Ireland. (Pl. 8)

Over high ground temperatures are lower than at sea-level, and snow may be able to survive on mountain-tops, when it cannot do so at lower levels. If climate in Ireland deteriorated, a north-east facing hollow in a mountain ridge would form a natural and sheltered trap for drifting snow, which would quickly thicken from a perennial snow-patch into a small lens of ice, capable of excavating a hollow or *corrie* in the rock of the hillside. Some lenses never expanded beyond this stage, but others could collect such an excess of snow that they could send a tongue of ice or *glacier* downslope. As the glacier moved along it entrenched itself and created a valley with a U-shaped cross-section, in contrast to the V-shaped river valley. If the ice-flow was really strong, the glacier when it reached lower ground could spread out into a bulbous lobe, as a *piedmont glacier*. The results of recent valley glaciation of this type are magnificently seen in the Dingle Peninsula.

Here there was not a sufficient area of high ground for a local ice-cap to develop. Farther to the south and centring on the Kenmare Estuary there was sufficient high ground, and the last of such caps formed here relatively recently. The high ground on which it lay was not continuous but was dissected into ridges and valleys, and these exercised a strong control on the directions of possible ice-movement. In places a tongue of ice forced its way across a ridge, gouging out a deep valley as it did so, as for example at the Gap of Dunloe. The ice-scoured country around the Upper Lake at Killarney gives further evidence of its erosive power, while the drumlins at Bantry, and the end-moraines around Killarney and Caragh Lake, show the materials that it transported and deposited.

VEGETATIONAL DEVELOPMENT IN WARM STAGES

Having summarized the developments that took place in cold stages in Ireland, we can now try to form a generalized picture of what happened in the warm episodes, which could be of minor or major duration.

When temperature rises at the end of a cold stage, the ground surface either emerges from below massive ice, or is released from the grip of frost, and soil development can start. The plants begin to return from the areas to which they had been dispersed by cold, and hardier types soon clothe the ground with vegetation. If when this point is reached the climatic trend is reversed, and the climate again gets colder, the plants will again retreat. Such minor episodes of amelioration – very many of which can be traced in the Pleistocene record – have been given the rather unsatisfactory name of 'interstadial', implying a minor phase of warmth characterized by vegetation which had not developed into closed woodland, as opposed to a major episode, the 'interglacial' or 'warm stage'. Closed woodland is the climax vegetation of north-west Europe today, and if we picture that the cold of the Pleistocene is over, and that we are living in the 'postglacial', then if a past stage of warmth was to merit the title of 'interglacial', corresponding in rank with the 'postglacial', it had to be of both sufficient warmth and length for closed woodland to develop in it.

For classificatory purposes therefore this first phase of vegetational development will be regarded as belonging to the cold stage, which may or may not be ending, and be called the Absence-phase (IWA) – implying that closed woodland is absent from Ireland. If amelioration continues, and the

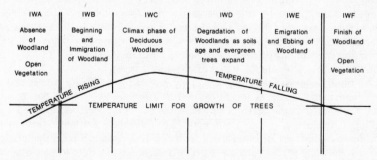

Successive phases of woodland development in a warm stage. See text for explanation of IWA etc.

trees return and gradually spread until they cover the whole countryside, then we enter on a true warm stage; if renewed deterioration sets in after only a short space of time, we have been merely concerned with yet another interstadial.

The events of a full warm stage are shown in diagrammatic form (p. 39); the stage is divided into phases, and each phase is given a label, e.g. IWX, in which I stands for Ireland, W stands for woodland, and X indicates the particular phase.

The return and the spreading of the trees are not simple functions of climate and of time. Even granted maximal conditions for expansion, trees will spread at different rates according to their methods of propagation. There is thus a period of immigration during which the woodlands cannot reach a position of stability, and this I call the Beginning-phase (IWB) – implying that woodland development is beginning as tree immigration proceeds. This phase opens when the first pioneer tree – in Ireland the juniper (*Juniperus*) – leads off an expansion of woodland that will continue without interruption until high forests are established.

Geographical barriers, such as mountain ranges and stretches of water, also affected immigration. As great ice-masses grew in cold stages they abstracted water from the oceans, and as sea-level fell Ireland would be joined to Britain, and Britain to Europe. Amelioration of climate reversed this trend, but at the beginning of the warm stage sea-level would still have been low, and immigration into Britain and Ireland would have been easy. But rising sea-level gradually re-flooded the old channels, and sooner or later natural immigration into Ireland was no longer possible.

The materials on which the soils of the warm stage developed had been constituted during the preceding cold stage first by the carrying away by ice or solifluction of the earlier exhausted soil, and second by fresh rock being comminuted by the grinding action of ice, or by subsoil being brought to the surface through the churning action of frost processes. Thus when the warm stage opened the soil parent materials were again rich in nutrient elements, and luxuriant plant growth could quickly lead to the development of deciduous woodland. In north-west Europe deciduous trees are thought of – perhaps illogically – as giving a richer aesthetic spectacle than coniferous trees, and so woodland composed of oak (*Quercus*), lime (*Tilia*) and elm (*Ulmus*), the *Quercetum-mixtum* or Mixed Oak Forest of some botanists, is regarded as climax woodland. Accepting this outlook, we can picture this phase with tall deciduous woodlands on deep forest soils as the climax and label it IWC, the Climax-phase – with climax-forest of deciduous trees.

As time progressed leaching gradually reduced the fertility of the soils, and there was a tendency to acidity, and to a replacement of the deciduous trees by conifers and heath, a process that may have been accelerated by falling temperature. Again on the perhaps mistaken aesthetic view that coniferous woods are of lower merit than deciduous, we can label this phase IWD – the Degradation-phase – with degrading soils leading to consequent 'degradation' of the woodlands.

Sooner or later the long-term cyclical fluctuation of the Pleistocene climate would start to draw the warm stage to a close, and temperatures would fall. All but the hardiest trees, in Ireland birch and pine, would be eliminated from the woodlands, and we have IWE, the Ebbing-phase – with ebbing of woodland, and emigration of all but the hardiest trees.

A still further increase in severity of climate would cause even the boreal woods to break up, and as continuous woodland is our criterion for a warm stage, here the warm stage must end. The woodlands are finished, but some hardy herbs and grasses will struggle on in clumps which are continually shrinking in size, until even they too may be eliminated as full polar desert conditions become established. Here we move past the golden spike to reach IWF – the Finished-phase – when the trees of the preceding warm stage have fled to distant refugia, and all vegetation is on the retreat, as the rigorous climate of the next cold stage develops.

There were a considerable number of warm stages during the Pleistocene, and if in each warm stage the vegetational cycle and the plants which composed it had repeated themselves identically, obviously study of the plant fossils in the organic deposits of a stage could not lead to the pin-pointing of the deposit as belonging to one particular warm stage rather than any other. But fortunately there were some variations in the vegetational developments of the different warm stages, and so detailed studies may reveal key characteristics by which the particular deposits of each warm stage may be identified.

During the warm stages peats and muds slowly accumulate, trapping successive generations of pollen-grains within their deposits as they grow in thickness, and studies of the contained pollen-grains are particularly useful in revealing vegetational differences, even on a small scale. To make such a study a vertical series of samples is taken at suitable intervals from the top to the bottom of the deposit, and statistical counts of the different pollens are made. Within the whole column of samples a sequence, of shorter or longer length, may give broadly similar pollen-counts, indicating relatively stable plant communities throughout the period of time represented by the accumulation of the sediment from which the sequence came. The counts will be dominated by certain pollens, presumably derived from plants that were prominent in the neighbourhood at the time, and so we can establish a type of biozone, a *pollen-assemblage-zone* (PAZ), for example a *Corylus-Pinus*-zone, from which we draw the inference that pine and hazel were then common in the local woodlands. A second sequence of samples immediately above the first may show increased amounts of *Quercus* and *Ulmus*, giving a further pollen-assemblage-zone, from which we can infer that relatively open woodland with pine and hazel had been replaced by denser woodland with tall deciduous trees (see figure on p. 97).

For many years systematic pollen-counts aimed only at recording the relative proportions of the different pollens in the samples, and interpretation of such counts could be very treacherous. If the amount of one pollen fell drastically in quantity, say pollen of elm due to an outbreak of disease, then the figures for the other pollens rose automatically to fill the gap, but it did not follow that the importance of the plants that produced them had increased in the local countryside. Today efforts are being made to determine the total number of pollen-grains contained in a unit-volume of a deposit, and to assess the time it took for the unit-volume to be deposited, and so form an impression of the 'absolute' amount of pollen contributed by different plants to the accumulating deposit in a given length of time. Although it is difficult to find deposits which make this kind of count possible, and there are still problems of interpretation, such absolute counts promise to give a great deal of more accurate information than the older relative counts. Under tundra conditions total pollen production by herbs and grasses is low, under closed woodland conditions pollen production by trees is high, and by making absolute counts it is possible to follow the expansion and contraction of the woodland cover as climate changed, as well as see how the different trees building up that cover waxed and waned in importance.

In addition to pollen grains, other small fossils such as diatom-skeletons and fungus-spores can be identified and counted with profit. Larger fossils, wood, epidermis, seeds, insect parts, mollusc shells, often loosely called 'macrofossils', may also be preserved, and their detailed study can give a great deal of valuable information. Vertebrate bones are also of help, but because of the mobility of the typical mammal, their interpretation is often difficult.

It is thus clear that even a small amount of organic material can yield a surprising amount of information to specialized treatment, while a deposit whose thickness is measured in metres may hold a complete record of a warm stage from the first replacement of the preceding tundra, through the full development of the woodlands to their final collapse and replacement by the succeeding tundra of the next cold stage. It may also be possible to form an impression of its absolute age by determining its surviving content of radio-active carbon.*

But even after an organic deposit obviously from a warm stage has been subjected to a most meticulous examination, some ambiguity may remain as to the particular warm stage to which it should be assigned. The deposits of the cold stages also present difficulties. In all of the cold stages the action of ice and frost produced broadly similar deposits, and their appropriate assignation is difficult. The younger deposits are not neatly stacked on top of the older ones, because a younger ice-sheet could cut away older deposits, and replace them by its own ones. An ice-sheet can simultaneously deposit till in one place and meltwater sands and gravels in another, and if the ice-sheet is moving, the two types of deposit may merge laterally into one another. Fossils are usually rare in cold stage deposits.

Thus it is exceedingly difficult to sort out Pleistocene deposits into their correct chronological sequence, and this difficulty obtains even within a single country, let alone on a continental or world-wide scale. Recently under the auspices of the Geological Society of London a determined effort has been

*Numerous dates based on radiocarbon age determinations (C-14 dates) are cited in this book. In recent years many efforts have been made to harmonize C-14 dates with the dates arrived at by counting the annual growth-rings of the Bristlecone Pine. All the dates in this book are 'raw' dates, that is to say they are the figures as issued by the dating laboratory, un-'corrected' in any way. They should be regarded as indicating an approximate age, and not a detailed date to an individual year; most are probably accurate to about one hundred years.

TABLE SHOWING STAGES OF THE LATER PLEISTOCENE IN THE BRITISH ISLES

BRITISH STAGES	IRISH STAGES	IMPORTANT SITES	NOTES
FLANDRIAN WARM	LITTLETONIAN WARM	Littleton, Tipperary	The record in the peats and underlying muds in a raised-bog at Littleton runs from 12,000 years ago to the present day
	10,000 BP		
		Nahanagan, Wicklow	A corrie moraine here records a short stadial or cold phase from 10,500 to 10,000 BP
		Woodgrange, Down	The lacustrine deposits here record an interstadial or warm phase that lasted from about 14,000 to 10,500 BP
	LATE	Armoy, Antrim	An end-moraine here marks the limit of a late advance. of ice from Scotland
		Kells, Meath	An end-moraine here marks the eastern limit of an ice-advance during which drumlins were formed
DEVENSIAN COLD	MIDLANDIAN COLD	Ballylanders, Limerick	An end-moraine here probably marks the southern limit of a late advance of ice from the Midlands
	26,000 BP	Derryvree, Fermanagh	Silt with organic remains, resting on till, and covered by till which is moulded in drumlin form, has been dated to 30,500 BP
	MIDDLE	Castlepook, Cork	A femur of Woolly Mammoth (*E. primigenius*) from a cave here has been dated to 33,500 BP
		Hollymount, Fermanagh	Silt with organic remains, resting on till, and covered by till which is moulded in drumlin form, is older than 41,500 BP
	50,000 BP EARLY	Hollymount, Fermanagh	The lower till here may be of Early Midlandian age
	70,000 BP		
IPSWICHIAN WARM	LAST WARM	No suitable type site yet discovered	
WOLSTONIAN COLD	MUNSTERIAN COLD	Garryvoe, Cork	Till deposited by ice moving eastwards from west Cork and Kerry rests on Ballycroneen till
		Ballyvoyle, Waterford	Till deposited by ice moving southeastwards from the Midlands rests on Ballycroneen till
		Ballycroneen Cork	Shelly calcareous till deposited by ice that had advanced down the basin of the Irish Sea has its western limit here
		Ballymakegoge, Kerry	Peats and silts under head record the end of the Gortian woodlands, and the opening of this cold stage. The deposits rest on a raised beach
HOXNIAN WARM	GORTIAN WARM	nr. Gort, Galway	A thick deposit of mud below till records the development of the Gortian woodlands. The mud passes down into muddy clay, which rests on sandy clay. The plant fossils show that the base of the muddy clay is the base of the warm stage
ANGLIAN COLD	PRE-GORTIAN COLD	nr. Gort, Galway	The basal sandy clay belongs to this cold stage

made to produce a correlation-table of the Pleistocene deposits of the British Isles in a chronological sequence of warm and cold stages. Seven cold stages were recognized, but of these only the three latest could be traced in Ireland. Thus only the upper part of the correlation-table has interest for us here, and a modified version is shown above. The table relates the Irish stages to those of Britain, and also lists some sites which have particular importance in deciphering the Pleistocene history of Ireland.

THE GORTIAN WOODLANDS

More than one hundred years ago a distinguished Irish geologist, G. H. Kinahan, discovered 'a peaty accumulation' below a thick cover of 'glacial drift' in a river valley near Gort in Co. Galway. Pine, spruce (*Picea*) and hazel were recorded, and Kinahan considered that 'the presence of such trees in Ireland during intra-glacial times' was proved by his discovery. In 1949 the deposit was re-investigated by Knud Jessen, Svend Andersen and Tony Farrington, who confirmed that it did indeed belong to a Pleistocene warm stage, almost certainly the same one as that in which the famous organic deposit at Hoxne in East Anglia accumulated, perhaps 200,000 years ago.

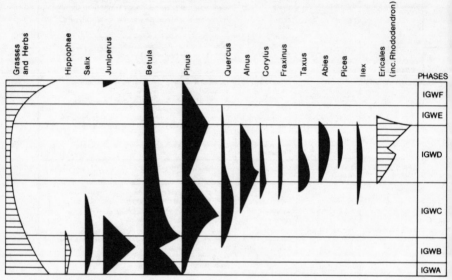

A schematic pollen-diagram to illustrate the phases of woodland development in the Gortian Warm Stage.

Although the Gort deposit gives its name to this warm stage in Ireland, it does not contain a record of the entire warm stage, as the upper part is missing, perhaps cut away by the later ice, which deposited till on top of it. Bill Watts has described other deposits which appear to belong to the same warm stage, but all these are incomplete also. However I have put together from these partial records a schematic pollen-diagram to suggest the course of woodland development in Ireland throughout the whole of the Gortian Warm Stage. As the woodlands of the warm stage in which we are living have been wrecked by the activities of man, it is of interest to see what the Irish landscape may have looked like at a time when we have no record of man in Ireland, though palaeolithic man was in England at this time, and indeed his implements are quite common at Hoxne itself.

When we are considering the events of this warm stage, we can picture that at its opening vegetation was scanty and sea-level was low, probably far below its present level. In the central part of the stage there were dense woodlands and sea-level was high, probably about 25 m above the level today. There is

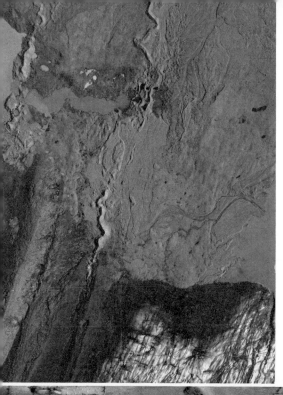

PLATE 7 *Left*, eskers being exposed as ice-sheet melts away, Breidamerkurjokull, Iceland. *Below*, bifurcating fossil eskers, nr. Ballinlough, Co. Roscommon. Discharge water flowed from bottom to top of picture. Note road on crest of esker in lower right-hand corner.

PLATE 8 North of Galbally, Co. Limerick, a rock ridge of Armorican origin formed the watershed between the Shannon and the Blackwater rivers. Ice from the midlands ponded meltwater against the north face of the ridge; the ponded water over-topped a low point on the ridge, and as it gushed southwards it cut a deep channel in the ridge. The watershed was thus breached, and some water which formerly went to the Shannon now turns south to the Blackwater.

no record of such a high sea-level in Ireland, but in England it is well documented. As climate worsened again, the woodlands broke up, and sea-level fell back. Such changes in sea-level are due to water being withdrawn from the oceans to build up ice-masses in cold stages, and returning to the oceans when the ice melts; changes in level brought about in this way are called *eustatic* changes.

The re-investigation at Gort was done by means of a special boring, and towards the bottom of the borehole there was a change in deposit from fine sandy clay below to muddy clay above. In the sandy clay pollen of herbs and and of birch (probably the dwarf form, *Betula nana*) were common, indicating the immigration of pioneer vegetation on to still unstable soils as the preceding cold stage was ending. This is the Absence-phase, and on the right-hand margin of the diagram this level is marked IGWA (G being inserted to stand for Gortian) showing the approach to the Gortian Warm Stage with woodland still absent. Thus it is clear that cold conditions preceded the Gortian Warm Stage in Ireland, and that we had here a cold stage which was probably the equivalent of the Anglian Cold Stage in Britain.

The Gortian diagram then shows an upsurge in pollen of *Juniperus*, presumably in response to a rise in temperature to a level sufficient to allow this tree to spread widely and to flower freely. This rise marks the beginning of woodland expansion, and the Beginning-phase (IGWB) opens the Gortian Warm Stage. *Betula, Juniperus, Pinus* and *Salix* are the most important trees in this early phase.

The Climax-phase (IGWC) starts when *Quercus* appears in strength, and the output of pine pollen falls back. We thus had climax-forest of *Quercus*, with smaller amounts of *Alnus, Corylus* and *Fraxinus* (ash), and of the evergreens *Ilex* and *Taxus* (yew). The climax woods of this Gortian stage were thus very different from those of the warm stage in which we are living – the Littletonian. In these later woods *Ulmus* and *Corylus* had much greater importance.

Abies then makes its appearance, and as it increases in quantity it is joined by *Picea*. Ericaceous pollen, among which that of *Rhododendron* is important, also appear in quantity. Here we see the trend towards soil acidity, encouraging coniferous woodland and heath, that marks the opening of the Degradation-phase (IGWD), when degradation is setting in. Fir and spruce did not establish themselves in the Littletonian woodlands in Ireland, although today they are widely planted. *Rhododendron ponticum* is also here today, but only as a result of introduction in the late eighteenth century. It is clear that once introduced it found conditions ideal on Ireland's acid soils, and it has run like wildfire through woods and over upland bogs. It is a classic example of a tree that had a wider distribution in an earlier warm stage, was then driven by cold far back into Europe – it now centres to the south and west of the Black Sea, with a few outlying localities in Spain and Portugal – and has since been prevented by geographical barriers from returning to areas where it formerly grew, and can again flourish after introduction by man.

At Gort itself the record ends at this level, but at Kilbeg in Waterford *Pinus* then climbs to high levels (and grasses and herbs also rise) while the

other trees, except for *Betula*, are eliminated. Here the Gortian woodlands
reach their final boreal Ebbing-phase (IGWE). Pine and birch then fall away,
juniper – now that the overshadowing trees have gone – makes a last fleeting
appearance, and values for herbaceous pollens rise dramatically. Here the
Gortian woodlands have vanished, and we have the Finished-phase (IGWF),
as open country with park tundra extends, and heralds the opening of the
following cold stage, the Munsterian, so called because its deposits are well
seen in the south of Ireland.

We can also see the transition from the Gortian Warm Stage to the Munsterian Cold Stage near Fenit, on the north shore of Tralee Bay in Co. Kerry,
and at this coastal site we have the possibility of bringing the climatic changes
of the times into relationship with sea-level changes. The fossiliferous deposits
rest on a beach sand, and this in turn rests on a wave-cut shore-platform.

The shore-platform is of considerable interest. Almost seventy years ago
Wright and Muff wrote a paper in which they described a 'preglacial' beach
along the south coast of Ireland. They used the term 'preglacial' because they
were unable to demonstrate that any glacial events had preceded the formation
of the beach, although it was clear that glaciation had followed its formation.
In their 'beach' they included two elements, a shore-platform backed by a
cliff cut in rock about 3 m above the level at which the modern waves are
cutting their platform, and beach gravels deposited either in the notch where
the platform meets the cliff, or abandoned on the lower stretches of the platform when sea-level subsequently fell. At first it was thought that only one
cycle was involved, and that the deposition of the beach gravels followed
quickly on the cutting of the platform, but it now seems more probable that
the shore-platform is a composite feature of considerable age, and that the
beach gravels may have been trapped on its bench-like form at a very much
later date.

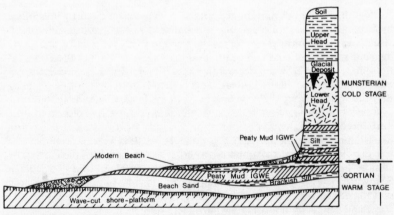

Diagrammatic section through the late Gortian and early Munsterian deposits
exposed in a cliff-section at Ballymakegoge, near Fenit, Co. Kerry.

Similar platforms are known in south-west Britain and north-west France, and in places in Brittany the platform is cut in Palaeogene rocks, so at any rate there is a lower limit to its age. It is also younger than the formation of the present valley system, because the platform invades the drowned mouths of the valleys. This is very well seen inside Cork Harbour, as Wright and Muff pointed out. Nowhere do we see the platform cut in glacial deposits, so in one sense Wright and Muff were correct when they spoke of it as 'preglacial'. On the other hand in many localities the platform is very well preserved and looks very 'fresh', so it is unlikely to be a feature of very high antiquity. (Pl. 10)

Near Fenit, at Ballymakegoge, there are extensive areas of the old shore-platform, almost unmodified by the modern waves. The overlying fossil beach is here sandy in facies, and may originally have lain in dune-like ridges. Between the ridges a brackish silt with remains of seaweed and salt-marsh plants was first deposited, and its high content of pine pollen showed that it belonged to the Ebbing-phase (IWGE), when the Gortian woodlands were taking on a boreal aspect as temperature dropped. Continuing fall in sea-level then left the site free from marine influence, and a freshwater peaty mud formed, containing pollen still indicating boreal woodland in the Ebbing-phase. The next layer is an inorganic silt with plant debris, including that of the northern moss *Polytrichum alpinum*, and derived pollen of fir, yew, holly and rhododendron belonging to the earlier woodland phase. This inorganic material was moved downslope by the freeze-thaw processes of the incipient Munsterian Cold Stage, and the pollen of the temperate trees, which had been in the old woodland soil, was carried down with the silt.

Peaty mud then formed once more, but now the pine, birch and juniper had disappeared, as there is none of their pollen in the mud, though there is some derived pollen. Here we have the Finished-phase (IGWF), the Gortian woods have disappeared, and we have moved into the opening of the Mun-sterian Cold Stage; the figure shows a symbolical golden spike at the transition. Solifluction at first must have been rather slow, because we have alternating layers of silt with derived pollen, and peaty muds which indicate treeless tundra. Solifluction then sets in in earnest, and coarser debris with stones up to 10 cm in length is moved downslope to form a thick deposit of head. Ice-wedge-casts in the head are evidence of a phase of permafrost. The head in turn is buried by a glacial deposit with striated boulders which shows that massive ice was now in the vicinity.

This site demonstrates that by the time the high-level Gortian seas had been lowered eustatically by the abstraction of water to the level of the modern sea, the fall in temperature had eliminated the warmth-demanding trees from the Irish forests, leaving only open stands of pine, birch and juniper. The sea may already have been cold enough to carry floating pack-ice with embedded stones and boulders, and if this was the case, then we have an explanation for the presence of the boulders, sometimes from far-distant sources, that are occasionally found among the beach deposits on the shore-platform. Boulders from the English Lake District are known on the corresponding shore-platform in Cornwall.

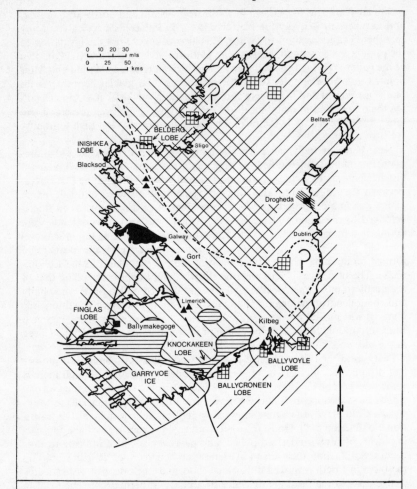

▲ DEPOSIT OF GORTIAN AGE

■ GLACIO-MARINE DEPOSIT

EARLIEST TILL FROM IRISH MIDLANDS

EARLY TILL WITH CONTENT OF MARINE CLAY

AREA COVERED BY EARLY ICE OF SCOTTISH ORIGIN

AREA COVERED BY LATER ICE OF IRISH ORIGIN

AREA PERHAPS NOT COVERED BY ICE

We have seen that the Gortian climax woodlands were very different from those of the current Littletonian Warm Stage, not so much in the difference in the trees present, as in the different proportions in which they were present. The later phases of the Gortian forests with fir, yew and alder, and smaller amounts of spruce are, of course, unrepresented in modern Ireland, and the European woods that most resemble them today are on the southern slopes of the Caucasus. Several of the trees of those later Gortian forests have been introduced by man into Ireland – fir, spruce, hornbeam, box (*Buxus*) and rhododendron – but it is unlikely that they could have reached the country unless assisted in this way.

In all about one hundred taxa of higher plants have been identified for this warm stage, and of these about twenty are not native in Ireland today. Three that are no longer here are essentially North American in their modern distribution, and show that as the Pleistocene progressed there was a progressive elimination from Europe of plants that had earlier grown freely on both sides of the Atlantic Ocean. Two such water-plants, *Eriocaulon septangulare* and *Naias flexilis*, still grow in the west of Ireland, and they are also recorded from the Gortian deposits. Today the west of Ireland has several unusual heathers, *Daboecia cantabrica*, *Erica ciliaris* and *E. mackaiana*, and these were also in Ireland in Gortian times.

THE MUNSTERIAN COLD STAGE

We can perhaps picture the Munsterian Cold Stage as beginning some 175,000 years ago, and lasting for some 75,000 years. In it both frost and ice were active, but we can say little about their relative importances at different parts of the stage. Head formed on an extensive scale, and there certainly was some permafrost, as shown by the ice-wedge-casts on the north shore of Tralee Bay.

Large ice-masses also formed, and most of Ireland was probably covered by ice in at least some part of the stage, though limited areas of higher ground in the south and west probably remained ice-free, rising as nunataks above the surrounding ice. The northern Midlands may have been the first part of the country to be buried by ice, because the stratigraphically lowest – and therefore perhaps the earliest – glacial deposit of this stage appears to be a till of inland Irish origin on the east coast near Drogheda.

An immense ice-mass then seems to have formed in Scotland, and as the ice radiated out to west and south it crossed the former sea floor and became charged with shelly calcareous marine muds and clays. In north-west Ireland, at Belderg in Mayo and also in Donegal, there is a shelly till which may well have been deposited by this invading Scottish ice, and we can picture a western Belderg Lobe. The southerly stream from Scotland poured down the basin of the Irish Sea, and as it moved down the Firth of Clyde it assimilated great quantities of the very distinctive fine-grained granite of which Ailsa Craig is

The location of Gortian Warm Stage sites, and extent of ice-masses of Munsterian Cold Stage.

formed; these erratics it carried as far as the south of Wales and the south of Ireland.

The Scottish ice filled the basin of the Irish Sea, sending a lobe south-eastwards deep into the Cheshire lowlands, and another eastwards up the Bristol Channel, almost as far as Bristol itself. It continued along the face of the high cliffs of Devon and Cornwall, and came to a halt against the northern limits of the Isles of Scilly. On the Irish side of the basin the ice pushed westwards across the low coasts near Drogheda, Dublin and Arklow; it overrode the Carnsore promontory in Wexford, and continued along coastal Waterford and Cork as far as Ballycroneen Bay, just east of Cork Harbour. Along the Cork coast its till acquires, in addition to marine shells and Ailsa Craig granite, a considerable content of chalk. The source of the chalk was for long a puzzle, but it is now known to come from the extensive areas of chalk that form the sea floor along much of the south coast of Ireland.

Such an immense mass of ice was, of course, of very considerable weight, and this had important consequences. A great deal of geological evidence suggests that the continents of the world are composed of rocks of relatively low specific gravity, and that they float like rafts on a substratum of higher specific gravity. If the load on a raft is increased, it sinks lower in the water; if ice is heaped up on a continent, it sinks lower into the substratum. When the ice melts away, the continent rises again, and often seems to return to its original level with remarkable precision. The 'preglacial' shore-platform is still almost horizontal today, and differs in height from the modern shore-platform by only a few metres, even though parts of it have been grossly deformed by an overburden of ice on at least two occasions.

The movement of the land-mass as it is loaded or unloaded with ice is said to be *isostatic*, and it can easily be seen that if fluctuations in ice volume are causing the level of the sea to rise or fall eustatically, and the level of the land to rise or fall isostatically, the net relative movement that will cause the sea to encroach on or recede from the margin of the land may be difficult to assess.

Still we must do what we can. Along the line of contact between the sea and the land beach deposits will often accumulate, and we may subsequently find these as raised beaches if the net movement of the land relative to the sea has been upwards, or as drowned beaches if the net movement has been downwards. Thus a beach above modern sea-level does not necessarily mean that the sea once stood at a higher eustatic level; it may have been formed when land isostatically depressed far below its present level was washed by the waves of a sea at a eustatic level below that of today. Provided the subsequent isostatic rise of the land outstripped the eustatic rise of the sea, the beach today will be raised above modern sea-level.

If we are to analyse such movements fully, we must find a stable point on the earth's surface from which we can measure on the one hand the eustatic changes in sea-level, and on the other the isostatic movements of those land areas that have been influenced by ice-masses. Archimedes said, 'Give me a stable place to base my lever, and I will move the world'; unfortunately modern geophysicists tell us that nowhere, even on a tropical oceanic island far removed from all influence of ice, will we be able to find a stable base for our measurements.

The Scottish ice-mass brought about an enormous downsinking of the earth's crust not only below itself, but also of the surrounding area, with the result that although sea-level had fallen eustatically far below its present level, an arctic fiord was still able to occupy the Irish Sea Trough in front of the advancing ice. Near Drogheda, and now at a height of 35 m above modern sea-level due to the isostatic rebound of the land on the disappearance of the ice, there is a series of glacio-marine deposits ranging from clays to bedded gravels, and containing fossils of arctic deep-water molluscs that imply that the fiord had a depth of about 100 m. The clays contain large erratics dropped from floating pack-ice or ice-bergs, which had calved off from the front of the advancing Scottish ice; in due course the ice obliterated the fiord and advanced over the deposits on its floor.

Ice of Irish origin then became important once more. It is not known when this ice first formed, but it now invaded areas that had formerly been occupied by Scottish ice. The centre of the ice-mass was perhaps in the mountains of Connemara, because granite from the north shore of Galway Bay was carried southwards, as far as Kerry and Cork, while granite from Blacksod was carried north-westwards across the islands of Mayo by what we can call the Inishkea Lobe. To the south the ice reached the Dingle Peninsula, depositing occasional boulders of Galway granite and quantities of limestone debris against its northern slopes; the valley of the Finglas River slopes north, and over one hundred years ago it was recognized that limestone boulders had been pushed up into the valley; I therefore call the ice here the Finglas Lobe. The ice-flow was deflected westwards by the Brandon massif, and the steepness of the north-facing cliffs here may owe something to erosion by ice. Rounding the corner the ice pushed into Smerwick Harbour, and may have come to a halt against Slea Head and the Blasket Islands. On its way south the ice passed over the Fenit area, and as we have seen, deposited till on top of the earlier deposits of head and their contained ice-wedge-casts.

To the south-south-east a lobe of the radiating Connemara ice reached almost as far as Midleton in Co. Cork; north of the town at Knockakeen and elsewhere big gravel deposits contain not only volcanic rocks from the Limerick area – which lay in the path of the advancing ice – but also occasional erratics of Galway granite; this was the Knockakeen Lobe. Still farther east a lobe pushed between the Comeraghs (which may have stood up as nunataks) and the Wicklow Mountains, and then expanded southwards down Waterford Harbour to Ballyvoyle near Dungarvan in a Ballyvoyle Lobe. On the way it disturbed several Gortian deposits; at Kilbeg the deposit was buried below till, at Ballykeerogemore, the deposit was kneaded and broken, while at Newtown on the west side of Waterford Harbour organic material was drawn out into wisps and lenses in the till. When the Irish ice advanced into the coastal areas that had been covered by the Ballycroneen Lobe of the Scottish ice, it stripped away much of the calcareous shelly till. At Garrarus on the Waterford coast west of Tramore a layer of head lies between the lower Ballycroneen till and the upper Ballyvoyle till; the head shows that the area must have had an ice-free spell prior to being covered by ice moving down from the Midlands. Deposits of the Ballyvoyle Lobe continue eastwards as far as Carnsore Point.

We can hope for some success in tracing these ice movements in the south of Ireland, because this part of the country was never again overrun by ice on a large scale; thus it is in Munster that deposits of this age are best seen, and so the cold stage is called the Munsterian. As soon as we turn up the east coast, north of Carnsore Point, we quickly run into the deposits of the later cold stage, the Midlandian, so called because its deposits are seen to good advantage in the Midlands. As a consequence the Munsterian deposits become much more patchy, either because they were eroded away by the later ice, or because they have become buried beneath younger deposits.

At Clogga, south of Arklow, an older till, presumably of Munsterian age, is to be seen below younger Midlandian till. The till is rich in Leinster granite from the mountains to the west, but has also a small content of silicified limestone, and this suggests – though Galway granite has not been recorded – that not all of Munsterian ice from the western centre was deflected by the Wicklow Mountains and forced to flow south-eastwards as the Ballyvoyle Lobe, but that some of it pushed right over the Wicklow Mountains bringing limestone from the Midlands out into the Irish Sea. If this is the case, the ice in eastern Ireland must have been at least 1000 m thick, and the ice in the west must have been substantially thicker in order to give momentum to the necessary flow. Such ice will also have moved westwards far out into the Atlantic Ocean, and some preliminary studies of sea-floor deposits here do suggest that material of glacial origin can be traced offshore for a very considerable distance.

There was another very much smaller ice-cap in the mountains of Kerry and west Cork. On the west and south it escaped seawards, but on the north it failed to override the Dingle Peninsula, and perhaps the high ground of east Kerry also. It advanced eastwards across the lower-lying ground of south Cork past the site of Cork city as far as Garryvoe in Ballycotton Bay. At Garryvoe till rich in erratics from the west rests on the chalky shelly till and outwash sands of the earlier Ballycroneen Lobe, which had advanced from the east. The Garryvoe ice-mass may thus be of approximately the same age as the ice-mass that radiated from Connemara.

As there were Munsterian ice-masses on the mountains of south-western and of western Ireland, it seems reasonable to think that there would have been one in Donegal also. There are some indications that this was the case, but the amount of evidence is still very scanty.

If we try to form a general picture of Ireland during the Munsterian Cold Stage, our main impression is of great masses of ice waxing and waning from time to time in different parts of the country, with only small patches of higher ground here and there remaining ice-free. Even before it was buried by ice, low-lying ground, even along the shore of the Atlantic Ocean, was experiencing cold polar desert climate with permafrost and ice-wedges, while on higher ground conditions will have been still more severe; under these circumstances only the hardiest of plants and animals could have survived.

Where then were the temperate trees and shrubs that had clothed Ireland during the Gortian Warm Stage? They can only have survived to the south or the west. To the south conditions warm enough for their survival probably did not exist north of the Pyrenees, though they could have found refugia in Spain or Portugal. What about the west? Sea-level probably fell by substantially more than 100 m during the Munsterian Cold Stage, and along much of western Europe the fall exposed broad expanses of the continental shelf on which severe climatic conditions would have obtained. But off the mountains of Kerry and Connemara the steeper slopes continue seawards, slopes that even with a lower sea-level might have continued to receive the full force of the Gulf Stream. Here ridges and valleys provided shelter, slopes drained the soils, the aspect was favourable, and oceanic waters provided a moderating influence. Could there have been small refugia with favourable micro-climates off these areas?

We have seen that there was a considerable range of species of heather in Gortian Ireland, and that several of the same species are in Ireland today. Have they returned from Spain and Portugal after each cold stage, or did they find refuge closer at hand? In Ireland today most of the localities for the rarer heathers lie west of the 5°C mean January isotherm, and this may be their limiting temperature. The glacial coast was perhaps 35 km west of, and 100 m lower than the modern coasts where the ice-wedge-casts are now seen. The presence of the casts implies a -12°C mean January temperature, and it seems difficult to conceive of a temperature gradient of more than 15°C in such a short vertical range, and such a gradient would appear to be necessary if the heathers were to survive. On the other hand in support of the concept of a refuge off the present coast of Connemara, where the offshore slopes are steep and the heathers have their main concentration, we may note that Donegal, similar in general terrain and vegetation to Connemara, but without steep offshore slopes, is today very much poorer in heathers.

THE HIDDEN INTERREGNUM

The terrestrial record of Pleistocene events tends to be episodic and disjointed, but there is every hope that the marine deposits on the sea floor will tell a more continuous story. Marine studies already indicate that the warm stage that preceded the present one in which we live began about 100,000 years ago and lasted until about 70,000 years ago. This warm stage is well documented in north-west Europe, where it is known as the Eemian Warm Stage, and numerous deposits are known in Britain also, ranging from Devon to Durham. Such deposits are particularly common in East Anglia, and a site near Ipswich was chosen to give its name to the Ipswichian Warm Stage. As a result we have quite a considerable knowledge of the flora and fauna, terrestrial, freshwater and marine, of this warm stage in north-west Europe, and can draw the inference that the climate, when at its most favourable phase, was rather warmer and more continental than at present; sea-level was perhaps about 7·5 m above today's level.

Compared with this detailed record our knowledge of events in Ireland at the corresponding time is deplorably meagre, as we do not know of any deposit which can be unequivocally allotted to this warm stage. One would think that as this warm stage is younger than the Gortian, its deposits would have had a better chance of survival than those of the older period, and the chances of discovery should be at least equal in the two cases. But we are in the embarrassing position of having too many Gortian deposits, and too few younger ones, so much so that many geologists ask, 'Are you sure your so-called Gortian deposits are not really younger, and perhaps of Ipswichian age?'

We have seen that the vegetational developments of the different warm stages tend to have a basic similarity, but we are fortunate that there were significant differences between the woodlands of the later phases of the Hoxnian and those of the corresponding phases of the Ipswichian. *Abies* is the key tree of the Hoxnian/Gortian phase, whereas *Carpinus* is the key tree of the Ipswichian/Eemian phase. In north-west Europe no deposit of Ipswichian/Eemian carries large quantities of *Abies* pollen, but very many of them have substantial quantities of *Carpinus* pollen. With two exceptions to be noted below, all Irish warm stage deposits carry substantial amounts of *Abies* pollen, so unless the vegetation of Ireland at this time was utterly different to that of the rest of north-west Europe, we must conclude that these deposits are indeed of Gortian age.

It could conceivably be argued that a deep strait of water separated Ireland from Britain during the Ipswichian, with the result that immigration from the east was blocked. If the essential elements of the Gortian vegetation had survived the Munsterian cold in refugia to the south and west, they could have reclothed the country once more when the warm conditions of the Ipswichian set in. In this way the vegetation of Ireland might have had an entirely different character to that of the rest of north-west Europe at this time. But as the Irish vegetation resembled that of Europe both in the earlier Gortian Warm Stage and in the current 'postglacial' or Littletonian Warm Stage, it is hard to believe that it can have been widely different in the intervening warm stage. Ipswichian/Eemian deposits rich in pollen of *Carpinus* are now known from north-west France to north-west England, and it would seem to be only a matter of time and chance before corresponding deposits are discovered in Ireland.

In the meantime we must make do with what we have. A well at Baggotstown, Co. Limerick, revealed a complicated and intriguing sequence of deposits, which can be outlined as follows:

DEPOSIT	POSSIBLE AGE
Till	Midlandian? Cold Stage
Thin freshwater mud, with much pollen of *Alnus* and *Pinus*, and lesser amounts of *Quercus*, *Corylus*, *Ilex* and *Taxus*	Missing warm stage?
Till	Munsterian? Cold Stage
Thick freshwater muds and peats, with pollen of *Abies* and *Rhododendron*	Gortian Warm Stage
Stony clay with erratics (till?)	Pre-Gortian Cold Stage

The presence of *Abies* pollen suggests that the lower organic layer must be Gortian in age, and the overlying till should be of Munsterian age. The upper organic layer, though very thin, is unlikely to be a disturbed part of the lower layer, because the pollen-count it presents cannot be matched in the lower layer. The pollen clearly derives from a temperate woodland in its Climax-phase, and can perhaps belong to the 'missing' warm stage. The site calls for urgent re-examination.

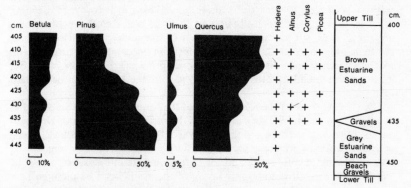

A pollen-diagram from warm stage deposit, possibly of Ipswichian age, at Shortalstown, Co. Wexford.

At Shortalstown, Co. Wexford, a farm drainage trench showed a mass of estuarine sand between an upper and a lower till. A pollen-diagram was prepared from the sand, and it shows a Climax-phase of deciduous woodland, with abundant pollen of *Quercus*; the diagram agrees very closely with the Climax-phase in the diagram from the English type-site at Ipswich itself. Unfortunately, as we have already seen, the early stages of woodland development in the different warm stages were very similar, and it is difficult to be emphatic that this Climax-phase must be Ipswichian and not Gortian. The main difference between the Shortalstown diagram and a Gortian one at a similar phase is the amount of *Ulmus* pollen present, even though the quantity is only small. Pollen of *Ulmus* is almost unknown from Gortian deposits, and no Gortian diagram shows such amounts of *Ulmus* pollen as are seen at Shortalstown. In the field the fossiliferous sand appeared to separate two different tills, rather than be an erratic lump of sand caught up in one till, and it seems reasonable to regard this deposit also as belonging to the 'missing' warm stage.

As well as pollen, Shortalstown yielded macrofossils, chiefly of plants and of marine molluscs. By the time we reach this relatively recent warm stage the flora and fauna of north-west Europe were not very different from what they are today, but Shortalstown did produce one important find. This was a seed of a plant now extinct in Europe, but still growing in the central United States, *Decodon*, the water willow, a member of the loosestrife family.

It did formerly grow in Europe, and its seeds are known fossil from the Neogene to the Lower Pleistocene. It is yet another example of an American plant that seems to have survived longer in Ireland than in the more continental parts of Europe.

During the central part of this warm stage sea-level will have been high, and evidence from estuarine and beach deposits in England suggests that at its maximum the Ipswichian sea-level was perhaps 7·5 m above its present level. Again evidence from Ireland is almost totally lacking, but a possible beach of this age occurs on the coast at Cahore, Co. Wexford. Below a Midlandian till there is a small deposit about 1 m thick of well-rounded pebbles with horizontal axes, suggesting a beach. Most of the pebbles are of local stone, but there are some erratics. The deposit rests on head, which in turn rests on solid rock. The deposit is about 3 m above spring-tide highwater mark, but it has to be remembered that along this part of the Irish coast the modern tidal range is very small.

The eroding force of the ice and frost of the Munsterian Cold Stage had in many parts of Ireland left rock exposed at the surface of the ground. Throughout the following warm period the rock was subject to chemical attack, a type of attack to which granite is particularly vulnerable. Earth movements bring about cracking in solid rock, and very often more than one set of cracks or *joints* intersect, so that the upper layers of the granite can be pictured as a mass of closely packed, if somewhat irregular, cubes, rather than as solid rock. Water percolates along the cracks, and from them its chemical attack moves out into the stone, being especially severe at the corners of the cubes.

The upper part of the rock thus becomes a weathered mush of loose debris, which contains within itself, like currants in a cake, the rounded blocks or *core-stones* of intact rock which had survived in the centre of the cubes. The contact between the weathered rind and the solid rock below is often irregular, again due to the influence of the joint-pattern.

When the Midlandian Cold Stage came on, and freeze-thaw processes again became active, the superficial weathered debris crept away downslope. The core-stones were left behind, littering the surface, while prominences on the irregular surface of the solid rock stood up as tors. If a granitic area escaped being overrun by ice, as was the case with two headlands at opposite ends of Ireland, the Bloody Foreland in Donegal and Carnsore Point in Wexford – and with the Three-rock Mountain south of Dublin, because it stood up above the ice – then the core-stones and the tors will still survive. Where the granite was overrun by ice, as was the case with Killiney Hill near Dublin, the core-stones have been carried off, and the upstanding tors have been drastically abraded and turned into elongated rounded bosses, the elongation being parallel with the direction of ice-movement. Such bosses of abraded rock, from which the direction of ice-movement can be deduced, are known to the geologist as *roches moutonnées*, because nineteenth-century observers thought their outline resembled that of a *moutonnée*, a type of sheepskin wig then in fashion. (Pl. 9)

THE MIDLANDIAN COLD STAGE

There would seem to be a consensus of opinion that the last cold stage, called in Ireland the Midlandian, because its deposits are well displayed in the Midlands, began about 70,000 years ago and ended 10,000 years ago. Over most of this range of time radiocarbon dating can be of great assistance, and the Geological Society correlation-table took advantage of this to divide the stage into three sub-stages – Early, from 70,000 to 50,000 years ago; Middle, from 50,000 to 26,000 years ago; and Late, from 26,000 to 10,000 years ago. This division is based on study of the numerous organic deposits belonging to the last cold stage that are known in Britain, Holland and Denmark, and the combination of biological data and radiocarbon dates arising from these studies has made it possible to suggest a temperature curve for this stage. On the assumption that climatic movements will have been essentially the same throughout north-west Europe, a version of this curve, adjusted to fit what we know of climatic events in Ireland, is given overleaf.

The cold stage probably began with fluctuating climate, but then there was a period between 55,000 and 50,000 years ago when the climate was very cold, and the question arises, 'Did ice-masses form at this time, or was it a period of dry polar deserts without ice?' In England the answer to this question is generally considered to be 'No', because there does not seem to be any evidence of ice-masses before about 20,000 years ago. In Ireland the answer is uncertain, largely because of lack of adequate information.

The boundary between the Early and the Middle part of the cold stage is placed at the rise in temperature that took place about 50,000 years ago. We now come to the cause of our Irish uncertainty. Much of Fermanagh is covered by drumlins which are probably of Late Midlandian age. At Holly-mount, near Lisnaskea, a river has cut a cliff in the flank of a drumlin. Beneath the till that is moulded into drumlin form there is a silt with washed-in vegetable debris derived from a tundra landscape; the vegetable debris was given a radiocarbon age of more than 41,500 years, and Professor Shotton, who carried out the dating in Birmingham, considers that the material may be of interglacial age. But the silt passed downwards into arctic clay, and this rested directly on unweathered calcareous till. If the deposit was interglacial, and the underlying till was thus of Munsterian age, it is not unreasonable to think that its surface should have undergone some weathering during the subsequent interglacial or warm stage. But the stratigraphical sequence – unweathered till, arctic clay, silt with tundra plant debris – appeared to be uninterrupted, and the till may belong to the cold spell at the end of the Early Midlandian, and the plant debris to a phase of warmth or interstadial in the Middle Midlandian.

Evidence from England suggests that there were several fluctuations in climate in the Middle Midlandian. In Ireland such a fluctuation or inter-stadial is recorded at Derryvree, also in Co. Fermanagh, only a few kilo-metres away from Hollymount. Here a drumlin was sectioned artificially in the course of a road-straightening operation, and again underneath till that had been moulded into drumlin form, there was a thin layer of mud and

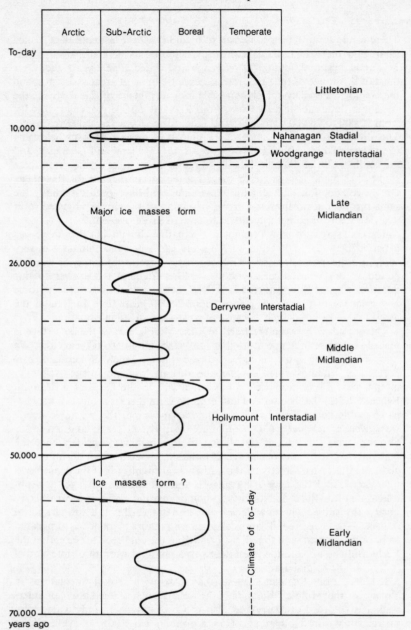

An outline curve to indicate possible temperature range during the Midlandian Cold Stage.

moss-peat containing a flora and a beetle-fauna of tundra aspect; the layer had a radiocarbon age of 30,500 years, and rested on a lower till whose surface showed no signs of either having been weathered or affected by frost action before the organic material was deposited on it. Again the problem arises – Is the lower till of Munsterian or of Early Midlandian age?

In contrast to other countries, almost nothing is known about mammalian life in Ireland during the Pleistocene. Only one cave, that at Castlepook, Co. Cork, has produced a substantial fauna, and here the bones did not lie as originally deposited, but had been re-distributed by later running water. Bones of the Late Pleistocene elephant, *Elephas primigenius*, the Woolly Mammoth, were very common, and ranged in size from those of adults to those of unborn foetuses. The cave also produced the only bones of the Spotted Hyena, *Crocuta crocuta*, ever to be found in Ireland. The cave contained some recent animal bones, brought in by modern foxes, but the Pleistocene fauna can probably be listed as follows:

Woolly Mammoth	*Elephas primigenius*
Brown Bear	*Ursus arctos*
Spotted Hyena	*Crocuta crocuta*
Wolf	*Canis lupus*
Arctic Fox	*Alopex lagopus*
Irish Giant Deer	*Megaloceros giganteus*
Reindeer	*Rangifer tarandus*
Horse	*Equus caballus*
Mountain Hare	*Lepus timidus*
Norwegian Lemming	*Lemmus lemmus*
Greenland Lemming	*Dicrostonyx torquatus*

A Mammoth bone from the cave has recently been given the radiocarbon age of 33,500 years, and thus the Castlepook animals may well have lived during the Derryvree interstadial. In England numerous finds of Woolly Mammoth have been made in the Severn basin and one find in a cave in north Wales, and radiocarbon datings give a range between 40,000 and 18,000 years ago; no younger finds are known, and the Woolly Mammoth may have failed to survive the last major advance of ice. If this is the case all the Irish finds of Woolly Mammoth may well fall in the same time range as those from Britain.

What did the Irish landscape look like when these herds of Mammoth were wandering through it? The Castlepook cave and two other caves with Mammoth remains are in the Carboniferous limestone of the Blackwater valley, where there will have been both shelter and fertile soil material, and we probably had rich grasslands with scattered copses of birch and willow, where the Mammoth and the Giant Deer browsed and grazed, and the Bear and the Hyena prowled around scavenging. The tree growth cannot have been dense, because the Giant Deer could not cope with closed woodland. On the other hand bare tundra would probably not have provided sufficient food for the Mammoth, and although the Pleistocene range of the Hyena went farther north than that of today, it is doubtful if it pushed up into the tundra zone. Climatic conditions in the Blackwater valley may have been

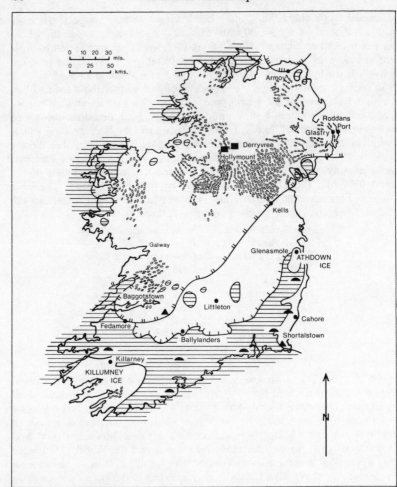

0 10 20 30 ┗━━━━┛ mls.
0 25 50 ┗━━━━┛ kms.

Armoy

Roddans
Port
Glasfry

Derryvree
Hollymount

Kells

Galway

Glenasmole
ATHDOWN
ICE

Baggotstown

Littleton

Cahore

Fedamore

Ballylanders

Shortalstown

Killarney

KILLUMNEY
ICE

N

○○○○○○	DRUMLINS
⊟	AREAS NOT COVERED BY ICE
┴┴┴┴	LIMIT OF FIRST ICE-MASS OVER MIDLANDS
ᴜᴜᴜ	LIMIT OF SECOND ICE-MASS OVER MIDLANDS
ᴜᴜᴜ	LIMIT OF LATE ADVANCE FROM SCOTLAND
▲	DEPOSITS OF PRECEDING WARM STAGE
■	DEPOSITS OF MIDDLE MIDLANDIAN AGE
⌐	PINGOS

specially favourable, but there is one old and enigmatic record that suggests that the mammoth may also have wandered farther north in Ireland. In 1715 during the construction of a mill near Belturbet the molar teeth and a substantial part of the skeleton of an elephant, almost certainly a Woolly Mammoth, were found. The locality is in drumlin country, and it is not impossible that when the foundations for the mill were being dug part of a drumlin was cut away to reveal, as at Derryvree, a Middle Midlandian organic deposit which contained the mammoth bones.

After 26,000 years ago more severe climatic conditions set in again, and this deterioration ushers in the Late Midlandian, when large masses of ice formed in the British Isles. As in the earlier Munsterian Cold Stage a stream of ice from Scotland moved down the basin of the Irish Sea. On its western flank as far south as Wicklow it was in contact with ice that had formed in the Irish Midlands, but from its eastern flank it was able to send a lobe south-eastwards into the Cheshire plain. This advance came to a halt in Staffordshire, where its till of Irish Sea origin rests on interstadial deposits of Middle Midlandian age. There is no sign of an earlier Midlandian till in this area, and it is for this reason that many English workers think that in the last cold stage ice-masses did not form before the beginning of the Late Midlandian. The main stream of ice continued down the Irish Sea to the vicinity of Carnsore Point in Ireland and of St David's Head in Wales, and recent submarine investigations have shown that to the north of a line joining these two points the sea floor is thickly covered with glacial deposits, whereas south of the line the deposits are much more patchy.

The Irish ice formed as an oval mass over the Midlands, with its long axis running approximately from Belfast to Limerick. We can trace its southern and south-eastern limits, but on the west its deposits lie below those of a still later advance, while in the north and east it was confluent with the Scottish ice. On the south it was halted against the northern slopes of the Galty Mountains, the Ballyhoura Hills, and the rock escarpment that limits the Limerick plain on the south-west. Lobes of ice pushed south at both ends of the Ballyhoura Hills, and the end-moraine of Ballylanders between the Ballyhouras and the Galtees gives its name to this advance. From each of these lobes escaping meltwaters carried gravels into the Blackwater valley. (Pl. 8)

On its south-east flank the ice encircled the Castlecomer plateau, which stood up as a nunatak. The ice also failed to override the high ground of County Wicklow, and big lakes were dammed up between the ice and the mountain slopes. As a result splendid examples of lake clays, glacial deltas, overflow channels and sub-glacial chutes can be seen in this area. North of the mountains and around their margin as far as Wicklow town the ice was confluent with the ice of Scottish origin in the basin of the Irish Sea.

The location of warm stage sites, possibly of Ipswichian age, extent of ice-masses of Midlandian Cold Stage, distribution of drumlins, location of Middle Midlandian interstadial sites, and some pingo localities.

The ice-masses then started to shrink, but after the ice in the Irish Sea had withdrawn a short distance from its limit near Carnsore Point, there seems to have been a standstill just north of Wexford town, because in the Curracloe area there is an enormous end-moraine of shelly sands and gravels, pitted by innumerable kettle-holes, both large and small. (Pl. 6)

An extensive melting-out followed, and much of the Irish lowlands probably became ice-free. The Irish ice-mass then re-established itself, but this time the axis had moved slightly north-west, and now ran from Scattery Island – largely built up of end-moraine – in the Shannon Estuary to Fair Head in Antrim. The lower Shannon basin was filled with ice, and from here the eastern margin ran north-eastwards through Kells to reach the modern coast-line at Dundalk. From Dundalk the edge ran round the north-west flanks of Carlingford Mountain and the Mournes, and out into the Irish Sea. North-east Ireland was covered by ice, but it is not clear how much was of Irish, and how much of Scottish origin. The two ice-masses confronted one another here, just like two opposing sets of forwards in a Rugby scrum, and the result-ing thrusting and wheeling has produced a series of glacial deposits more than usually confused.

To the north-west the ice must have been rather thinner, because on the whole it failed to overrun higher ground, and rather followed the lower corridors wherever they offered an escape route. Thus the present sites of Galway Bay, Clew Bay, Sligo Bay and Gweebarra Bay were all occupied by lobes of ice. As we have seen the higher ground of the Bloody Foreland was not covered.

For some quite unexplained reason the ice of this later advance at some stage of its development moulded the underlying deposits it gave rise to into drumlins, so much so that Francis Synge has been tempted to call it the Drumlin Advance. Numbering thousands, they were often aligned in serried ranks, giving rise to the so-called 'basket-of-eggs' topography. In areas of lower topography they blocked the surface drainage routes and were often separated by standing water. Thousands of years later when separated by water and covered by dense woodland, they provided a severe obstacle to man's lines of communication. As the sea at the time the drumlins were formed was far below its present level, many were formed below modern sea-level, and are today being attacked by the waves, as in Strangford Lough and Clew Bay. (Pls. 6, 22)

At some phase of the Midlandian small ice-caps formed in the mountains of Wicklow, and of west Cork and Kerry, and it is of interest that even the small southern ice-cap succeeded in forming drumlins of its own, as can be seen around the head of Bantry Bay. In Wicklow, where Farrington has described the Athdown Mountain Glaciation, the local ice was still capable of advance after the lowland ice had retreated, because granitic outwash from the mountains rests on the arctic clays that had been deposited in temporary lakes dammed up in the mountain valleys by the ice from the Midlands. In Cork and Kerry the ice that stretched to Killumney in the east, to Killarney in the north and to Waterville in the west did not reach that part of Limerick that was glaciated by ice from the Midlands, and it is not possible to say what the time-relation between the two ice-masses was. It is tempting to think that the Killumney ice-mass in the south-west was contemporaneous with the Athdown ice-cap in the Wicklow Mountains. There were also active corrie and valley glaciers in the mountains of the Dingle Peninsula at some phase of the Midlandian.

If we return to the lowlands, we can find today within the area formerly covered by the later ice-mass extensive deposits of the type associated with the ablation of 'dead' ice, that is eskers and irregular mounds of morainic sands and gravels. This suggests that the snow supply was cut off relatively abruptly, and that the ice gradually disappeared with very little disturbance of the englacial material. The Scottish ice-mass may have retained some vigour after the Irish one had collapsed, because a final advance from Scotland brought ice once more to the Antrim coast and up the Bush valley as far as Armoy, where there is a prominent moraine. (Pls. 6, 7)

We have seen that in the Munsterian Cold Stage there was a substantial depression of the basin of the Irish Sea underneath the accumulated weight of ice. Similar downward movement, though on a smaller scale, took place during the Midlandian Cold Stage, so that as the ice disappeared from north-east Ireland the sea, though still at a glacial level many metres below its present one, was able to flood in over the depressed land, and form beaches at its margins. Subsequent isostatic recovery has raised the oldest of these beaches to a height of 20 m above modern sea-level. There are younger beaches at lower levels, and a start has been made on the work of relating beaches at different levels to stages of ice retreat. Unfortunately the beaches have not yet produced any fossils which might be of help in dating them. (See figure overleaf and Pl. 10).

When the Midlandian ice finally disappeared, many of the areas it had covered presented an essentially 'young' landscape, that is they showed either features associated with recent ice scouring and moulding, or features associated with ice deposition – unweathered till, steeply sloping drumlins, and sharp-sided eskers. What of the areas that were not glaciated during the Midlandian, but had been covered by Munsterian ice, and where similar 'young' features must have existed immediately after the retreat of that ice? Such features were in the 'periglacial' zone of the Midlandian, and were subject to attack by the freeze-thaw processes of that cold stage. Where solid rock was concerned, water could easily percolate into cracks, and then expanding as it froze prise off blocks and fragments which crept away down-slope to accumulate as scree or head at lower levels. In the case of uncon-solidated deposits, their vulnerability depended largely on the relative amounts of clay, silt, sand and gravel that they contained. Sands and gravels are not easily affected, and some eskers and kames of Munsterian age still stand with quite steep slopes. But where clay and silt dominated, freeze-thaw processes could mobilize the materials, and given the necessary degree of slope great solifluction-flows would be set in motion, only coming to a halt in lake-basins, valley-bottoms and similar places where the necessary gradient was no longer available. On these stretches of flatter ground polygonal patterns and involutions would develop.

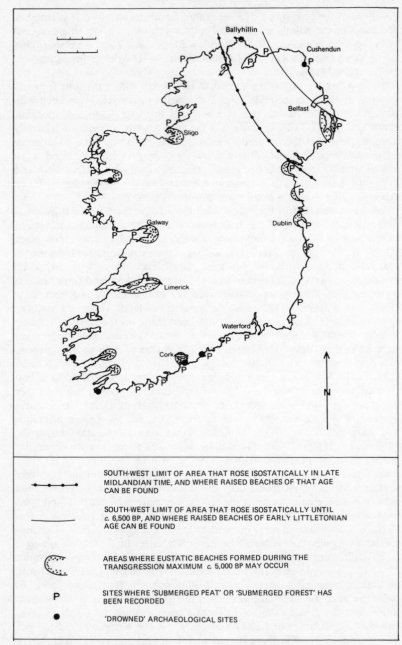

SOUTH-WEST LIMIT OF AREA THAT ROSE ISOSTATICALLY IN LATE MIDLANDIAN TIME, AND WHERE RAISED BEACHES OF THAT AGE CAN BE FOUND

SOUTH-WEST LIMIT OF AREA THAT ROSE ISOSTATICALLY UNTIL *c.* 6,500 BP, AND WHERE RAISED BEACHES OF EARLY LITTLETONIAN AGE CAN BE FOUND

AREAS WHERE EUSTATIC BEACHES FORMED DURING THE TRANSGRESSION MAXIMUM *c.* 5,000 BP MAY OCCUR

P SITES WHERE 'SUBMERGED PEAT' OR 'SUBMERGED FOREST' HAS BEEN RECORDED

● 'DROWNED' ARCHAEOLOGICAL SITES

Late coastal changes in Ireland

Thus in the areas, largely in Munster, where freeze-thaw and not glacial conditions dominated during the Midlandian Cold Stage, there is on the whole an 'older' smoother landscape, where sections usually show erected stones, involutions and head, whereas farther north where there was Midlandian ice the topography is 'younger' and more irregular, and sections rarely show the churning action of frost. This concept of areas of 'Newer Drift', with steep slopes and open lake-basins, as opposed to 'Older Drift' with more gentle slopes and only rare open-water lakes, was much used by older generations of glacial geologists. It then fell rather into disrepute, but second thoughts suggest that it should not be too lightly discarded. The contrast in the two landscapes is sometimes quite striking. Midlandian ice advanced down the Shannon Estuary as far as Scattery Island in midstream and Ballylongford on the south shore. Within the Midlandian limit around Ballylongford we have hummocky topography and well-drained soils; outside the limit – and with an abrupt change – we have smooth slopes of poorly-drained soils, heavily infested with rushes (*Juncus* spp.). (Pls. 10, 25)

In the Midlandian Cold Stage much of the south of Ireland was never covered by ice, and most of the rest of the country was probably only physically covered by ice for relatively short periods. Was there any plant or animal life at this time? Our evidence from lowland Fermanagh shows that both 40,000 years ago at Hollymount, and 30,000 years ago at Derryvree, there was a sparse treeless vegetation of tundra type with beetles characteristic of a cold climate with very severe winters. Some of the northern plants recorded in Middle Midlandian Fermanagh, such as

Arenaria ciliata	Fringed Sandwort
Dryas octopetala	Mountain Avens
Oxyria digyna	Mountain Sorrel
Salix herbacea	Least Willow
Saxifraga oppositifolia	Purple Saxifrage

still maintain a precarious foothold in Ireland.

The most important modern habitats for such plants in Ireland today are the cliffs and screes around the limestone blocks that rise to over 500 m in Co. Sligo, principally those around Ben Bulbin. These blocks were probably not overridden by ice at any phase of the Midlandian, and provided nunatak refuges for northern plants at times of ice advance. Slieve League, a quartzite peak with screes that rises to 600 m on the north shore of Donegal Bay, was also a nunatak and also has northern plants. If these plants could survive on nunataks in the north part of the country, they will also have survived in suitable habitats in the ice-free areas of Munster. (Pl. 1)

Thus 'cold polar desert' is perhaps too stern a term by which to describe Ireland during the Midlandian Cold Stage, if by 'polar desert' we mean a '*tabula rasa*' from which all life has been swept away. At the peaks of cold there may have been very little life, but for much of the stage the landscape will have been strewn with scanty patches of arctic-alpine plants, with some beetles in ponds and patches of vegetable debris. In the interstadial represented by the Castlepook fauna conditions must have been relatively genial, at least in areas with favourable aspect and fertile well-drained soils. If they were to live and breed in the country, the Woolly Mammoths must have had access to substantial quantities of rich fodder. It may have been possible for the hardier reindeer to survive in Ireland throughout the cold stage.

THE ABSENCE OF LARGE MAMMALS AND OF PALAEOLITHIC MAN

In marked contrast to Ireland, where we have only one limited mammalian fauna of Middle Midlandian age at Castlepook, many parts of the world have fossil remains of rich mammalian faunas which often assist in deciphering Pleistocene events. In England good assemblages are known from several warm stages, while the Irish record is blank. Most of the mammalian finds come from river gravels, or from cave deposits. Much of the south of England was never covered by ice, and river gravels containing mammalian bones continued to build up through much of the Pleistocene. In Ireland the ice cover was extensive, even in Midlandian times, and nearly every major valley outside the ice limit served as a meltwater discharge channel into a sea whose level was much below that of today, so that any earlier gravels the valleys may have contained were scoured away. Ireland has no interglacial gravels such as those of Ipswichian age in Trafalgar Square in London, which have produced abundant remains of lion, hyena, rhinoceros, elephant and hippopotamus.

The Carboniferous limestone of Ireland contains many caves, but most of the limestone is at a relatively low altitude. All the limestone areas were probably overrun by ice during the Munsterian, and by far the greater part was again overrun during the Midlandian. When the ice stagnated, and meltwater was draining downwards, many cave systems served as escape routes for meltwater, and any deposits they contained were in part grossly disturbed and in part completely carried away. Nevertheless when all this has been said, it must be admitted that there are in the Lee and lower Blackwater valleys in Cork many cave systems which it would seem could have provided shelter for Ipswichian mammals, and where the bones might have escaped disturbance. But despite sporadic excavation over the past hundred years, no temperate mammalian faunas, such as those that occur in the caves of Devon, have been found.

Much of the cave excavation of the late nineteenth century was directed towards the discovery of 'Early Man', and it must at once be said that all the excavators went disappointed. In the first half of this century there was a revival of interest in the search, and various claims were made. Limestone flakes from Co. Sligo were claimed by Reid Moir and Burchell to be the handiwork of palaeolithic man, but were dismissed as entirely natural by Charlesworth and others. Kilgraeny Cave, Co. Waterford, produced human remains in apparent association with bones of the Giant Deer, but a later re-examination of the cave showed that the deposits in some places had been considerably disturbed. Radiocarbon dating of some of the human bones claimed to be early indicated that they were Neolithic, rather than Mesolithic or Palaeolithic in age.

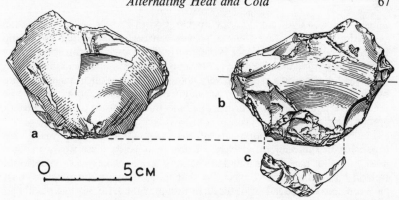

Palaeolithic flint flake from near Drogheda, Co. Louth: **a**, bulbar surface; **b**, dorsal surface; **c**, striking-platform.

A recent chance find has drawn attention to the problem once more. When examining the glacial gravel of Irish Sea origin and of Munsterian age that occurs in a big quarry near Drogheda, Co. Louth, I picked up from its stripped surface a large coarsely struck flint flake, which showed some signs of having been rolled and abraded by running water. It cannot be claimed that the object was *in situ* when I found it, but it would strain credibility to think that someone had dropped it on the recently stripped gravel surface a short time before my visit. Also the rolling is most easily explained if the flake belonged to the gravel, and had been rolled along with it.

On the assumption that the flake did belong to the gravel, I brought it to Gail Sieveking in the British Museum. He is satisfied that although the flake is no more than a piece of knapper's waste, it was struck by a technique that was in vogue in southern England in palaeolithic time. Palaeolithic implements are common in the south of England, but thin out rapidly northwards; a few have been found in central England. The Drogheda flake shows that the palaeolithic hunters pushed still farther north-westwards, out into what is now the basin of the Irish Sea. When in Munsterian times ice was advancing southwards from Scotland the flake – along with stones and other debris – was first picked up by the ice, and was subsequently washed out of the melting ice by currents which deposited it in gravel on the Irish coast.

While the occurrence of this worked flake in Co. Louth cannot be claimed to establish the presence of palaeolithic man in Ireland, it does show that in Britain he wandered sufficiently far to the west to reach the basin of the Irish Sea.

THE WOODGRANGE INTERSTADIAL, AND THE RE-INVASION OF IRELAND BY PLANTS AND ANIMALS, INCLUDING THE GIANT DEER

Some scanty vegetation, chiefly northern grasses and arctic-alpine herbs, probably persisted in Ireland throughout much of the Midlandian Cold

Stage. About 14,000 years ago an amelioration of climate set in, and as the vegetational changes that followed have been best documented by Gurdip Singh in a pollen-diagram from Woodgrange, Co. Down, we can speak of the Woodgrange Interstadial or Warm Phase; it was no more than an interstadial as it was followed by a return to very cold conditions. Pollen-diagrams from other parts of Ireland show corresponding developments, though with some regional variation, and two further diagrams in addition to that from Woodgrange are illustrated (p. 71).

The vegetational developments of the interstadial were not merely an expansion of the plants that were already in Ireland; there was a massive immigration of new plants – and also of animals. Such easy movements into Ireland imply that land connections that made immigration possible must have replaced the glacial strait that had occupied the Irish Sea basin and had built up beaches round its margins. How was such a reversal possible? What was sea-level doing?

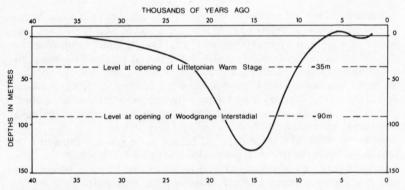

An outline curve to indicate possible course of sea-level during the Middle and Late Midlandian Cold Stage, and in the Littletonian Warm Stage.

It is now possible to build up a generalized curve for sea-level movements during the past 40,000 years. In the Midlandian Cold Stage the final big build-up of ice came very late, and the curve shows the steep eustatic fall in level as water was withdrawn from the oceans to be locked up as ice on land. In the British Isles the last ice may have reached its maximum about 20,000 years ago, but the ice-mass over North America, which was much larger than that of Europe, only reached its maximum later, about 15,000 years ago, and the curve shows that it was then that the sea reached its lowest level, about 130 m, say 450 ft, below that of today. From that low level it rose steadily until about 5000 years ago, when it stood about 4 m *above* its present level. Since then there have been minor oscillations, not as yet clearly understood, ending up – temporarily at least – at the present level.

The curve suggests that 13,000 years ago sea-level was still about 90 m (300 ft) below its present level, and at first sight it would seem that if we wish to see where the connections with Britain were, we need only take an Admiralty Chart of the waters around Ireland, and see how much land would appear if sea-level were lowered by 90 m. The result is a bridge to Scotland via Islay, a bridge to the Isle of Man and Anglesey and on east to the English mainland, and a third bridge from Wicklow to the Lleyn Peninsula. But before we become too dogmatic, we must first remember that what we measure today is the position of the sea floor after isostatic recovery had finally ended, and the topography of the sea floor after it had been modified by wave-action as the basin was being re-flooded.

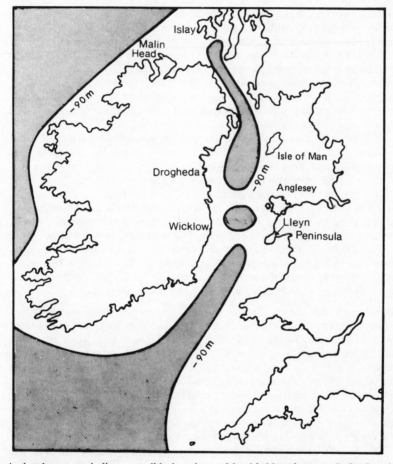

A sketch-map to indicate possible locations of land-bridges between Ireland and Great Britain during the Late Midlandian Cold Stage and the early Littletonian Warm Stage.

Late-glacial beaches, which give clear evidence of considerable isostatic recovery have not been traced south of Drogheda. From a relatively low level here they rise progressively northwards to reach their highest level, about 20 m above present sea-level, at Malin Head, the most northerly point of Ireland (see figure on p. 64). In the Woodgrange Interstadial the sea floor between Malin Head and Islay must have been far below its present level, and the land-connection will have been correspondingly narrower than the map suggests, if indeed it existed at all. (Pl. 10)

But between Wicklow and the Lleyn Peninsula subsequent isostatic uplift has been much smaller, and the ridge on the sea floor, almost certainly of morainic origin, will have stood above sea-level. North of the ridge the sea floor drops into a basin, and then rises again to a level less than 90 m below present sea-level. The Solway Firth, Morecambe Bay and Liverpool Bay would have been dry, with the Isle of Man rising as a mountain above relatively flat ground. A ridge stretched from west of Anglesey to the east coast of Ireland. To the north of this ridge lay the southern end of a deep trough which ran north between Down and Galloway and continued on below the North Channel almost as far as Islay. The origin of this trough, whose floor in places is 200 m below present sea-level, is not clear; it may be tectonic, it may be due to glacial erosion, or it may be due to tidal scour. There will have been a water-barrier here.

It is clear that movement into the Isle of Man presented no difficulty, because by 12,000 years ago at least eighty plant taxa had already reached the Isle of Man, and many more were pushing in; a large number of beetles and the Giant Deer were also present. Ireland's richest Woodgrange flora comes from a site near the Leinster coast at Mapastown, Co. Louth, and the plants – and the beetles – must have moved on easily into Ireland. The bridges of glacial material probably carried a varied pattern of soil materials, across which a wide range of plants and animals could quickly reach Ireland.

The schematic pollen-diagrams shown opposite have been drawn up to give some indication of vegetational development in Ireland during the warm Woodgrange Interstadial and the following cold Nahanagan Stadial, and to show that there was regional variation within the general pattern.

Woodgrange, Co. Down. This is the type-site for the Woodgrange Warm Phase or Interstadial. The basin which holds the deposits lies at sea-level between drumlins. The record probably begins about 15,000 years ago when conditions were arctic or sub-arctic, and there was an open vegetation with patches of grasses, sedges, flowering plants and scrub willows, producing on the whole only small amounts of pollen. There was then a marked increase in pollen output as improving climate enabled the plant cover to spread and develop a meadow-like aspect, with species of dock (*Rumex*) prominent in the meadows; we can speak of a Gramineae-*Rumex* pollen-assemblage-zone. This is the first phase of the Woodgrange Interstadial, lasting perhaps from 14,000 to 13,000 years ago. Juniper was then favoured by the continuing rise in temperature, and it was able to spread widely and flower freely, and we have the *Juniperus* pollen-assemblage-zone, which perhaps lasted from 13,000 to 12,000 years ago. Some of the plants recorded have today 'a remarkably

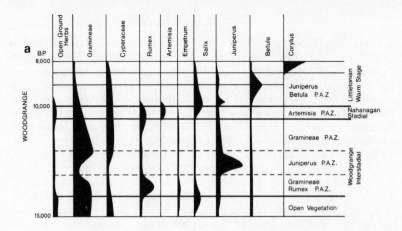

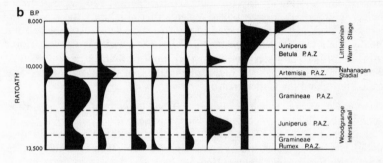

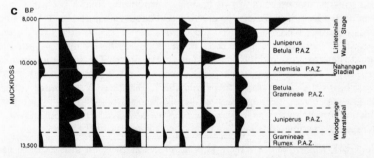

Pollen-diagrams to show the development of vegetation in the Woodgrange Inter-stadial and in the Nahanagan Stadial at a, Woodgrange, Co. Down (after G. Singh), b, Ratoath, Co. Meath (after Sylvia Peglar), and c, Muckross, near Killarney, Co. Kerry (after Elizabeth Huckerby).

southern, central or western European distribution', as Knud Jessen remarked over twenty years ago. Recent detailed studies by Russell Coope of an insect fauna of this phase from Shortalstown in Co. Wexford show that it closely resembles insect assemblages from England and Wales that date from about the same time. These faunas suggest a climate at least as warm as, or at times even warmer than that in the same areas at the present day. Finds of birch fruits show that tree-birches were in Ireland at this time, and if temperature had continued to improve, birch probably would have expanded into extensive woods. Instead the grasslands re-expand, and there is beetle evidence to show that temperature was now falling back. This is the Gramineae pollen-assemblage-zone, extending perhaps from 12,000 to 10,500 years ago. Climate then deteriorated rapidly, ending the Woodgrange Interstadial and ushering in the Nahanagan Cold Phase or Stadial. Periglacial conditions returned in strength on the lowlands, the continuous plant-cover broke up, and *Artemisia* (Mugwort) became common, giving its name to the pollen-assemblage-zone. *Salix*, probably *herbacea*, *Rumex* and arctic-alpine plants became more common. About 10,000 years ago climate started to improve again, and juniper expanded and flowered freely once more. This time there was no reversal, and continuing improvement allowed the birch to overshadow the juniper, and a peak in birch pollen replaces that in juniper; the grasses and herbs fall back as the trees spread in the *Juniperus-Betula* assemblage-zone. Finally at about 8500 years ago the hazel arrived in Ireland; *Corylus* cannot grow in northern latitudes, and its arrival confirms that the improvement in climate 10,000 years ago was indeed the opening of the current warm stage (called in Ireland the Littletonian).

Ratoath, Co. Meath. This basin lies at 100 m in an undulating till landscape. Here the record does not begin until the Gramineae-*Rumex* assemblage-zone is established, perhaps about 13,500 years ago. As the Woodgrange Interstadial proceeds, juniper shows a dramatic rise, and then falls away as the grasses rise to very high values. Here we have the late glacial grasslands at their greatest extension, and this basin has produced remains both of Giant Deer and of Reindeer. Today the area is again under rich grass, but is fattening herds of cattle, where it once fed the Giant Deer. The low values for *Betula* show that there cannot have been birch woods in the vicinity. Again the climate deteriorates, and the Nahanagan Stadial opens. The vegetation breaks up; sedges replace the grasses, and *Artemisia* and the open-ground herbs flourish. As the climatic tide turns and the Littletonian Warm Stage opens, the grasses show a fleeting recovery before being overshadowed by juniper, which in turn gives way as it is crowded out by extensive birch woods in which there are also some willows. The birch then gives way to the hazel.

Muckross, Killarney, Co. Kerry. This basin lies at 20 m on thin till on limestone. As at Ratoath, the record begins in the Woodgrange Gramineae-*Rumex* assemblage-zone, and the vegetational picture is very similar, except that *Empetrum* (Crowberry) is rather more common. This is probably a reflection of the western and relatively oceanic location of the site, as *Empetrum* is still more common in the sites investigated by Professor Jessen at Roundstone in Co. Galway. The subsequent rise in juniper is at this site accompanied by a rise in birch, and in the later part of the interstadial there are substantial amounts of birch pollen as well as grass pollen, and here we can speak of a *Betula*-Gramineae assemblage-zone. Thus in contrast to the other two sites there must have been a considerable expanse of birch wood in the Killarney district at this time. In the Nahanagan Stadial birch pollen falls away but that of the grasses holds its own level. Sedges and open ground herbs increase strikingly, but the amount of *Artemisia* pollen is small. This appears to be a local phenomenon, as in other diagrams from the Killarney area, *Artemisia* shows typical values at this level. Juniper then shows its peak at the opening of the Littletonian Warm Stage, and is quickly crowded out by birch and willow, which in turn give way to invading *Corylus*.

It is evident that there were rapid changes in the Irish landscape as the Midlandian Cold Stage was ending. About 14,000 years ago a wave of green spread over the countryside as meadows rich in docks and other herbs replaced the open vegetation. Juniper thickets then invaded the meadows only to fall back as grasslands became dominant once more. In the Killarney area the grasslands were interspersed with birch woods, but at both Ratoath and Woodgrange they were virtually treeless; at Ratoath they provided rich fodder for Giant Deer and Reindeer. The plant cover then collapsed as conditions of severe frost made a fleeting return for a period of about 500 years. About 10,000 years ago the return of the modern vegetation began in earnest.

It was in Ireland, during this grassland phase of the Woodgrange Interstadial, that that magnificent animal, the Irish Giant Deer (*Megaloceros giganteus*), reached the zenith of its success, only to be struck down, like Lucifer in full flight, by the abrupt climatic deterioration which followed. That deterioration restored freeze-thaw conditions, which broke up the plant-cover and allowed sand and clay (often containing remains of arctic plants) to be washed down into lake-basins. As a result the Woodgrange muds and peats in which the remains of the Giant Deer are typically found are usually sealed by a layer of sandy clay, an observation first made two hundred and fifty years ago.

A letter of 1725 from Downpatrick, Co. Down, states, 'Under this appears a stratum of blue clay, half a foot thick, fully mixed with shells; then appears the right marl, commonly two, three or four feet deep, and in some places much deeper, which looks like buried lime, or the lime that tanners throw out of their lime-pits, only that it is fully mixed with shells – such as the Scots call "fresh-water wilks". Among this marl, and often at the bottom of it, we find very great horns, which we, for want of another name, call "Elk-horns". We have also found shanks and other bones of these beasts in the same place.' The shells referred to are those of freshwater molluscs, and investigations in the same area many years later by Arthur Stelfox revealed fossil molluscan faunas of great interest, including arctic types no longer living in Ireland.

The same stratigraphy was also well known to Williams, an energetic nineteenth-century taxidermist and dealer in natural history specimens, and the illustration which he contributed to Millais's book on *British Deer and their Horns* is shown overleaf. The method of probing shown is the same that was used by country folk to locate buried timbers in bogs at times when wood was short in Ireland. The stratigraphy was again confirmed in 1934 by Knud Jessen when he worked at Ballybetagh Bog in Co. Dublin, a site long

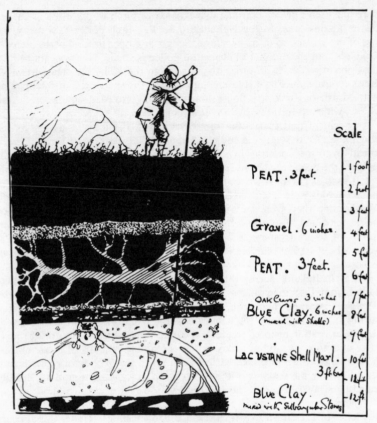

Scale

PEAT. 3 feet.

Gravel. 6 inches.

PEAT. 3 feet.

OAK Cones 3 inches
Blue Clay. 6 inches
(mixed with Shells)

Lacustrine Shell Marl.
3 ft 6 in

Blue Clay.
mixed with Subangular Stones

- 1 foot
- 2 feet
- 3 feet
- 4 feet
- 5 feet
- 6 feet
- 7 feet
- 8 feet
- 9 feet
- 10 feet
- 11 feet
- 12 ft.

Finding bones of the Giant Deer.

famous because of the large quantities of remains of Giant Deer and of reindeer that it had produced for Williams and other collectors. Since 1934 about twenty-five further finds of remains of Giant Deer have been investigated in the field, and in each case the remains were at the same stratigraphical horizon. Radiocarbon dating now enables us to put a date in years on the lake-mud in which the bones are entombed; a mud from Knocknacran was given an age of 11,300 years and a mud from Shortalstown 12,150 years, ages which are compatible with the Woodgrange Interstadial. (Pl. 31)

What is the record of the Giant Deer outside Ireland? Its ancestors appear in early Pleistocene deposits in western Eurasia, but a related form appears as far away as China. In the later Pleistocene the Giant Deer was widely spread through Europe, northern Asia and northern Africa. In western Europe, as in Ireland, it seems to have become extinct about 10,000 years ago, but there are suggestions that it survived in Syria and southern Russia almost until the birth of Christ. It was in England during the Hoxnian Warm Stage, and was also there when the Giant Deer was undergoing its final expansion in Ireland, though numbers in England appear to have remained very much smaller. A Swedish find was dated to 11,330 years ago.

As far as western Europe is concerned, we can picture the Giant Deer as a restless wanderer throughout much of the later Pleistocene. He could not go north to the tundras, because there he could not get sufficient nourishment to sustain him, nor south to the forests, because there the spread of his antlers would impede his movements. He lived on the intervening grasslands, which became poorer to the north, and interspersed with bushes to the south. With every climatic shift these belts of vegetation would be correspondingly displaced, and as the grasslands wandered, so the Giant Deer had to wander also. He was in Ireland about 30,000 years ago, he was then expelled by Late Midlandian ice, and about 13,000 years ago he returned for the last time.

What did he look like? He was a splendid deer, standing about 2 m high at the shoulders, and over 3 m to the tips of the antlers. Only the male carried antlers, and these could have a span of almost 3 m, and a dry weight of about 30 kilogrammes. The antlers were shed annually, and had to be grown again, to a still larger size, each spring. The necessity to produce so much bony tissue so rapidly must have placed a tremendous physiological strain on the animal, and necessitated the consumption of large amounts of nutritious vegetable matter, rich in calcium. Though heavy in weight and impressive in appearance, the antlers were structurally very feeble, with elongated points mounted on the edge of a thin curved plate. They would have been useless in combat, and their only function can have been to impress. Like a Monarch of the Glen, the master stag of the herd would stand on some hillock in full view of the younger males and slowly raise and lower his magnificent antlers, and trust that at least on that occasion his status would go unchallenged. (Pl. 11)

What did he want? Two things, rich and abundant food, and freedom from predators. The soils of Ireland in the Woodgrange Interstadial were rich in fresh and unweathered mineral matter, especially calcium carbonate, and the plant cover must have been equally rich, at least for a short time, until the nutrient minerals had either been absorbed by the plants, or washed out of the soil by weathering. In the warmer part of the interstadial there would have been an abundance of rich grass and bushes, ideal food for the Giant Deer, and even in the later phases when grass-covered prairie, largely uninterrupted by trees and bushes, would have been the rule, there probably was sufficient sustenance for the herds.

A distribution-map of the remains makes this relationship with fertile soils quite plain (see figure overleaf), even when we allow for the selective nature of such records. If an animal is to leave fossil remains, it must die in circumstances that will make preservation possible. Countless Giant Deer doubtless died in open country without leaving any evidence behind them; it is only those whose remains were dragged into caves by wolves or foxes, or those which were drowned in lakes or ponds that provide us with fossil material. In Ireland lakes and caves tend to be on the lowlands, and this must influence

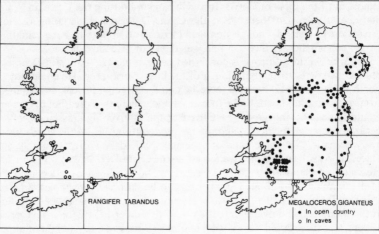

Localities where remains of *Rangifer tarandus* (Reindeer) and *Megaloceros giganteus* (Giant Deer) have been found in Ireland.

the pattern of fossil distribution. But the map does make abundantly clear the way that finds are concentrated in the Limerick region; today Limerick is still noted for the richness of its grasslands which make it one of the centres of the Irish dairy industry. Records are also abundant in Co. Down, which today supplies Belfast with its liquid milk, and in Co. Meath, now an important region for fattening cattle. By contrast the mountainous regions of Donegal, Mayo and Kerry with their poor and acid soils are empty of records. The blanks in the Midlands are probably due not to the lack of fossils, but to the fact that thick accumulations of peat have buried the remains beyond reach of casual discovery. Lowland areas with rich grasslands were frequented by the Giant Deer, the infertile parts of the country were avoided.

Ponds and lakes have provided many records. How did so many come to be drowned, often a large number in the one lake? The lake-margin will have been floored by soft muds and clays, concealed beneath a floating mat of succulent water-plants. An animal might come down to drink or to feed, and find one foot becoming embedded in the mud. The struggle to extricate the trapped foot might lead to the others becoming enmired, and occasionally the desperate trampings are recorded by disturbances in the muds immediately below the skeleton. For the males the heavy antlers will have made balance especially precarious, and if the animal once went down, it will have found it hard to regain its feet. Death would quickly follow.

Predators offered little threat. There is no record of the lion (*Felis leo*) from Ireland, and this animal had probably disappeared from England long before this later interstadial began. There will have been wolves and arctic foxes, but while these will have preyed on old animals and sickly calves it is unlikely that they will have offered much threat to the herds. Man was still absent from Ireland, and there were no bands of specialized hunters like those who followed the reindeer herds in northern Europe. The Giant Deer must have found conditions in Ireland almost idyllic, and proceeded to expand in numbers accordingly. Conditions in England must have been very similar, and it is not easy to see why the Giant Deer should be so common in Ireland, and by comparison so very rare in Britain, except in the Isle of Man where numerous finds have been made.

Though records of its remains are very much less common, the reindeer was also in Ireland at this time, and its distribution is generally similar to that of the Giant Deer. There are no records of other mammals from open country in the interstadial.

THE FINAL COLD SNAP

It has long been known that the uninterrupted return of warmth that marked the opening of the postglacial – or Littletonian Warm Stage – in which we live, was immediately preceded by a short spell of final cold, but until recently it had not been realized both how short it was, and how cold it was. Radiocarbon has been able to tell us that the cold spell began about 10,500 years ago and that it ended about 10,000 years ago, and it therefore had a duration of not more than 500 years.

Lough Nahanagan is a corrie lake at about 400 m in the Wicklow Mountains. It lies at the head of Glendasan, a valley that has been glaciated on more than one occasion. The corrie was probably occupied by a substantial ice-mass in the cold phase at the opening of the Late Midlandian, and a big moraine was thrown across its mouth. The modern lake behind the moraine has been developed as part of a pumped-storage generating system, and during the course of construction it was necessary to drain the lake temporarily. As water level fell, it revealed a series of very small moraines banked against the hillside. These were studied in detail by Francis Synge and Eric Colhoun, who soon found that the moraines had got lumps of organic mud embedded in them. The mud had a radiocarbon age of 11,500 years, a pollen picture that suggested the transition from the *Juniperus* to the Gramineae pollen-assemblage-zone, and macroscopic remains of arctic-alpine plants. It was clear that the mud had formed in the Woodgrange Interstadial in an earlier lake held up by the main moraine, and had then been ploughed up by the ice of a smaller later glacier that re-occupied part of the pre-existing corrie, and formed the small inner moraines. As this was the first site to demonstrate that the cold spell was severe enough for glacier ice to form in Ireland, the cold phase has been named the Nahanagan Stadial. In Scotland a small ice-cap formed on high ground at this time, and its ice advanced as far south as Loch Lomond. But the volume of ice formed was small, and it is unlikely that the continuing upward rise of the land by isostatic recovery and of the level of the sea by eustatic release of meltwater was seriously interrupted.

Other evidence also points to severe cold. Both at Howth in Co. Dublin, and at Old Head, near Louisburgh in Mayo, solifluction moved till downslope where it buried organic deposits of Woodgrange age. There may even have been permafrost; Late Midlandian outwash gravels in Co. Tyrone are

penetrated by ice-wedge-casts, which can only have formed after the gravels
had been deposited. They may have formed in the Nahanagan Stadial, and
if so they indicate a mean annual temperature of less than −5°C. Pingos
may have formed in Wexford at this time; at Camaross it was difficult to
locate any early sediments in the pingo basins, but in one basin deposits had
only started to form late in the Nahanagan Stadial. Pingos in Wales tell the
same story. Again very severe cold is indicated.

The fossil evidence is similar. At Drumurcher, Co. Monaghan, a basin in
between Late Midlandian drumlins yielded a muddy silt, dated to 10,500
years ago, which contained remains of about 100 species of beetle. Many of

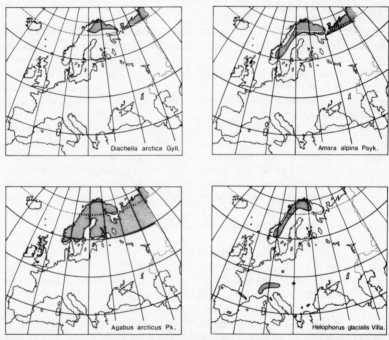

The modern distribution of some beetles which were in Ireland in the Nahanagan
Stadial.

the beetles indicated an arctic or sub-arctic regime, such as occurs today in the
lower alpine regions of the mountains of Scandinavia or the tundra regions
of the far north. Modern distribution-maps for four beetles typical of those
discovered at Drumurcher make this clear; *Diacheila arctica* is today confined
to the high north; *Amara alpina* extends south down the mountains of
Scandinavia, and also occurs in the higher Scottish mountains; *Agabus
arcticus* is widely distributed in the north of Europe and of Britain, and has
outlying stations in Ireland; *Helophorus glacialis* was, when climate was cold,

widely distributed throughout western Europe, and still maintains a precarious foothold in the mountains of Scandinavia, the Alps and the Pyrenees.

The Drumurcher silt also produced the first seed so far found in Ireland of the Arctic Poppy (*Papaver radicatum* s.l.); today the distribution of this plant is strictly arctic circumpolar, and Great Britain, too, has only produced one fossil seed, from a deposit of comparable age in Berwickshire.

In south-west Ireland arctic-alpine plants were growing at low levels around Killarney, and at modern sea-level at Waterville, so the open tundra vegetation stretched right out to the shores of the Atlantic Ocean.

All this evidence clearly points to very cold conditions, and thus in the curve on p. 58 the temperature is shown as plunging very steeply down in this stadial. The Woodgrange grasslands broke up and disappeared, and with them the Giant Deer disappeared also. We do not know if the reindeer survived the Nahanagan Stadial in Ireland, but he certainly survived it somewhere, perhaps far south in Europe, and from there, as the postglacial forests re-advanced inexorably northwards driving the tundras before them, the reindeer kept pace with the tundra till it stabilized itself in northern latitudes. And there the reindeer still survives, if only by the courtesy of the Lapps and Eskimos, who have learned that it is better to manage your meat supply than to exterminate it.

It is only very recently that we have come to realize exactly how severe conditions were during the Nahanagan Stadial, and we have not yet realized the implications of that severity for many forms of animal and plant life. When we are asking ourselves if there could have been nearby refugia where some life could have survived when the Midlandian and the Munsterian ice-masses were at their maxima, we must also ask what forms could have survived the last episode of cold.

3

Ireland before Man, 10,000 to 5500 years ago

THE GEOLOGICAL SUB-STRUCTURE

A brief recapitulation*

THE dominant features of the rocky skeleton of Ireland that we see today – the distribution of upland and lowland, the details of the hills and valleys – had probably taken on their basic outlines ten million years ago. In older geological time dramatic events had taken place in Ireland; layers of rock were crumpled into hills and valleys; molten rock, rising from lower depths, was injected into rocks nearer the surface, or burst up through them to appear as a lava flow or a volcano. For much of the time climate was distinctly warmer than today. But gradually Ireland became more and more quiescent. The earthquakes that must formerly have been frequent completely died away; the last appearance of molten rock was perhaps twenty million years ago; the last major earth movements may have been of the same age.

If we could see the country as it was ten million years ago, it would be strangely different from what we know today. It would be densely wooded, but the trees composing the forests would be very different from those of modern Ireland, though some of them can still be coaxed to grow in the almost frost-free areas of south-west Cork and Kerry. They continue to flourish in the Appalachians and the mountains of China, but were driven out of Ireland by a progressive fall in temperature. Few modern Irish soils are more than 1 m deep, but these earlier woodlands were rooted in soils whose depths extended to tens of metres. Long exposure to wet tropical conditions had brought about profound chemical changes in the superficial rocks, and had buried them deeply beneath a thick mantle of highly weathered and often brightly coloured clays. Very little sound rock was exposed at the surface, even on slopes and hill-tops.

About two million years ago when it became cold enough for temperatures to fall below the freezing-point of water for long periods, the landscape was changed dramatically. As water freezes and thaws, it contracts and expands the surface layers of the soil; thawing loosens the soil particles, and when they are free to move, they creep away downhill. As a result the weathered soil material gradually moved downslope into the lake-basins and the valleys, and from there the rivers carried much of it into the sea. Where the contact between the weathered mantle and the sounder rock below varied in depth,

---

*This brief recapitulation, inserted for the use of those readers who wish to begin at this point, endeavours to outline the basic features of Chapters 1 and 2.

PLATE 9 *Above*, during the last warm stage the granite of the Three Rock Mountain, Co. Dublin, was partly rotted by chemical weathering to some depth. The mountain was a nunatak in the Midlandian Cold Stage, and freeze-thaw activity moved the rotted material downslope, leaving masses of solid rock standing up as tors, and rounded core-stones scattered about. *Below*, Killiney Hill, Co. Dublin, also of granite, was overrun by Midlandian ice, which carried away the rotted material, and abraded the solid rock, turning upstanding blocks into streamlined *roches moutonnées*. The ice was moving from left to right; it cut away the upstream side of the rock in the foreground, leaving it smoothed and rounded, but plucked blocks off the downstream side, giving it sharp outlines. The rock behind shows the same shape.

PLATE 10 *Above*, at the foot of low cliffs, a flat platform, cut in rock by wave-action, extends seawards at Sandy Cove, nr. Kinsale, Co. Cork. The modern waves could not have cut this platform, and it was probably cut at a time when sea-level was a few metres higher than to-day. It appears to be older than the glacial deposits of the region. *Below*, nr. Malin Head, Co. Donegal, Ballyhillin village lies along the curved crest of a Late Midlandian beach, raised by isostatic uplift to about 20m above modern sea-level. From the crest the beach gravels slope seawards, with unfenced strip-fields on them. When about 5000 years ago sea-level rose eustatically about 4m above its present level, its waves cut cliffs in the earlier beach gravels; more gravel was laid down as the waves retreated.

upstanding bosses of more solid rock survived as tors, after the looser debris around them had been carried away. (Pl. 9)

When in addition to temperature being low there were heavy falls of snow, gradually the unmelted snow consolidated into ice, and great masses of ice built up into dome-like forms from which wide glaciers flowed away across the surrounding countryside. Where the ice crossed weathered rock, it quickly assimilated the rotted debris into itself and carried it along. The ice often cut down into the sound rock below, creating a polished and striated surface on it, and adding freshly-ground rock debris to its load.

Thus about two million years ago when cold in Ireland became really severe the landscape was profoundly altered. Warmth-demanding trees with a long record of growth in Ireland were swept away. On higher ground fresh rock appeared as the rounded outlines of the deeply weathered tops were sharpened, and the slopes were steepened, both by the gouging action of ice and by the mass-movements brought about by the freeze-thaw processes. On lower ground the effect was reversed, because it was here that the melting ice-sheets and the earth-flows dumped their loads. Irregularities in rock topography were masked by a relatively even-surfaced layer of glacial deposits, river valleys were obliterated, and in many areas the surface-waters had to find escape routes past masses of closely packed drumlins. Is Upper Lough Erne a river, a lake or a mass of partly submerged drumlins? Below Carrick-on-Shannon, the Shannon enters into a field of drumlins; one inter-drumlin route carried more water than any other, and man has selected this route, deepened it, and made it the river-channel. In this sector the Shannon has no valley, in any recognized sense of the word; it launches its water into one end of the drumlin field, and trusts that it will emerge at the other.

But on the whole the major features of the landscape that we see today are controlled by the underlying rock, and not by the unconsolidated glacial materials that have been dumped on top of it.

The major landscape features of Ireland

At the heart of Ireland the low-lying Central Plain is largely floored by Carboniferous limestone, with small areas of higher ground formed either of younger rocks still *in situ* on top of the limestone, or of deformed older rocks projecting up through it. The younger rocks contain all that is left of Ireland's once extensive coal deposits, now reduced by erosion to tiny pockets around Castlecomer and Arigna. The older rocks appear in the higher ground around Lough Derg, and in the Slieve Bloom Mountains. The limestone itself is largely hidden by glacial deposits, but here and there, chiefly in Roscommon and Galway, it does appear at the surface. Its former protective mantle was stripped off by the ice, and the modern rains are dissolving it away.

Around the Central Plain there is an almost continuous rim of higher ground. In the north-west, from Connemara to Inishowen, older metamorphic and granitic rocks stand up in hilly ground which still bears a strong north-east/south-west fold pattern. The hills have been etched by glacial action, and in some places the great ice-masses to the south-east thrust tongues

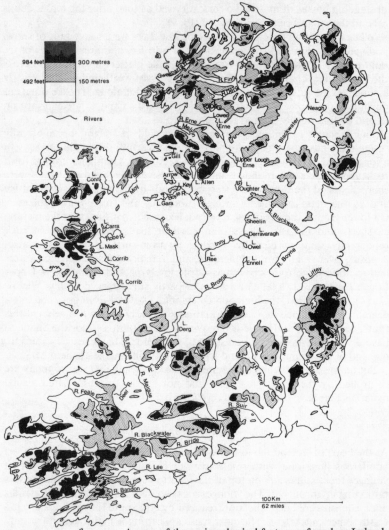

984 feet ⬛ 300 metres
492 feet ▒ 150 metres

〰️ Rivers

L. Conn
L. Carra
Robe R.
L. Mask
L. Corrib
R. Corrib
R. Moy
R. Gill
L. Arrow
Key R.
L. Gara
Boyle R.
L. Allen
R. Shannon
L. Melvin
L. Erne
Lower L. Erne
R. Erne
R. Finn
R. Derg
Gweeba...
Foyle
R. Bann
L. Neagh
R. Lagan
Belfast R.
R. Blackwater
R. Bann
Upper Lough Erne
L. Oughter
R. Blackwater
L. Sheelin
L. Derravaragh
L. Owel
L. Ennell
Inny R.
L. Ree
R. Suck
R. Brosna
R. Boyne
R. Liffey
R. Barrow
Slaney
R. Nore
L. Derg
R. Shannon
R. Fergus
R. Maigue
Deel R.
R. Feale
R. Suir
R. Blackwater
R. Bride
R. Lee
R. Bandon
R. Laune
Bay

100 Km
62 miles

A map of the major physical features of modern Ireland.

of ice across the higher ground, and these gouged out great trenches as they passed through the hills.

The north-east corner has the youngest rocks in Ireland, where high-standing sheets of volcanic lava protect beneath themselves the chalk and other relatively young sedimentary rocks. This striking geological structure is splendidly seen in Cave Hill, which overhangs the city of Belfast. Over the rest of Ireland these young rocks have largely been stripped away by erosion.

The central area of the lava flows has sagged into a great depression which still holds Ireland's largest lake, Lough Neagh, under whose waters can be found deposits extending back through many millions of years.

Over most of Down, and in a wedge of rolling country stretching south-west from it as far as Cavan, we have older slates and sandstone, again with a north-east/south-west trend; the rocks are usually buried by glacial deposits, often in drumlin form. Surrounding Carlingford Lough, the Mourne Mountains, Carlingford Mountain and Slieve Gullion are surviving evidence of young centres of great igneous activity, of the same age as the outpourings of lava farther north. Earlier tropical weatherings had penetrated deeply into the granite of the Mournes creating rounded outlines, and when cold stripped the debris away, massive tors were left behind on some of the tops.

The limestone of the Central Plain, also heavily mantled by glacial deposits, reached the Irish Sea between Dundalk and Dublin, but in the south-east corner, from Dublin to Dungarvan, we come again to higher ground of older slates, sandstones and volcanic rocks, all with a north-east/south-west trend. In the central axis of the area granite rises into the Wicklow Mountains, and although this granite is very much older than that of the Mourne Mountains, it has the same rounded outlines and the same scatter of tors, so well seen on the so-called Two-rock and Three-rock Mountains that overlook the city of Dublin. (Pl. 9)

The extremity of the corner in Wexford, south-east of Forth Mountain – which itself carries splendid tors – is composed of glacial deposits. Without these deposits to build the region up above modern sea-level, we should have had the sea lapping against cliffs on Forth Mountain, and an offshore archipelago of islands – Greenore, Tuskar, Carnsore, Kilmorequay, the Saltees. As it is the Tuskar Rock and the Saltees remain islands, while Greenore, Carnsore and Kilmorequay are still linked to the mainland. But wave attack is constantly eroding the cliffs of glacial material in their vicinity, and given sufficient time they, too, will again become offshore skerries.

South-west of a line from Dungarvan to Killarney, and again in the Dingle peninsula, we are beyond the limits of the last big build-up of ice on the Central Plain, and so are beyond the younger glacial deposits that clutter up much of the northern part of the country. Here on lower ground the contemporary freeze-thaw activity shifted much of the older glacial deposits not only down the slopes but also out along the valleys to levels below the modern sea. On higher ground glaciers did form, producing corries, arêtes and through-valleys such as the Gap of Dunloe. As a consequence rock-forms, rather than glacial deposits, tend to dominate the landscape.

In this area the solid rocks have a different grain, trending east to west, rather than north-east/south-west, as is the rule in much of the rest of the country. Great east/west ridges of sandstone and slate, rising into Ireland's highest ground, are separated by long valleys, in some of which strips of down-folded Carboniferous limestone have survived. The city of Cork lies in such a valley. East of Killarney we have the southern limit of a great belt of higher ground built up of upper Carboniferous shales and sandstones with tantalizing wisps of coal, a belt that stretches north across the Shannon

Estuary almost to the shores of Galway Bay. South of the Shannon the combination of heavy clayey soil and wetness due to elevation have encouraged the growth of bog, making this region scenically one of the dreariest parts of Ireland. Crossing the Shannon we come into the area that was covered by ice during the last glaciation, and young glacial deposits and drumlins introduce some variety into the landscape.

Approaching Galway Bay the shales and sandstones end abruptly, and at one of the most dramatic scenic changes in Ireland we reach the bare and dry limestone hills of the Burren, with their fantastic vegetational mixture of Alpine and Mediterranean plants. Around the shores of Galway Bay the limestone drops in level, and here the Central Plain meets the Atlantic Ocean.

THE COURSE OF SEA-LEVEL

About 10,000 years ago cold conditions came to an end, and the Littletonian Warm Stage opened. Sea-level had continued to rise from its low glacial level as more and more of the world's ice melted, and had probably recovered to within 35 m (100 ft) of its present level, when the warm stage opened (see figure on p. 68). Animals and plants quickly moved back into Ireland once more, and it is obvious that there must still have been land connections with Britain and Europe to enable them to do so. But we are faced with the difficulty that if sea-level today were to drop by no more than 35 m, a broad and continuous stretch of water would remain between Ireland and Britain.

As the ice that had formerly occupied the basin of the Irish Sea withdrew northwards, it left behind it glacial deposits of very irregular topography, which sank in some places into deep hollows which quickly filled with water, and rose in others into high morainic ridges, which served as routeways for immigration into Ireland (see figure on p. 69). These deposits were progressively drowned by the rising sea, and their topography was drastically modified both by wave erosion when the basin was being re-flooded, and by the strong tidal currents which developed as soon as the transverse morainic ridges were breached by the rising sea, and are still active today. Subjected to these attacks the unconsolidated sands, gravels and clays of the ridges were quickly washed away, leaving only their truncated ends which still project as headlands on the coasts of Louth and Meath on the one hand, and in Cumberland and the Isle of Man on the other.

If we look at the form the basin has today, we see a belt of gravel stretching south from Scotland through the Isle of Man to Anglesey. East of the gravel, from the Solway Firth to the Mersey, sands brought in by tidal currents and by river action are still accumulating, and the floor in this area has been built up to higher and higher levels with the passage of time. Much of St George's Channel is floored by sand which is kept in motion by tidal currents which draw it along the sea bed in ribbons and streams. Off the east coast of Ireland to the north of Dublin there is deeper water, and the finer particles of clay and mud have opportunity to settle here.

For how long did the land-bridges remain available as entry routes into Ireland? At Cushendun, Co. Antrim, a freshwater peat which formed 8500 years ago was later buried beneath beach gravels thrown up by the rising sea; the beach gravels started to form 7500 years ago. Evidence from other parts of the Irish Sea basin suggests that 8500 years ago sea-level was no more than 20 m below its present level, and it seems almost certain that by this time all land connections must have been severed. They were certainly gone 7000 years ago, because at Termonfeckin on the Louth coast, in the area of one of the postulated land-bridges, peat which formed at about this time is buried beneath a beach deposit. We shall probably be prudent if we picture that there was a period of not more than 1500 years, from 10,000 years ago when climatic amelioration stimulated migration, until 8500 years ago when land connections were severed, during which the movement of animals and plants into Ireland was relatively easy. But we need not worry that such a period was unduly short for the recolonization of Ireland, because the pollen content of the peat at Cushendun shows that 8500 years ago woods of pine, hazel, elm and oak were already established in north-east Ireland, and a radiocarbon date from Belle Lake, Co. Waterford, shows that oak and elm were growing there about 9000 years ago. (Pl. 13).

Sea-level continued to rise, and about 5500 years ago it probably stood about 4 m above its present level.

THE COURSE OF CLIMATE

At about 10,000 years ago temperature in north-west Europe reached the limit that enabled closed woodland to develop, and the Littletonian Warm Stage opened. Temperature continued to rise, and probably passed the present level, for there is some evidence that about six or seven thousand years ago the average July temperatures were 1° or 2°C warmer than at present. Evidence from Lough Neagh and other lakes suggests that lake levels were

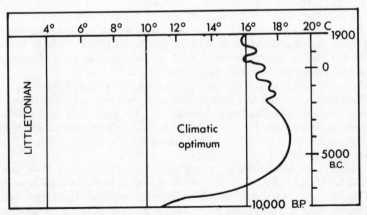

Possible course of July temperature during the Littletonian Warm Stage. (After Johs. Iversen).

lower than at the present time, and the climate may have been rather drier. This period has been referred to as the postglacial climatic optimum, and credit for its discovery is often given to Praeger, who towards the end of last century noted that the estuarine clays and raised beaches formed in the north of Ireland at this time contained a molluscan fauna with species which do not live so far to the north at the present day.

Robert Lloyd Praeger (1865–1963) was one of Ireland's most distinguished naturalists, who during a long working life made many important discoveries, and increased our knowledge of field botany in Ireland very substantially, but he did not discover, and never claimed to have discovered, the climatic optimum. The attribution arose from the fact that W. B. Wright had, like many others, a great admiration for Praeger, and when in 1936 he published the second edition of his book, *The Quaternary Ice Age*, he dedicated it to Praeger – the Discoverer of the Climatic Optimum. The discovery had in fact been made as long ago as 1865 by T. F. Jamieson, when he was studying the molluscan fauna of the estuarine clays of central Scotland. Praeger refers to Jamieson's work in his own paper, and would, were he alive today, be most anxious to see that honour is given where honour is due. I do not make this correction with any intent to lessen Praeger's standing. Born with a love for natural history in his blood, he qualified as an engineer, and one of his first jobs was on the excavations for dock constructions in Belfast. These excavations gave a wonderful opportunity for molluscan studies, and Praeger made the most of it, and published a series of brilliant papers. However, botany called more strongly than geology, and most of his subsequent work was primarily botanical. But he never overlooked the importance of fossil evidence, and he realized that Ireland's bogs and lakes must hold great quantities of seeds and other plant parts, whose identification would throw much light on the history of Irish vegetation. He thus made, and lodged in the National Herbarium, a collection of the seeds of all the plants regarded as native in Ireland. This was done long before organized studies of the fossil material were even thought of, and it must have given Praeger enormous satisfaction when, together with Tony Farrington of the Royal Irish Academy and Adolph Mahr of the National Museum, he organized Knud Jessen's visits to Ireland, and was able to see Jessen making full use of the collections of reference material he had put together many years before.

From this optimal level temperature then appears to have fallen back. It is not easy to document the change in Ireland, but pollen studies of certain temperate plants in Denmark, notably ivy (*Hedera*), holly and mistletoe (*Viscum*), suggest decreases of a degree or two in both summer and winter temperatures. In Sweden hazel could no longer grow as far north as it had previously done.

Temperature is only one parameter of climate. What are we to say about the other features of the Irish climate? Some would hold that there is no such thing as climate in Ireland, but only an irregular sequence of different weather patterns, with the emphasis on frontal systems bringing wind and rain. Ireland is an outpost in the Atlantic Ocean, and maritime influences predominate. Harsh frosts are rare; only the very centre of the country will know

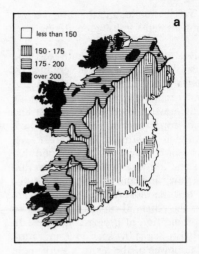

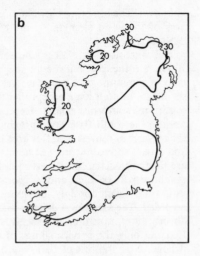

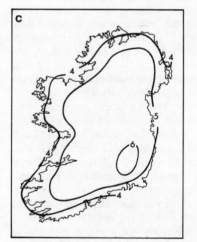

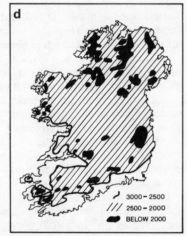

Some Irish climatic features: **a**, number of rain-days *per annum*; **b**, greatest number of successive days likely to occur without rain; **c**, saturation-deficit for the month of July, when the drying property of the air is greatest; **d**, accumulated temperatures in day-degrees *per annum*.

more than one day in the year when temperature will not rise above freezing point throughout the twenty-four hours. High summer temperatures are rare: 33°C is the highest ever recorded. The annual range is only 9°C in the south-west and 10°C in the east.

The great frequency – especially in the west of the country – of winds of moderate to severe intensity is a notable feature, and days of calm are almost unknown. The air being blown along is usually humid, and the disagreeableness of the wind strength is rarely compensated for by good drying conditions.

The amount of rainfall is not excessive, 1400 mm in the south-west and 700 mm in the east, but the number of days on which it falls is very high. A map of the number of rain-days *per annum* will in a crude way almost also serve as a rainfall map, except that it under-represents the rainfall along the south and south-east coasts. Depressions move along the south coast and up into the south Irish Sea, bringing occasional days of heavy rain though the number of rain-days in this area is not high. Continued droughts are rare, and a map shows the greatest number of consecutive days without rain that are likely to occur. Numerous rain-days and infrequent droughts mean that humidity will be high and evaporation low, and another map shows the saturation deficit for July, the month when the most favourable values are recorded. The saturation deficit indicates the potential capacity of the air to absorb more moisture, and so gives an indication of drying conditions. In England only the eastern shores of the Irish Sea show such low saturation deficits; over the rest of that country the power of the air to absorb more moisture is very much higher. Visitors from England to the west coast of Ireland often comment unfavourably on the late hour at which the local farmers begin their hay-making operations. They overlook the fact that noon on the clock in Greenwich is eleven o'clock by the sun in Connaught, and noon summer time is ten o'clock by the western sun. Several hours of morning sunshine are necessary before the local poor drying conditions can bring the grass into a condition in which it can safely be cut or turned.

The high humidity brings about extensive cloud cover and a poor sunshine record. Plants such as the primrose and the wood-sorrel that in England grow in woods and shady places find in the west of Ireland that the clouds provide an adequate sun-screen, and live on open and treeless hillsides. People living in Ireland are not exposed to strong insolation, and if they migrate to Australia or other areas with high sunshine records they are very prone to skin-cancers and other forms of skin irritation.

Irish immigrants contrast the harshness of the Australian light with the softer colours of the Irish landscape. Australian air is almost free both from water vapour and industrial smog, and it is these two elements that give to Irish air that slightest of haziness that appeals to the Irish eye. Winds from the east increase the haziness and mute the landscape colours; winds from the north-west bring clearer air with sunshine and drifting clouds, and at once the landscape springs to brilliance. Variations in wind and cloud come rapidly in Ireland, and the never-ending change in the strength of the light and the value of the colour tones brings delight to the eye – and despair to the brush – of the artist.

The cloud cover cuts down the amount of sunshine that can actually reach and warm the soil, and growth is correspondingly slowed. The actual amount of heat that probably reaches the ground can be evaluated and represented cartographically on a map. Such a map shows a strip along the south and south-west coast that is relatively favoured, though only to the same modest degree as the extreme west coast of England; the other parts of England are much warmer. The rest of the lowlands of Ireland receive less heat, and anywhere the ground rises, the amount of heat received drops again. Growth conditions in Ireland for many plants thus will always be slow and difficult.

We can, as seen above, make some effort to trace the course of temperature in Ireland in the past. We cannot easily pin down the other climatic features in the same way, but maritime influences will always have prevailed.

THE BEGINNING OF SOIL DEVELOPMENT

If this were a standard text-book on Irish geography, we would at this point have a map which presented an outline of the soils of Ireland. But at the time about which I am speaking, 10,000 years ago, most of the soils which we know today, and which the soil surveyor can record and enter up on his field map, had not yet developed, the numerous lake-basins left behind by the ice had not been overgrown by fens, and there had been no formation of peat. Here we can only indicate the trend of soil development on different parent materials as time went by.

We have seen that the effect of cold was to refresh the soil parent material, either by the deposition of rock debris freshly crushed by ice action, or by freeze-thaw disturbance and sludging bringing subsoil to the surface where it replaced, or at least diluted, the materials that had been deeply weathered during the preceding warm stage. At the opening of the Littletonian the replacement of a dry cold climate by a warm moist one meant, first that water was now free to bring about chemical changes, second that the high humidity reduced evaporation, and third that vigorous plant growth both by its foliage above ground, and by the humus its decaying debris was contributing to the upper layers of the soil below ground, checked water from flowing away along the surface, and encouraged it to sink down into the ground instead.

The classical processes of soil formation thus started anew under the influence of primary base status, texture and organic activity. As the water moved down from the surface it could carry easily-soluble substances (including humus) in solution, and the very fine insoluble clay particles in suspension, and so remove or *leach* material from the surface layers, giving rise to the *leached-* or A-horizon of the pedologist. The materials carried down from above tended to be deposited below in an *enriched-* or B-horizon, while the as yet unaltered material below is styled the C-horizon. In this way the three main soil horizons of the pedologist began to appear.

To begin with everything was C-horizon, and in some areas there was little change, particularly if the primary material was rich in clay particles. Bodies of water that had been dammed up by ice often filled up with finely divided clays, and such glacial lake clays are not uncommon in Ireland. Clays could also accumulate where river currents slackened, and at the foot of slopes down which clay particles were moving under the influence of gravity. The upper Carboniferous shales of north Kerry, Clare and Kilkenny, and the tills derived from them, are very rich in clay; in Leitrim the drumlins are built up of stiff clayey till; on the south-east coast Midlandian ice moving in from the basin of the Irish Sea incorporated large quantities of marine clay in its till.

Because the spaces between the clay particles are very small, movement of groundwater through such materials is extremely slow, and there is in consequence no development of soil horizons; a wet water-logged soil, known as a *gley*, results, irrespective of the chemical composition of the parent materials. The typical gley is found on low-lying land and is known as a *ground-water gley*. Decomposing plant material may accumulate on the surface of the soil; if the plant layer remains thin, i.e. does not thicken into peat, then the soil is described as a *peaty gley*. If the primary parent material is over-rich in clay, then water will fail to penetrate it no matter what may be the shape of the ground, and we will have a *surface-water gley*, as for example on the flanks of a drumlin built up of clayey till.

If on the other hand the parent material was poorer in clay and coarser in texture, water could move downwards, and a well-drained soil, more favourable to plant root systems, could gradually develop. By means of a map we can attempt to indicate the initial distribution about 10,000 years ago of poorly-drained and well-drained soils, and also the much greater extent of lakes at that time, because they had not yet been overgrown by fens and bogs.

As the Littletonian proceeded trees returned to the country, and gradually a high forest of deciduous trees built up climax woodland where the primary soil materials allowed such development. If there were open-textured parent materials on limestone the establishment of the forest went hand in hand with the development of a *brown forest soil*. The surface layers of such a soil consist of an intimate mixture of well decomposed humus and mineral matter. The humus is only a few centimetres thick, and there is no sharp dividing line between it and the mineral soil immediately below. In such a soil horizons do not develop prominently; the amount of humus decreases with depth, and the black colour changes correspondingly first to brown, and then merges gradually into the colour of the underlying glacial deposit or rock, where the soil ends. Where the rock was near the surface, the soil profile could only be shallow. Because of the way man subsequently interfered with the woodlands, we cannot find any typical brown forest soils in Ireland today. If change has only been slight, the surface humus will have disappeared, but many of the other soil properties will have remained, and the soil becomes a fertile *brown earth*, which in Ireland is quite often shallow. With more profound change, the development of horizons will have become more pronounced.

Where the parent glacial material was not strongly calcareous, the chemical action of the groundwater could be more marked, and there was a tendency for substances to be leached out of the top layer – the A-horizon – and carried away in the groundwater, or deposited lower down in the profile in the B-horizon. If small quantities of iron were washed down, the A-horizon tended to be bleached to a paler, ashy colour, a feature described as *podzolic*,* while the B-horizon, because of enrichment there, took on a strong brown colour, and we have a *brown podzolic* soil. Human interference does not appear to have affected these soils greatly.

*Based on the Russian *pod*, meaning *under*, and *zola*, *ash*.

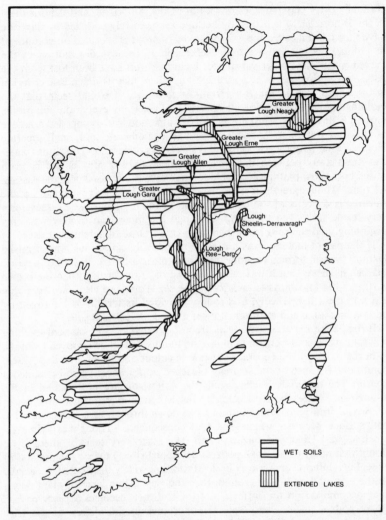

A map to show areas where the very high primary clay content causes the soil to remain poorly drained and wet at all times. At the opening of the Littletonian Warm Stage the lakes on the lowlands were much larger than they are to-day; the map endeavours to indicate the extent of these lakes before they were reduced in size by the growth of fens and bogs.

If the parent material was calcareous and had some content of clay, or of minerals that would break down into clay on weathering, then the movement or flow of groundwater down the profile over a long period of time would gradually carry clay particles down out of the A-horizon, and deposit them in the B-horizon, which thereby became progressively enriched in clay. We have thus the soil called the *grey-brown podzolic*; it is so-called on account of its colour, bleached above and deeper below, because in addition to the movement of clay, other substances including iron have been lost from the A-horizon, bringing about podzolization, but in fact its diagnostic criterion is the added clay in the B-horizon. At first sight it would seem that the building up of a layer of fine clay particles at a certain level in the soil profile must impede the downward movement of water, and lead to impeded drainage of the soil. But the clay particles tend to agglomerate into small separate blocks, rather than form a continuous sheet, and under most conditions water can drain away between the blocks. Studies of fossil soils buried beneath raised bogs show that the accumulation of clay has increased with the passage of time. Today grey-brown podzolic soils are widely developed on the calcareous deposits of the last glaciation in the midlands, where they form very fertile soils. Ten thousand years ago the movement of clay was only beginning, and the soils must then have had a rather different character.

If the parent material was not more than feebly calcareous and of mixed texture, the soil formed resembled the brown earth in that it did not develop marked horizons, but it was more acid and of lower fertility than the brown earth, and is known as an *acid brown earth*. Woodland clearance probably did not affect it markedly, and today, provided its fertility is improved by adding limestone and fertilizer, it gives a good agricultural soil.

If the parent material is non-calcareous and rich in sand, marked leaching will take place, and iron, aluminium and humus will all be removed from the A-horizon, which will become very pale in colour and be left in a highly acid condition. Because of the strongly bleached appearance the soil is called a *podzol*. The materials leached from the A-horizon are precipitated in the B-horizon, where the iron often forms a continuous impermeable layer, known as 'iron-pan'. Water cannot move down through such a layer, and the soil surface becomes water-logged in consequence. Though experimental work suggests that podzolization can take place very quickly, there is no doubt that many of the Irish podzols developed slowly over a long period of time. Such infertile and poorly drained soils are widely distributed, especially in the west and on higher ground. Like the gley, a thin layer of plant debris may accumulate on the surface, and the soil then becomes a *peaty podzol*. Peaty podzols have a very special importance in the history of the Irish landscape, because they provided the substratum on which blanket-bogs later developed.

Base status and texture are not the only factors affecting soil development. Topography, including altitude, slope and aspect, is also very important. In low-lying areas rivers are sluggish, and there may be lakes of varying sizes. On higher ground temperature is lower and winds are stronger, and these factors influence plant growth, especially tree growth. We can thus picture three main landscape units: (1) the lowlands, which are given an arbitrary upper limit at 150 m (approximately 500 ft), which is the height above which tillage is rarely practised in Ireland today; (2) the uplands above 150 m (often today covered by blanket-bog); and (3) what can be conveniently called the 'wetlands' and will include rivers, lakes, fens, raised-bogs, and extensive areas of gley soils on the lowlands. These three landscape units had different patterns of vegetation, and their later uses by man differed widely, and wherever it is appropriate they will be discussed separately. And we must remember that the difference between them is not fixed and immutable. If climate improved woodland (and tillage) might move higher up the mountain slopes; if climate deteriorated and blanket-bog spread, fertile lowland areas might be turned into infertile wetlands.

THE RETURN OF THE FLORA AND FAUNA

We can now retrace our steps to about 10,000 years ago, and ask ourselves what will happen when the Littletonian thermostat is given a vigorous upward turn? In the Nahanagan Stadial we had plants and animals requiring open habitats, but capable of surviving relatively adverse climatic conditions. Now these must face rising temperatures and strong competition; some will survive the change and hold their own, others will become extinct in Ireland, a few will find refuge on cliffs on the sea-shore or on mountain-tops. Where are their competitors? We can picture them strung out across Britain and on into continental Europe, as well as down the Atlantic coast of France, standing in their places like the starters in a handicapped gold rush. When the 'off' is given, they spring into action, each determined to stake out his claim. And this is a race against the clock, because there is not more than 1500 years to go before a water-barrier will have to be crossed if they are to reach Ireland, the Outpost of Europe, as Grenville Cole called it many years ago.

We can emphasize this with a diagram (see overleaf) which suggests an outline of north-west Europe, as it might appear if viewed from an aeroplane over the Atlantic to the north-west of Ireland. We see the drowned margin of the Continental Shelf, with the British Isles rising above it, and the deep trough cut into it off the Norwegian coast. We see the remote position of Ireland.

And we must remember that for many plants from the continent as they were moving north-westwards towards Ireland, the goal was becoming less inviting. Soils were less rich, temperature was falling and cloud cover was increasing, and many had no inclination to reach northern England, let alone push on into Ireland. Of the 260 flowering plants of continental affinity that entered Britain, less than half continued on into Ireland. Many years ago Sir Cyril Fox drew a line from Tyneside to Exeter separating lowland Britain with its soft rocks, base-rich soils and low rainfall from highland Britain with its harder rocks, less fertile soils and higher rainfall. For many migrating organisms this was their limit, not the line now occupied by the Irish Sea.

A second path led up the west coast of Europe, and at least one plant – the Strawberry Tree (*Arbutus unedo*) – travelled its full length from the Mediterranean to the islands of Lough Gill in Sligo. But many fell by the wayside on this route also, because again less than half of the 105 flowering plants of Mediterranean/Atlantic affinity that reached Britain succeeded in

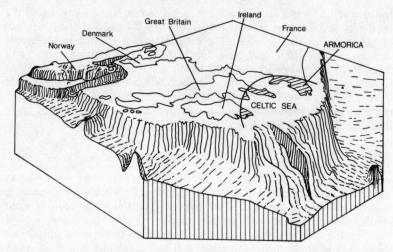

Ireland the Outpost. A schematic diagram (after B. Larsen) to illustrate Ireland's relationship to the European land-mass and to the continental shelf. Four promontories, linked by the similarity of the type of rock of which they are composed and by the earth-movements to which those rocks were subjected, are united into Armorica, a land now largely drowned below the waters of the Celtic Sea. The four promontories, south-west Ireland, south-west Wales, Cornwall, and Brittany, show some remarkable resemblances in geomorphology, archaeology, history and land-use.

reaching Ireland. But there was a coastal strip along which movement into Ireland was possible, as is convincingly demonstrated by the modern distribution of a shore-living bug, *Aepophilus bonnairei*. The modern headquarters of this insect, which lives in rock-crevices near low-tide-mark and can neither swim nor fly, are on the Atlantic coast from Morocco to Portugal. It could not have survived the cold of the Nahanagan Stadial in the British Isles, and when warmth returned at the beginning of the Littletonian Warm Stage it marched north up the French coast, skirted the embayments that then occupied the English Channel and the south of the Irish Sea, and made its way on to the Atlantic coast of Ireland.

In climates such as that of north-west Europe today, trees are the dominant plants, and the trees that did arrive in Ireland gradually expanded and transformed the landscape, as unending woodlands obliterated the open countryside. And with the trees came the shrubs, lianes and herbs which tolerate and sometimes require the cover of deciduous trees, together with the mammals and other animals of the woods. Today Ireland has a population of plants and animals of woodland ancestry, but a population which is very much poorer than that of Britain.

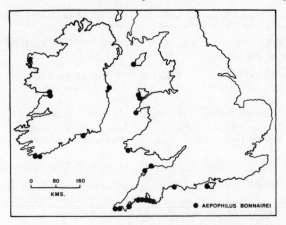

The modern distribution of *Aepophilus bonnairei*, a shore-dwelling bug, which is most likely to have reached Ireland in early Littletonian time by moving along a continuous coastline that stretched from the Atlantic coast of France to Ireland.

THE FLORAS OF IRELAND AND GREAT BRITAIN COMPARED
(after Webb)

Species native to Ireland		*Species native to Britain*	
Native in Britain also	889	Native in Ireland also	889
Naturalized in Britain	3	Naturalized in Ireland	51
Absent from Britain	15	Absent from Ireland	409
Total	907	Total	1349

Why should the shortfall among the flowering plants amount to nearly one third of the British species, with similar shortages among the ferns, mosses, etc.? Setting aside the matter of more difficult access, Ireland is much more homogeneous and uniform than Britain, and the range of habitats available to satisfy different plant communities is correspondingly restricted. Ireland extends only through four degrees of latitude as against ten for Britain; the mountains are lower and their masses smaller; except in the north-east there are no calcareous sedimentary rocks of young geological age, such as are dominant in south-east England.

Woodland communities and mountain communities of alpine facies are noticeably weaker in Ireland. Causes of social and historical origin explain the shortfall in woodland forms; the managed semi-natural woods that are such a feature of southern England are virtually unknown in Ireland. With regard to mountain vegetation, the Irish hills in their equable Atlantic setting were not high enough to allow true tundra communities to survive, as they have done on the higher Scottish summits. Irish summits, corries and ledges carry a vegetation which is markedly lowland in aspect, and arctic-alpine survivors are not only few in number, but markedly scarce as well. The greater part of the surface of Ireland is covered by grassland, moorland and bog, communities which do not encourage floral diversity.

The different animal groups also show deficiencies, as great or greater than those of the plants.

THE LAND MAMMALS OF IRELAND AND GREAT BRITAIN COMPARED

Species native to Ireland		*Species native to Britain*	
Extinct	3	Extinct	4
Native in Britain also	11	Native in Ireland also	11
Naturalized in Britain	0	Naturalized in Ireland	3
Absent from Britain	0	Absent from Ireland	14
Total	14	Total	32

Similar shortfalls are recorded among the birds (Ireland 354; Britain 456) the reptiles (Ireland 1; Britain 4), and the amphibians (Ireland 2; Britain 6), as well as among the less well known invertebrate groups.

LITTLETONIAN DEVELOPMENTS BETWEEN 10,000 AND 5500 YEARS AGO

The current, or Littletonian, warm stage is, we believe, merely another interregnum in continuing cold, and we can follow its development – as far as it has proceeded – in the same way as we followed earlier warm stages. Below we see the phases of woodland development into which it can be divided, and also two curves, one to indicate the movement of temperature

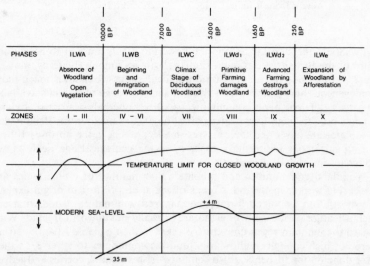

Phases of woodland development in the Littletonian Warm Stage in Ireland. An older scheme of zones is also shown (see Mitchell, 1965).

PLATE 11 An artist's impression of the Giant Deer in life. The antlers though huge were frail, for show rather than combat. The stag would take his stand on a hillock, and slowly move the antlers up and down in order to display them fully and discourage rivals.

PLATE 12 The Geeragh, nr. Macroom, Co. Cork, now drowned beneath a reservoir. Here the Lee expanded into a network of streams and wooded islets, uninvaded by grazing animals. Much of lowland Ireland looked like this before fens and bogs clogged the waterways, and man and his animals damaged the woodlands.

and the second to indicate the movement of sea-level. We can also draw a schematic pollen-diagram to indicate the order in which the trees arrived in Ireland, and give some indication of their relative importances, as shown by the amounts of pollen they produced. The amounts indicated are 'raw' figures, that is to say they are the numbers counted, and ignore the fact that some trees are much more lavish producers of pollen than others, and so give an impression that they were more important in the woodlands than their numbers warranted. It is possible to introduce corrections to allow for the relative pollen productions of the different trees, but that has not been done in this simple diagram.

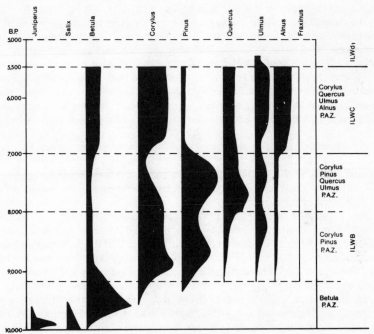

A schematic pollen-diagram to illustrate the early development of the Littletonian woodlands in Ireland.

i Beginning-phase (ILWB) and immigration of woodlands 10,000 to 7000 years ago

As we have already seen, the Littletonian Warm Stage opens at 10,000 years ago when rising warmth brought the Nahanagan Stadial to an end, and allowed the juniper to flower freely once more and mark the start of woodland immigration in the Beginning-phase. The beetles of the Nahanagan Stadial suggest a July average temperature of only 10°C such as is found in the Scandinavian mountains today, and they are rapidly replaced by relatively thermophilous forms which indicate a July average of 15°C, which is the same as that of today. Temperature was therefore not a limit on the movement of plants and animals, and immense migratory movements must have begun. Willow was at first an important producer of pollen along with the juniper, and then both of these trees were quickly shaded out by the expansion of the birch woods. We have thus a *Betula* pollen-assemblage-zone which lasted from 10,000 years ago till about 9250 years ago, by which time pollen of hazel is appearing in the pollen counts, and indicating the arrival of this bush or small tree. Pollen of pine appears virtually simultaneously with that of hazel, and both climb rapidly to high values, as the birch trees are overshadowed and disappear beneath the higher canopy. In modern woodlands both pine and hazel tend to play second fiddle to the other trees, but at this early stage in the absence of competition they will have run riot everywhere, with the pine perhaps especially favouring the drier soils, except where these were on limestone. The hazel will have flourished on the limestone, and on wetter soils. Lake-muds are full not only of its pollen, but also of fragments of its nuts, and sheets of dense hazel scrub must have been abundant throughout Ireland. Oak and elm, and alder also, had reached the country about 9000 years ago, but at first they were not able to displace the pine and hazel, and we have a *Corylus-Pinus* assemblage-zone from about 9250 until 8000 years ago.

A visitor to Ireland at this time would have seen endless sheets of trees interrupted only by the water of lakes and river-channels. Such country has almost totally vanished, though some fragments did survive until recently in the valley of the Lee; they are now submerged beneath the waters of a hydroelectric scheme. (Pl. 12)

Just south of Coleraine, high bluffs dominate the River Bann at Mount Sandel. Such a strategic site has been occupied by man throughout the millennia, and Peter Woodman has recently shown that it is here that we have the earliest record of man in Ireland, dated by radiocarbon to between 8700 and 8600 years ago. The site appears to have been occupied by people who used small flint points, or microliths, and small axes made from flint flakes. Such implements indicate people living in a Mesolithic style, hunting and trapping small game and fish, but without any knowledge of farming. (Pl. 13)

The stone axe is produced by removing appropriately shaped flakes from the blank originally chosen, the blank being either a pebble, or an already struck flake of flint or some stone of suitable texture. Flake-axes and microliths are found in late Mesolithic sites in Denmark, and we cannot overlook Denmark in our search for the original home of the first men to reach Ireland. There is also an early Danish Mesolithic, and this spills over into eastern England, where it perhaps finds its finest flowering at Star Carr, occupied about 9500 years ago. This wonderful site, discovered by John Moore and excavated by Grahame Clark, was on the margin of a lake which was then at a rather lower level, and the damp conditions created by a later rise in the water-table had enabled bone and wood to survive. So here we had, what we have yet to find in Ireland, a Mesolithic dwelling-site with all its appurtenances. There were antler harpoons, both finished and unfinished, and as if this was not enough, carefully-cut antler head-dresses, which were used either as stalking-aids in actual hunting, or in ceremonies intended to promote success in the chase. There were also containers made out of birch bark.

The Star Carr folk had an impressive range of implements of flint and stone. Their axes (and adzes) were made from pebbles, not flakes, and are known as core-axes; in addition to variously trimmed flakes and microliths they also had the burin, a chisel-like and invaluable tool, especially for the cutting and working of bone. Core-axes occur in southern England, Wales and west Scotland, on sites dated between 7000 and 6000 years ago, and they also occur, though rarely, in Ireland on sites which appear to be still younger in age. But our real dilemma is this: primitive people obviously needed the best tools that were available to them; if relatively advanced folk were in Yorkshire about 9500 years ago, and were from there pushing slowly westwards, surely they needed to carry along with them all the technological information that was available? Yet knowledge of the burin seems not to have reached Ireland, though this tool must have been as valuable as the steel chisel is to the modern carpenter.

Star Carr was probably a residential site or a base camp, and this is the type of site we have not yet found in Ireland. Mount Sandel may be such a site, because on the whole it has produced finished implements rather than work-site debitage, and circles of holes for large posts suggest the existence of substantial houses; but it is situated on a dry hill, and not in a wet swamp, and will not produce the organic materials that were found in such profusion at Star Carr. (Pl. 13)

But whoever they were, so far the Mount Sandel people stand alone in Ireland as the only known users of microliths in quantity. Did some tragedy befall them, and did they die out after only a short time had elapsed? In Britain microliths are known on west coast sites from Wales to the Hebrides, and it is curious that finds of microliths are so rare in Ireland.

ii Further forest development, and the establishment of man in Ireland

By 8000 BP the oak and the elm were beginning to overshadow the hazel on the heavier soils, and the amount of hazel pollen falls. The pine may have been forced back on to the sandier and drier soils, but it continued to produce very substantial amounts of pollen, which indeed tended to increase in quantity. Here we have the *Corylus-Pinus-Quercus-Ulmus* pollen-assemblage-zone, which lasted from 8000 to 7000 years ago. At this time the climate in general may have been rather dry. Under these circumstances the alder, a tree of wet soils, may have been restricted to the margins of lakes and rivers, and this may be why its pollen makes only a trifling appearance in the pollen record. Ash will have been in the country also, but was perhaps confined to dry limestone soils, a habitat which was not sufficiently extensive to enable the ash to make an effective contribution to the pollen rain. The yew will also have been in Ireland, but its pollen is relatively fragile and difficult to recognize in fossil form, and has hitherto been largely overlooked by many workers, including myself. More recent studies show that it was a much more important component of the early woods than has hitherto been supposed.

These are the trees that did reach Ireland; what others fell by the wayside? It is not easy to understand why the small-leaved lime (*Tilia cordata*) failed to reach Ireland, as it accompanied the oak and elm in their advance as far as south Wales, and Ireland had plenty of limestone soils on which to receive it. The hornbeam and the field maple (*Acer campestre*) did not advance seriously beyond south-east England. The beech (*Fagus sylvatica*) is more of a problem; introduced by man in the eighteenth century, it has spread widely and sets ripe seed throughout Ireland, where it finds the moist conditions very much to its taste. It had reached south-east England by this time, but its continued westward advance may have been too slow for it to reach Ireland. Its survival areas may have been relatively far away, so far away that its rate of advance could not carry it into Ireland before Ireland was severed from Britain.

Did other trees arrive, and then fail to survive? It is commonly pictured that climate at the opening of the Littletonian Warm Stage was relatively continental, and this may have meant that killing-frosts occurred later in spring than they do today. Within the range of plants that a botanist recognizes as a single species, there will be forms or *ecotypes* that have different ranges of tolerance for various factors, and it may have been that only those tree ecotypes that were sufficiently frost-hardy were able to hold a permanent position in the Irish woodlands.

It is one of the paradoxes of the modern Irish spring that some introduced trees, such as the horse chestnut (*Aesculus hippocastanum*) and the sycamore (*Acer pseudoplatanus*), which today are natives of more southern lands, put out their young leaves earlier than the native oak and ash, and are taking advantage of the sunshine while the Irish trees are still in bud. It may be that the modern Irish trees are the descendants of ecotypes that held back their leaves until the late killing-frosts were over, while other forms that put out their leaves earlier were eliminated. In the more oceanic Irish climate of to-day, the horse chestnut and the sycamore escape killing-frosts, and are able to flourish.

It was during the thousand years of this assemblage-zone that man became firmly established in Ireland, settling first at the north-west corner of Lough Neagh where the Lower Bann makes its exit towards the sea, and a little later on the east Antrim coast at Cushendun. The oldest charcoal from Peter Woodman's excavations at Newferry on the Bann is 8150 years old. Many years ago Hallam Movius excavated implements from estuarine gravels and silts in the raised beach at Cushendun, and charcoal and wood collected at the same time have now been dated by radiocarbon to an age of 7500 years. The sites provide a well-defined if restricted range of implements (among which the microlith, so common at Mount Sandel, is very rare, and the burin is unknown); typical implements are especially common in the raised beach gravels at Larne, Co. Antrim, where they have long been collected and studied, and hence the people who made and used them are known as Larnians. A map shows the Larnian sites so far discovered in Ireland, with an indication

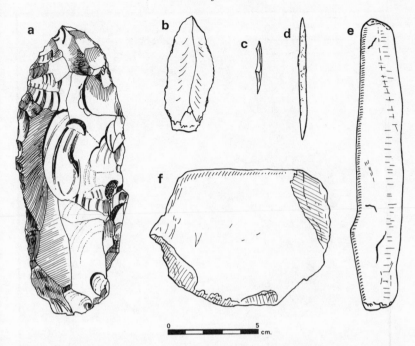

Types of Larnian implement: **a**, core-axe (chert), Lough Iron, Co. Longford; **b**, leaf-shaped flake (flint); **c** and **d**, points (bone); **e**, rubber (stone); **f**, chopper (stone), all from Rockmarshall, Co. Louth.

of the time at which they were occupied; the site at Mount Sandel is also shown (p. 102 and Pl. 13).

Who were they, these Larnians, and where did they come from? They had no knowledge of agriculture, and so they must have lived by hunting and fishing; they had no knowledge of the arts of making pottery or polishing stone, and so they had not attained the level of Neolithic culture. By the time they reached Ireland the country had been re-smothered in trees, and they could not range wide prairies in search of herds of big game, as the Palaeo-lithic hunters had done. They seem to have had axe-like implements of chipped stone, but they either could not, or did not, use these for forest-clearance as the Neolithic people used their hafted polished stone axes to open up cultivation-patches in the woodlands. They were hunters and fishers of Mesolithic status, restricted by their inability to clear large areas to roaming along the shores of lakes and rivers and along the coasts, hunting small game and catching fish, and collecting nuts and seeds, as seasonal opportunity offered.

They do appear to have made small clearings. If we make very detailed pollen-counts at critical levels in deposits associated with Mesolithic activities,

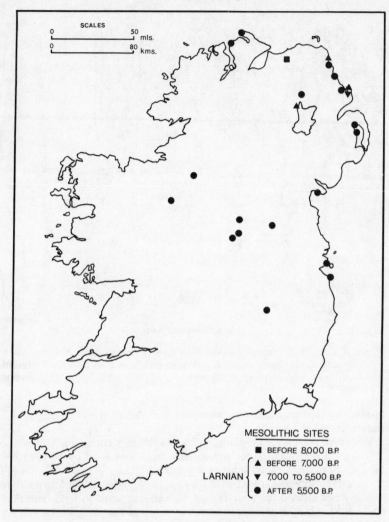

The location of mesolithic sites in Ireland.

we can see small irregular movements in some values that suggest that some artificial interference with the woodlands was taking place. A seasonal camp-site may have been semi-permanently fenced, and a stockade would have been necessary to keep wolves and foxes, and an occasional wandering bear, at bay. Such a camp-site would from time to time be abandoned, and it would soon be noted that deer came to browse on the young trees and bushes that started to recolonize the site. Deer haunt the margins, rather than the depths of the forests, and it would be quickly realized that an artificial clearing would attract deer into positions where they could be easily trapped or shot.

Dependent as they were on hunting and collecting for their proteins and their carbohydrates, the Larnians must have led a semi-nomadic existence as the seasonal pattern of abundance of various foodstuffs led them on from one location to another. Such a pattern of life dominated the Maoris of the extreme south of New Zealand at the time when they first came in contact with white settlers. The Maoris had a wider range of implements than the Larnians, but were like them essentially food-collectors. For carbohydrate they largely depended on bracken rhizomes, and on the starchy roots and young stems of the *Cordyline* (still known in New Zealand as the Cabbage Tree). They had a permanent village site, from which foraging parties travelled to places where they could live comfortably for several weeks, gathering and preserving seasonally abundant foods. For one such group the following yearly pattern in search of protein has been recorded – September and October, up to Tuturau for lampreys at the Mataura Falls; November, on to the Waimea Plains to get eels; December, back to Tuturau to dry food; January, to the coast to catch fish and collect seaweed; February, making seaweed bags; March, to the offshore islands; April, catching and smoking seabirds; May, return from the islands; June, bringing presents of smoked seabirds to friends and relatives; July and August, catching forest birds.

In Ireland we can see parts of the Larnian way of life, but not as yet the full sequence. Lough Neagh was then at a lower level, and there were sand-banks and bars both at Toome Bay, where Lough Beg is cut off from the main lake, and at Newferry where the Lower Bann flows out of Lough Beg. Fishing parties taking seasonally-running salmon and eels occupied the sand-banks, and almost certainly smoked fish there. After about 7000 years ago the Bann became more prone to seasonal flooding, and each year the water-meadows which flanked the river accumulated thin sheets of diatom-frustules which gradually built up into a thick layer of diatomite. In places the diatomite contains large spreads of ash, and some of these produced clusters of leaf-shaped flakes which the excavator, Hallam Movius, suggested might have been hafted together to form some sort of multi-pronged fishing implement – such as is still all too frequently (and illegally) employed in many parts of Ireland.

Flint was very valuable for the manufacture of implements, and this was most easily obtained on the Antrim coast, where not only are there outcrops of chalk, but the glacial deposits and beach gravels are full of derived flint nodules. Larnian groups would visit the shores, and give a preliminary dressing to suitable flint blocks, leaving sheets of debris behind them. Sea-level was still rising, and the knapping-floors were overwhelmed by the waves, and the debris embedded in beach deposits and spits, now raised above modern sea-level. Curran Point in Larne Harbour – which has been much built over – is such a spit which has long been famous for its content of man-worked flints. Excavating here in 1935 Hallam Movius opened up a pit 5 m square and 5 m deep, and from it he obtained over 15,000 pieces of humanly struck flint, but unfortunately relatively few finished implements. Sustenance was easy on the sea-shore, because both fish and shell-fish were readily available, and where the camp-sites were high enough to escape destruction by the sea, kitchen-middens of oyster, limpet, periwinkle and other shells have survived. It would not have been possible to cure shell-fish, crabs and lobsters, but sea-fish could have been salted and dried in the way that continues in Iceland to the present day. There great acreages of wooden fish-racks are employed in the drying and smoking of cod and other fish, and a substantial trade is carried on in the export of such preserved fish to Nigeria and other African countries which are short of protein. Porpoises and small whales would occasionally be stranded, or might under favourable circumstances be driven ashore, and after they had provided an immediate feast the rest of the flesh could be smoked, as mutton is smoked in Iceland today. Such was the way in which the coastal Aborigines of Australia were living when white folk first arrived there, and we are fortunate to have some paintings from which, if we ignore the difference in climate, we can form some impression of the Larnian way of life. Most early people have light boats, and in the currachs of the Atlantic coast of Ireland, we can imagine we see the descendants of Ireland's first boats. (Pl. 14)

Rather later in time, about 5400 years ago, the same type of activity was taking place on the lakes in the Irish midlands. On the shore of Lake Derra-varagh, just where the Inny enters the lake, there were extensive fens which were visited by people living in Larnian fashion. Chert (a black variety of flint which occurs in many Carboniferous limestones in Ireland) outcrops on the shores of the lake, and this was used for the manufacture of implements. There will have been open channels in the fen through which the river entered the lake, and water-lilies growing in the open water beyond the edge of the fen. In the fen-peat there were the ashes and charcoal of numerous isolated fires, and associated with these were chert flakes, hazel-nut shells and charred and uncharred seeds of the yellow water-lily (*Nuphar luteum*). We can picture parties of Larnian folk coming here in Maori style in early autumn, setting traps for fish in the fen-channels, collecting and perhaps parching water-lily seeds, gathering hazel-nuts and giving a preliminary dressing to blocks of chert, carrying away the semi-worked pieces to be finished elsewhere.

Where did the Larnians come from? Normally one tries to track down the origin of a group by comparing the types of implements it used with those of contemporary groups in neighbouring lands, but unfortunately the Larnians are only known by a very limited – though characteristic – range of relatively simple implements in flint, chert and stone (p. 101). They must also have had implements of wood, bone and antler, but of this almost nothing has survived. At Toome Bay on Lough Neagh some pieces of worked wood had got broken and were then used as firewood, but of the charred scraps it was only possible to say that they clearly had once been worked for some special purpose. A kitchen-midden on the shore of Dundalk Bay produced two small bone points, which were probably used as fish-gorges; a cord was attached to the point, not in the centre but towards one end; the point was baited and lowered into the water; an approaching fish would be given full opportunity to draw the bait well into its mouth; a quick jerk was then given to the cord, in the hope that the point would turn at right angles, so that its ends would jam in the sides of the fish's mouth, and enable the fish to be drawn from the water.

Most implements were made by a flaking process. Suitable rounded pebbles of flint would be collected on the sea-shore or from glacial gravels; one end would be struck off, and a flat surface produced; by striking blows at the perimeter of this surface, elongated flakes would be detached; two forms of these were most sought for, parallel-sided blades or knives, and leaf-shaped flakes, to be used as pointed knives, or mounted in a shaft to serve as an arrow- or spear-head. The Larnians were aware that a thin edge could be strengthened by removing small flakes at right angles to the edge, by the so-called 'retouching' or 'reworking' technique, and flakes were turned into scrapers and borers. In the same way one edge of a flake could be blunted, so producing a 'backed' knife. Core-axes were occasionally made, by striking flakes off a chosen pebble until it was reduced to the desired shape. Flat pebbles, either elongated or rounded, were used for pounding or scraping, with the result that the edges either flaked away or became facetted.

As already noted we urgently need to find residential sites, where we shall find the tools with which sophisticated objects in wood and bone were fabricated, and not just the waste fragments which were discarded by the thousand. And we need wet sites, where organic materials and objects fashioned from them will have survived, together with food debris and other potentially informative rubbish.

We may then be in a position to learn where not only the Larnians, but also their predecessors at Mount Sandel, came from, and the routes they took to get here. Did they come from north-west Europe, and move up the basin of the Irish Sea, or did they start from Scandinavia, cross the still dry floor of the North Sea into northern England and then through south-west Scotland across a still narrow North Channel into the north of Ireland? When they did reach Ireland, they had the island to themselves for some 3000 years, during which time they seem to have done little more than stagnate in cultural isolation.

iii Climax-phase (ILWC) of deciduous woodlands, and initiation of raised-bog growth, 7000 to 5500 years ago

In organic deposits which were accumulating about 7000 years ago, the pollen-counts show a dramatic change at this level, which must reflect a radical alteration in the woodlands. Alder rises from the meagre values it has hitherto shown, and pine falls back to a much lower level, and just as this change is taking place hazel for a time drops back to low values, but then recovers again. Related changes can be traced throughout north-west Europe, and it may be that the climate had become more oceanic and wetter, enabling alder to compete successfully on the damper soils, and forcing pine more exclusively on to the poorer soils. Temperatures remained high, with, as already noted, July temperatures perhaps $1°$ or $2°C$ warmer than at present.

Dense, tall deciduous woodland dominated by alder, oak and elm occupied the better lowland soils, with birch and pine still probably holding their own on the uplands. The Climax-phase of woodland stability, with a *Corylus-Quercus-Alnus* assemblage-zone, became established, and then persisted for about 1500 years until it was suddenly damaged by the activities of the first Neolithic farmers.

We cannot overlook the fact that natural soil development may also have been a factor in the establishment of the climax woodlands. But when we try to trace out the history of soil development in Ireland, we come up against the problem that man himself has been interfering with the soils for at least half the time that has been available for soil development, because it was about 5500 years ago that the natural progression was broken by man starting to clear trees away, in order to create clearings for his farming operations.

The opening five thousand years of the Littletonian Warm Stage must have seen a hand in hand development of the forests and of the soils on which they grew. The early shallow-rooted birches were progressively displaced by bigger and bigger forest trees with deeper and deeper rooting-systems, and deep soils will have formed. It was a very intimate relationship, because if on the one hand the more deeply penetrating roots and their accompanying microflora and fauna promoted soil development, on the other the inherent texture and base status of the soil in turn affected the competitive powers of the different tree genera, and thus influenced the composition of the woodlands. Due to the variety of Ireland's basic rock structure, and to the different flow-paths followed by different ice-masses, the parent material of the soils developed on glacial deposits varied widely, and so the forest pattern could not be monotonously uniform – as our pollen-diagrams often suggest – but presented a mosaic of concentrated stands of different trees, the specific trees involved being related to the soil parent material.

It is hard for us to picture the majesty and silence of those primeval woods, that stretched from Ireland far across northern Europe. We are accustomed to an almost treeless countryside, and if we can find anywhere some scraps of 'native' woodland, we are disappointed by the quality of the trees. For thousands of years man has been roving the Irish woodlands seeking for 'good' timber for houses, ships and other uses. As a result all the well-grown 'good' trees have long since disappeared, and what are left are the progeny of 'bad' trees, rejected by earlier carpenters. If we visit the National Museum we can see wooden shields, 1 m in diameter, worked from a slice taken from the trunk of a well-grown forest alder. We could not find in Ireland today a single alder tree capable of supplying a blank for such a shield. In some remote parts of Europe scraps of upland valleys have escaped the logger's attentions, and there we can recapture something of the vanished dignity of the Irish forests.

Throughout the period of the Beginning-phase (ILWB), from 10,000 to 7000 years ago, the great stretches of open water that were established after cold conditions had ended were being progressively reduced in area by the growth of marginal fens and marshes. This was the first link in a chain of development that led to the building-up of raised-bogs. Plants capable of spending their entire life largely submerged, such as bladderwort (*Utricularia*) and hornwort (*Ceratophyllum*), established themselves in shallow waters, and as their debris together with silts and clays further reduced the depth, plants

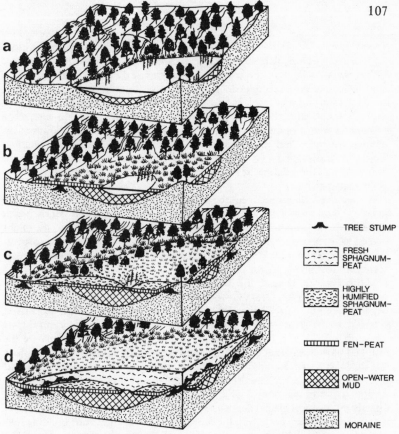

a

b

c

d

TREE STUMP

FRESH
SPHAGNUM-
PEAT

HIGHLY
HUMIFIED
SPHAGNUM-
PEAT

FEN-PEAT

OPEN-WATER
MUD

MORAINE

Four stages in the development of a typical Irish raised-bog: **a**, an open-water lake lies in morainic country which is covered by forest; an island of moraine rises in the lake, on whose floor open-water mud is accumulating.

b, fen plants, originally growing round the lake-edge, and whose decaying debris builds up fen-peat, extend in two directions: out into the lake as accumulating mud makes its margins shallow, and inland into the forest, burying the tree-stumps with its peat.

c, the same process continues, and as the fen-peat thickens, its surface becomes less rich in nutrients, and is invaded by the acid bog community, dominated by *Sphagnum*-moss. Nourished only by rain-water, the bog community slowly builds up a dome-like mass of highly humified *Sphagnum*-peat. As the bog grows, the local water-table rises, and the fen-peat creeps still higher up the surrounding slopes, killing more trees as it advances. The flanks of the dome of peat are relatively dry, and some trees can grow there.

d, some change in conditions allows the *Sphagnum*-peat to form more quickly, and the dome, now composed of fresh *Sphagnum*-peat, grows up still higher. The trees on the flanks of the older raised-bog die, and are buried by peat. The island, which had been getting smaller and smaller as bog growth continued, is finally overwhelmed by peat, and its trees disappear.

with floating leaves such as the pondweeds (*Potamogeton*) and the water-lilies (*Nuphar, Nymphaea*), colonized the margins. Soon the margins were invaded by the reedswamp plants, the bulrush (*Schoenoplectus lacustris*), the reed (*Phragmites communis*), the sedge (*Cladium mariscus*) and many others, and the accumulating vegetable debris, gradually consolidating into fen-peat, built itself up to water level. In the fen species of *Carex* (Sedges) and of grass are dominant, and there are flowering plants, such as marsh cinquefoil (*Potentilla palustris*), marsh marigold (*Caltha palustris*), cuckoo-flower (*Cardamine pratensis*) and meadowsweet (*Filipendula ulmaria*). At Ballyscullion Bog, Co. Antrim, first investigated by Jessen, and later re-investigated with the aid of radiocarbon dating by Alan Smith, such fen-peat was forming at least 9000 years ago.

If the water-table remained constant in level, willows and birches might invade the margin of the fen; as peat rich in sedge and wood debris began to build up, the wooded area would extend and other trees such as pine might invade its drier surface, and gradually a thick layer of wood-peat was formed. Such a development took place at Ballyscullion Bog, as is shown in the cross-section drawn up by Jessen (opposite).

If the water-table rose, the drainage of the surrounding slopes would be worsened, and the fens and fen-woods could creep up the surrounding slopes beyond the limits of the primary basal fen. Bob Hammond examined such a situation in the great areas of bog that now occupy much of the central lowlands of Ireland, and I have constructed a sketch-section to summarize his results. I have to say that the construction is my work, and I hope that it does not do injustice to Hammond's evidence. Here over a wide area there had been an early lake, and the open-water lake-mud is seen at the base of the section. On the right-hand of the section wet fen-wood is seen growing directly on the local glacial deposits 8500 years ago, and when the lake margin was invaded by fen vegetation, the fen spread in both directions building fen-peat out over the lake-muds on the one hand, and up the slope on top of the wood-fen-peat on the other. On the left-hand of the section, where the slope is steeper, the wood-fen-peat took a longer time to extend upwards, and its base is correspondingly younger, having only started to form about 5000 years ago.

Lakes continued to shrink as fens and fen-woods extended, and as the fen-peat thickened the plants on its surface found it more and more difficult to maintain their necessary supply of inorganic material from the underlying mineral soil, and the way was open for plants that could thrive on minimal amounts of inorganic nutrients to colonize the surface of the peat (p. 107, c).

The moss *Sphagnum* was ideally suited for this purpose, for it can grow vigorously when nourished only by rain and by the very small amount of nutrient material contained in the rain. *Sphagnum* has a remarkable capacity for capturing and storing rain-water. Many of its cells are like small hollow boxes with an aperture through which water can enter as into a trap; it is then held in the trap until needed for further growth. We can picture that the fen-surface was irregular and that rainfall was increasing. Pools will have formed in the fen hollows, and vigorously growing *Sphagnum*-species, such as *S.*

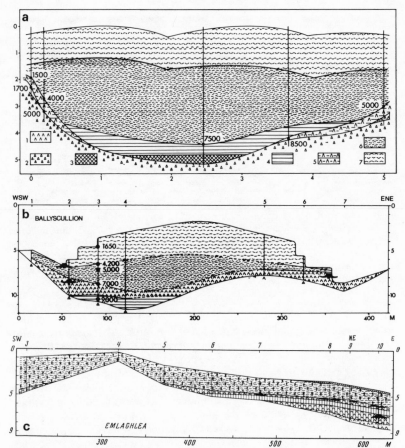

Sections through Irish bogs: **a**, schematic cross-section of large raised-bog complex in the Irish midlands to illustrate its progressive expansion as time elapsed (based on work by R. Hammond).

b, cross-section of the raised-bog at Ballyscullion, Co. Antrim, as drawn up by Knud Jessen, with added radiocarbon datings by Alan Smith.

c, cross-section through blanket-bog at Emlaghlea, Co. Kerry. 1, wood-peat; 2, glacial deposits; 3, open-water mud; 4, fen-peat; 5, wood-fen-peat; 6, *Sphagnum*-peat (highly humified); 7, *Sphagnum*-peat (slightly humified).

fuscum, will draw on the water, and build themselves up into a small mound or hummock. There is a limit to the height of the hummock, whose top becomes very sensitive to periods of dryness. As soon as the top becomes reasonably dry, it is invaded by lichens and by ling (*Calluna vulgaris*). As rain continues, the hummocks themselves now provide the high points between which water gets trapped, and shallow pools form between them. Aquatic *Sphagna* which

The Irish Landscape

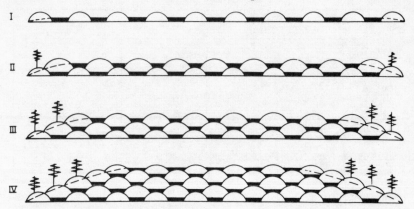

A diagram to illustrate one possible scheme of upward growth by a raised-bog, by the alternating development of pools and hummocks. The black shading indicates the wet pools, with *Sphagnum cuspidatum*, and the arcs represent the hummocks, with *S. fuscum* and *imbricatum*. The broken line indicates the water-table, and shows the way it rises as the bog grows upwards. (Redrawn by P. D. Moore and D. J. Bellamy after S. Kulczynski).

grow submerged, such as *S. cuspidatum*, invade the pools and build up a muddy layer which shallows the pools. The deer-grass (*Trichophorum cespitosum*), the cotton-grass (*Eriophorum angustifolium*), the beak-sedge (*Rhynchospora alba*), and the sun-dews (*Drosera* spp.) – which supplement their nutrient supply by catching insects – come in round the margin of the pond until the hummock-building *Sphagna* take over, and a new hummock rises over the former pool, while the tops of the old hummocks await flooding to form the next generation of pools. As the hummocks and pools scattered over the bog-surface replace one another cyclically, capillarity carries the water-table up with them, and the *Sphagnum*-peat rises into a dome or raised-bog nourished only by rain-water, forming the so-called ombrogenous-bog. (Pl. 15)

Such is the hummock-pool picture of raised-bog growth. But the picture is probably an over-simplification. If climate remained constant, could the oscillation between hummock and pool continue? Many people think that under constant conditions a uniform vegetation dominated by the vascular plants and lacking in vigorous *Sphagnum* growth would cover the bog-surface. Given constant climate, will the bog dome attain a certain degree of convexity, and then come into a standstill phase?

The bog can only grow because the rate of accumulation of vegetable debris exceeds the rate of decay. Most of the decay appears to take place in the top 20 cm, because below that level conditions are waterlogged, anaerobic and acid, with the result only very few decomposing organisms can operate. If growth is slow, there is time for attack on the surface materials, which partly break down or *humify*, producing brown degradation-products which culminate in jelly-like or liquid humic acids. If growth is rapid, the plant debris passes quickly beyond the reach of decay, and can survive in a remarkably undamaged condition. Efforts are made to correlate the degree of decay, or *humification*, with climate, strong humification being equated with relatively warm, dry conditions, and weak humification with relatively cool, wet conditions.

If climate moves towards warmth and dryness, the pools dry up, growth slows down, trees invade the bog margins, humification proceeds, and a rind of well-decayed peat covers the bog. If cold wet conditions return, the bog surface is flooded, the trees are killed and their stumps buried, muddy *Sphagnum*-peat is formed, the hummock-pool complex is renewed, and fresh unhumified peat starts to build up (p. 107, d). Such a stratigraphical change is said to record a 'regeneration' of the bog, and is sometimes spoken of as a 'recurrence-surface', at which there was a recurrence of peat-growth. In the past many efforts have been made to correlate recurrence-surfaces from one bog to another in an effort to reach a record of climatic change, but these on the whole have not been successful. (Pl. 31)

Raised-bogs, which were building up highly humified *Sphagnum*-peat, had certainly started to form, both in the midlands and in the north of Ireland, not less than 7000 years ago. It was at about the same time that alder started to expand in the Irish woodlands, and both phenomena may be due to increased wetness, that enabled water-tables to rise and allow the fens to expand, and the alder to invade the wetter soils. Because the *Sphagnum*-community can flourish when nurtured only by rain, it is tempting to think that increased wetness meant increased rain, and that this was the factor that triggered off the growth of the ombrogenous raised-bog. But the inhibiting factor that prevents the development of the *Sphagnum*-community may not be rainfall below a certain level, but rather the inability of the *Sphagnum*-community to oust other communities as long as the latter are continuing to receive at least the minimum amount of inorganic nutrients necessary for their growth. In other words it was the thickening of the fen-peat, to the point where the roots of the fen-plants could no longer draw sufficient inorganic nutrient to make healthy growth possible, that gave the *Sphagnum*-community its opportunity.

Two lines of evidence point in this direction. Raised-bog peat seems to find it impossible to start to form directly on inorganic soil; there must always be an insulating layer of fen-peat. Thus a peripheral band of fen vegetation always lies between the plants of the mineral soil and the plants of the raised-bog community, and unless the band advances secreting the insulating layer beneath itself, then the raised-bog cannot expand laterally, though it can grow upwards into a dome. The fens that lay in the poorly-drained ground between drumlins often provided nuclei for raised-bog growth, and from such nuclei the surface of the bog would rise like a rising tide to surround and eventually engulf the drumlins. But at all times a ribbon of fen, whose plants drew their nourishment from the drainage water from the mineral soil of the drumlin, lay between the slopes of the drumlin and the rising dome of the bog. (Pl. 15)

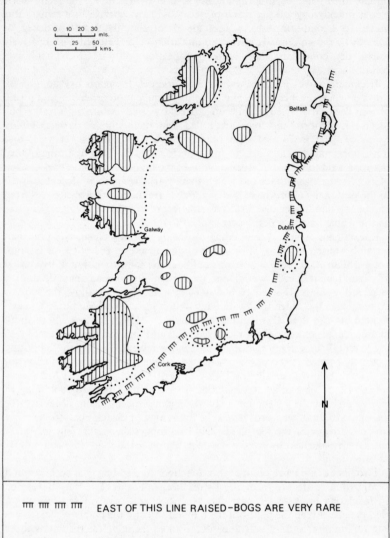

The distribution of bog in Ireland.

PLATE 13 *Above*, this mesolithic site at Mount Sandel, nr. Coleraine, Co. London-derry, dated to about 8650 years ago, gives us our oldest record of man in Ireland; it revealed huts, axes, microliths, and bones of birds and fish. *Below*, the raised beach at Cushendun, Co. Antrim, which contains mesolithic flint implements in Larnian style, has been isostatically uplifted to 8.5m above modern sea-level.

PLATE 14 *Above*, Aran Islands, Co. Galway. The currach, which still survives along the western seaboard, must have an ancestry going back through thousands of years in Ireland. *Below*, this scene of aboriginal life in New South Wales about 1820 could well represent Larnian life in Ireland, 5000 years ago. In the foreground men are spearing fish and catching lobsters; the group on the cliff-top are pointing to shoals of fish; light boats are drawn up on the shore; debris from the meal round the fire will form a kitchen-midden.

Today we have the impression that raised-bogs are very rare or absent near the coasts of east and south-east Ireland and that this reflects the dryness of these regions. But even here we can find the townland name 'Redbog' usually associated with low-lying ground, and here there will formerly have been raised-bogs which were cut away for fuel in days when the population was much higher than it is today. Few parts of Ireland have an annual rainfall of less than 750 mm, but although an area of the midlands between Athlone and Birr has no more rain than this, it is an area that is buried beneath some of the largest and deepest raised-bogs in Ireland.

The raised-bog system, once its growth had been initiated, may have been more or less self-perpetuating. It could trap water directly from the air, and build its own water-table up above that of the surrounding countryside. As it expanded it built up a natural dam across valleys which had previously been free to discharge surface water. The raised-bog can be likened to an enormous bag of water, and though we have very little knowledge as to whether there is a slow circulation of water within the bag, or as to whether water leaks out of the bag into the surrounding countryside, it is obvious that such a mass of saturated material may well have important effects on the water-table in the area surrounding it. The drainage of the neighbouring woodland floors may be further impeded, and the ground made still wetter.

Whatever may be the complicated factors that initiated bog-growth, domes of highly humified *Sphagnum*-peat had started to develop at least 7000 years ago. Climate was still relatively favourable, and bog-growth was slow. This type of accumulation continued till at least 5000 years ago.

In the next section we shall see the havoc that the first farmers wrought in the woodlands when they arrived in Ireland about 5500 years ago. But the acme of the Irish forests had probably passed with the climatic optimum. On the lowlands the expanding bogs were starting to engulf them like an inexorable tide. On the uplands increased exposure was probably enforcing a retreat to lower levels.

4

The First Farmers, 5500 to 1650 years ago

THE NEOLITHIC FARMERS AND THEIR MEGALITHIC TOMBS 5500 TO 4000 YEARS AGO

ABOUT 5500 years ago the amount of elm pollen being deposited in lakes and bogs underwent a drastic reduction throughout north-west Europe, and the cause of the fall has been a matter of considerable controversy. Elm is a relatively demanding tree, both in climate and in soil, and as there is some evidence that climate was now falling away from its 'optimum', some botanists suggested that climatic deterioration was the cause of the elm decline. Others pointed out that from time to time elm is vigorously attacked by disease, just as is happening in western Europe today, and claimed that a wave of such disease brought about the reduction in elm pollen.

It was Johannes Iversen in Denmark who first recognized about 1940 that the diminution in elm pollen was accompanied by the appearance of pollen of herbs that even today are still farming weeds, such as ribwort plantain (*Plantago lanceolata*), dock (*Rumex*) and nettle (*Urtica*), and that these phenomena must indicate forest clearance followed by farming which he styled 'landnam', using an old Scandinavian word for 'land taking'. It was quickly realized that such developments had taken place throughout north-west Europe, and radiocarbon datings place the event in the centuries before 5000 BP. Recent work in Co. Tyrone by Arthur ap Simon and Jon Pilcher shows that there the first attack on the woodlands took place as early as 5500 BP, and that is the date I am using here to end the Climax-phase (ILWC) when the Irish woodlands were at their finest development, and to begin the Damage-phase (ILWd₁) when they began to suffer from sporadic attack by invading farmers.

This event was studied closely by Alan Smith in a bog at Fallahogy, Co. Londonderry, where he combined detailed pollen-counts with numerous radiocarbon datings, and a version of the diagram is produced here. In this type of diagram the pollen-values are represented as free-standing columns, which expand or contract in width as values increase or diminish. A scale divided in units representing 10% of all pollen counted is shown along the base of the diagram, and along any horizontal line the total intercepts of the columns should add up to 100%. After the pollen-counts had been made, Professor Smith adjusted their values to accord with observations that some tree genera produce, area for area, very much more pollen than others. The aim is to make pollen-values relate to the areas occupied by the different trees, and not just report the crude pollen-values. This is the only diagram in this book in which such an adjustment has been made.

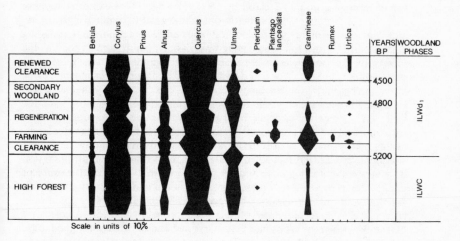

A schematic pollen-diagram from Fallahogy, Co. Londonderry, to illustrate a cycle of Neolithic land clearance.

At the base we see the Climax-phase continuing, with *Corylus*, *Quercus*, *Ulmus* and *Alnus* providing the bulk of the pollen, and the grasses only able to make a trifling contribution to the pollen-rain. Then the attack on the elm trees begins (here dated to 5200 years BP), and some hazel must have been removed also, as these pollens drop in value, while that of the grasses rises. A period of agriculture lasting about 350 years follows; grass rises to higher values, and some plants, notably plantain, dock and nettle rise to weed status in the cultivation-plots; bracken may have grown more freely. The natural fertility of the surface soil of the patches was quickly reduced, and when the farmers abandoned them, they were invaded first by hazel, and then by the forest trees. The grasses and weeds were gradually suppressed, and secondary woodland was established.

During the period of secondary woodland the deep roots of the trees penetrated down to levels where the soil was still rich in nutrients. These substances were drawn up into the leaves and wood of the tree, and when tree-debris was incorporated into the forest humus, the surface layers of the soil regained much of their lost fertility. The farmers could thus return to an area they had earlier abandoned. They did return at Fallahogy after another 350 years had elapsed, and at the top of the diagram we see the opening of the next farming phase.

Such in outline is the story that the pollen record tells us, and now we must ask ourselves, 'Do we believe it?' The Neolithic way of life, with its cultivated crops, its domestic animals, its pottery and its polished stone implements, began in the Middle East, and had reached south-east Europe before 7000 BP. How was it enabled to make a 'great leap forward' and spread apparently almost simultaneously throughout the whole of north-west Europe, so that it had reached even into Ireland by 5500 years ago? One can only suppose that the conditions of the 'climatic optimum' greatly favoured agriculture, and that the farming population was constantly increasing and radiating outwards. In central Europe farming was on open plains, and as soon as the forests of the north-west were reached, agricultural practices must have changed substantially. Woodland had to be cleared, and soil exhaustion came more quickly under the leaching effect of western rain. When the patch was exhausted there was still virgin forest ahead, and so you moved on, not back in search of an earlier clearing that had recovered. Can we picture a wave of agriculture advancing ever northwards and westwards through the woodlands, just as a fairy ring of toadstools advances outwards in a meadow?

Humphrey Case has recently discussed the problems of Neolithic migration in a very enlightening way, and he points out that communal movement implies the transposition of men, women, children and infants, together with breeding and milking livestock and seed-corn. Such an Odyssey could only take place at a certain time of the year, probably between August and November, when the crops had been harvested and there was still good grass and leaf-fodder along the route. The route to be followed would have been well prospected because once the crops had been sown, a limited number of able-bodied men could have gone out in scouting-parties, carrying some food but also existing in Mesolithic style by hunting and food-gathering.

From the chalk-cliffs of Calais the identical lands across the English Channel could easily be seen, and such a crossing was not too daunting or difficult for scouting-parties, but what about the livestock, the cattle, the sheep and the pigs? Until recently currachs were built in western Ireland with nothing more than lengths of timber, wooden pegs, rods of hazel or willow, hair twine and hides, though today more modern materials are used. These boats are about twenty feet in length, and in calm weather can carry up to twelve people, or a ton and a half of potatoes, or a cow with its legs tightly roped together. (Pl. 14)

Case discusses the type of boat that might have been available to Neolithic travellers, and comes to the conclusion that lightness and manoeuvrability were more important than size. A currach-type boat about thirty feet in length, with eight oarsmen and a helmsman, carrying about three tons gross weight might have been near the ideal size. With space for the crew and two dogs, and bedding for the stock, its load for a sea passage might have been two adult cows and two calves, or about six pigs, or ten sheep or goats. Because of the difficulty of watering stock on a voyage, such trips must of necessity have been short. Skin-bags or vessels containing water would add to the load of an already overcrowded boat; in any case the cattle would have been lying trussed on their sides, and could only have been given water with considerable difficulty. Case thinks that stock if well watered beforehand might hold out for two days, but that they would get restless and dangerous as their thirsts developed. They might also die quickly from a build-up of gases in the rumen. It is clear that sea voyages would have to be planned with some care, and that undue hold-ups had to be avoided.

We speak of not putting all our eggs in one basket, but this is exactly what

Neolithic folk were doing as they loaded their stock and their seed-corn into their skin boat on the shore of the English Channel or the Irish Sea. They could not have afforded not to know exactly where they were going, and what the beaches, tides and currents would be like at their landfall. Case thinks that there must have been a lot of coming and going, the location of elm-rich woodlands where the soils would be fertile, and perhaps the establishment of stock and crops on the far shore, before the final migration of the whole community. There was too much at stake to take a chance on *terra incognita*. Given these considerations we are almost inevitably driven to the conclusion that the first landings in Ireland must have been on the coasts of Antrim and Down, which are clearly visible from Britain. Scouting-parties may well have reported that here alone in Ireland there were ample supplies of flint. Tidal currents run strongly in the North Channel, but the distance is short, and advantage could be taken of spells of fine weather. Once ashore, there was much to be done. First the elm-woods were turned to; twigs and leaves were harvested to provide fodder to carry the stock through the first critical winter, and the trees themselves were ring-barked to kill them.

One of the things we have to believe is that a very limited number of immigrant farmers could so drastically reduce the output of elm pollen. I believe that this was only possible if in the primeval woods the elms were concentrated in dense stands on patches of good soil, and that the farmers, who were aware of this relationship, killed the trees by ring-barking them. All the farmer wanted to do was to allow the sun's rays to reach his crops without being intercepted by a canopy of leaves, and a dead tree casts little shade. He was going to till the soil with a polished stone mattock, not with a plough, and the fact that the ground was still encumbered with tree stems and roots would call for the expenditure of less additional labour than the cutting down and burning of the tree trunks themselves. So I picture that quite a small group of men could sweep through an elm-wood quickly ring-barking the trees, and so indeed putting an end to the production of elm pollen. In any case the soil of the tillage-patch thus created was going to become exhausted quite quickly, and it would have been stupid to put into land that was only going to have a short life the immense amount of effort necessary to produce neat fields, free of tree trunks and stumps.

Carl Sauer puts this point of view very well; he says, 'Primitive agriculture is located in woodlands. Even the pioneer American farmer hardly invaded the grasslands until the second quarter of the past century. His fields were clearings won by deadening, usually by girdling, the trees. The larger the trees, the easier the task; brush required grubbing and cutting; sod stopped his advance until he had plows capable of ripping through the matted grass roots. The forest litter he cleaned up by occasional burning; the dead trunks hardly interfered with his planting. The American pioneer learned and followed Indian practices. It is curious that scholars, because they carried into their thinking the tidy fields of the European plowman and the felling of trees by ax, have so often thought that forests repelled agriculture and that open lands invited it.'

Stockades had to be erected to protect the cultivated plots from grazing animals, and the breeding stock from their numerous enemies. First of these were the animal predators, the wolf, the lynx, the fox, none of which had seen slow-moving domesticated animals before, and would regard them as natural gifts from the gods. Second, there were those less lucky immigrant farmers who had lost some of their vital stock on the voyage, or whose bull was sterile, or whose heifers were barren, who were desperate and would stop at nothing. And then there were the Larnians, amazed by the newcomers, with their strangely different way of life. What were the contacts – hostile or friendly? I believe that friendly trading relations were established, and that the higher standard of living of the farmers raised that of the aborigines, who at first rapidly increased in numbers, and then were assimilated into the Neolithic communities. Both the coastal Larnians in Co. Dublin, and the lakeside settlers in Co. Westmeath, are dated after the arrival of the Neolithic people, and had gained polished stone axes from them. Perhaps the Larnians established fishing villages in the vicinity of Neolithic settlements, and traded fish for corn and stone axes.

When the stock was safe, attention could be turned to housing for the colonists. At Ballynagilly, Co. Tyrone, the Neolithic settlement was on a low hill of light soil, at an altitude of about 200 m; the top of the hill was crowned by the remains of a substantial house. This was almost square in shape, with 6 m sides, and had been built by erecting radially-split oak planks in a foundation trench; it had probably burned down, and charred plank remains gave a C-14 date of 5165 BP. Within the house post-holes indicated how the roof had been supported, and there were also two hearths and a refuse-pit with pottery and other debris.

Neolithic houses were also discovered at Lough Gur, Co. Limerick, during the extensive series of excavations carried out in that area by the late Seán Ó Ríordáin, whose untimely death was such a blow to archaeological studies in Ireland. Both rectangular and round houses were revealed, and charcoal from the base of a post-hole gave a C-14 date of about 4500 BP: an artist's impression suggests what the houses may have looked like. As at Ballynagilly, most had a hearth and a refuse-pit inside them: the pits may have started as store-places, and only been used for refuse later. Besides protecting their stock, the settlers had to protect their seed-corn against damp and weevils, as well as against thieves, and what better place than beside the constantly-attended hearth could be found?

When the necessary energy had been expended on the homestead, patience and resolution were the next qualities needed. In animal husbandry patience extending over years, until the foundation-stock had been built up to a level at which it could be safely cropped, and resolution to ensure that no matter what hardship, what famine came, the long-term breeding-stock would not be sacrificed to meet a short-term crisis, however severe it might be. In plant husbandry not only had the seed-corn to be guarded, but when sown it had to be defended during daylight hours against pigeons and sparrows. When it appeared above ground new enemies – deer, wild boar and hares – as well as the local farm beasts had to be guarded against night and day, and careful weeding was necessary if the return was to be as high as possible. Children

Reconstructions of the types of Neolithic houses excavated by S. P. Ó Ríordáin at Lough Gur, Co. Limerick.

and old folk, of course, could carry out much of this work, but the total amount of labour required in the growing-season must have been very great. If the crop was a light one, resolution was again needed to carry an adequate seed-stock through to the next season.

Taken all in all rare qualities of leadership were needed if the immigrant group were to survive the first few years of transplantation.

We can now jump forward one hundred years or more to the point where the farming communities are established in Ireland, and ask ourselves, 'What equipment have they got, what do they do with it, and what are they doing to the landscape?'

We can take the polished stone axe first because it was with this tool, suitably mounted in a wooden handle – occasionally preserved in bog-finds – that the farmers were enabled to establish mastery over their environment to a degree that was not possible to their Mesolithic predecessors. They were now able not only to eradicate trees on a large scale but were also able to work big pieces of wood, and as we have seen build substantial houses. If the axe was mounted with the edge at right angles to the shaft, it would serve as a digging-implement or *mattock*, and there are early pictorial representations both in Egypt and in Italy which show the mattock being used in cultivation.

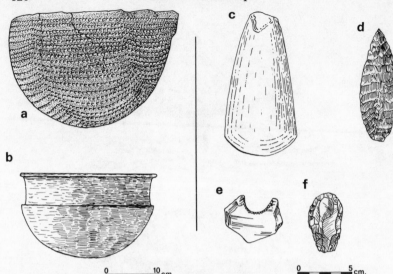

Some typical Neolithic objects: **a**, decorated round-bottomed bowl, Mound of the Hostages, Tara, Co. Meath; **b**, plain shouldered bowl, Browndod, Co. Antrim; **c**, polished axe, stone, Dunloy, Co. Antrim; **d**, javelin-head, flint, Bann Valley; **e**, hollow scraper, flint, Tamnyrankin, Co. Londonderry; **f**, end-scraper, flint, Ballynagard, Co. Antrim.

These Neolithic people knew that in addition to flint certain types of fine-grained rock were suitable for the making of such axes, and it was not long before 'factories' were established where outcrops of such rocks occurred. We have seen that in Palaeogene times volcanic lavas in the north of Ireland were weathered under tropical conditions to clayey residues, and when more lava was poured on top, the residue was sometimes baked to a china-like texture, producing a rock known as 'Porcellanite', eminently suitable for the manufacture of axes. In Antrim this rock outcrops at Tievebulliagh on the mainland and on Rathlin Island, and at each outcrop roughed-out axes and debris indicate the former existence of an axe-factory. Axes produced here were of special character, and were distributed widely as the distribution-map shows. These Irish factories have not been dated by C-14, but factories in the Lake District and in Scotland indicate an age around 4500 BP, and the Irish ones were probably operating at the same time.

There are several types of flint implements with trimmed edges, obviously used in scraping and planing, and flakes with a concave working edge – the so-called 'hollow scraper' – useful for stripping bark and buds off slender stems, which could then be used in basket-work or as shafts for arrows. Thin, carefully worked, lozenge-shaped pieces in various sizes were arrow or javelin heads, and, though not yet found in Ireland, Neolithic bows of yew wood have been found in bogs in Somerset.

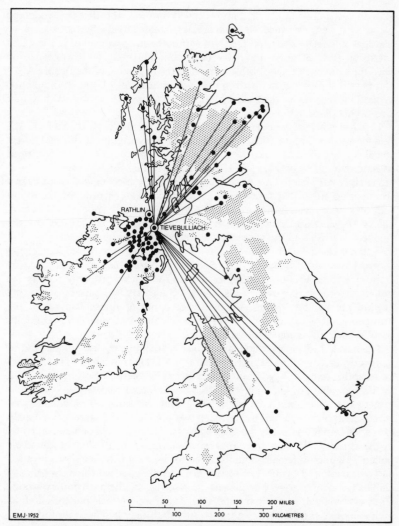

The distribution in the British Isles of polished axes of porcellanite originating from the 'axe factories' on Rathlin Island and at Tievebulliagh, Co. Antrim. (After E. M. Jope).

But evidence for agriculture is slight. There are no small flint blades which might have been mounted along an ox-jaw or a curved piece of wood to be used as a sickle, and stones whose shape suggests they might have been used for grinding corn are very rare. This, combined with the abundance of cattle bones on the dwelling-sites, would suggest that in the early stages emphasis was on cattle-grazing rather than on cereal farming, and that the woodland clearances were designed to give grazing areas rather than tillage plots. Cattle would feed eagerly on the shoots of bushes and regenerating trees, and extensive areas of grass may have been rare. This may be the explanation why grass pollen in the Neolithic – and also the beginning of the Bronze Age – shows only low values in the diagrams (see figure on p. 137), even though the general movements of the pollen curves make it clear that forest disturbance was taking place.

In what sorts of woodlands did they find themselves? In 5300 BP the midden-users living on Dalkey Island, an outcrop of granite, still had access to oak-woods, if we can take the small number of pieces of charcoal identified as representative – oak 11, ash 1, holly 1. But when the houses on the limestone slopes at Lough Gur were occupied, the firewood tended to be drawn from bushes rather than forest trees, as the charcoal list (in order of frequency) indicates hazel, ash, hawthorn (*Crataegus*), holly, oak, whitebeam (*Sorbus*), cherry (*Prunus*) and pine. Here the dry limestone soil is indicated by the frequency of ash and the absence of alder. Megalithic tombs on slaty soils in Leinster yielded hazel, willow or poplar (*Populus*), oak, whitebeam, hawthorn, birch, alder, ash, ivy, elm, elderberry (*Sambucus*) and cherry. Apart from clearance, the low ranking of ash and elm here probably reflects the non-calcareous nature of the soils, and the elderberry will have been growing around the habitation-sites, where the dumping of refuse had raised the nitrogen content of the soil. It will be noted that in the last two examples hazel is the most common charcoal.

The hazel at all times found conditions in Ireland very favourable, and in its first expansion in the Beginning-phase (ILWB) its contribution to the local pollen-rain seems to have been greater than elsewhere in Europe (p. 97). In the Climax-phase of high forest (ILWC) it was forced back, and its contribution to the pollen-rain falls below 50%. But as soon as a woodland area which had been cleared by farmers was abandoned, hazel immediately expanded into it, in exactly the same way as it had expanded on its first arrival in the country. We had thus an area of hazel scrub, producing abundant pollen. If the scrub remained undisturbed for long enough then it was invaded and overshadowed by the forest trees, just as had happened when the primary climax woodlands were establishing themselves. In these secondary woodlands elm and ash were often important, and if we see their pollens climb to high values in our diagram, we can be sure that there had been a substantial reduction of farming in the vicinity.

But the high forest never re-established itself to the extent that it seriously depressed the output of hazel pollen, and the pollen record shows that at all times from the first woodland disturbance more than five thousand years ago, until the Tudor clearance in the late sixteenth century, there must have been very extensive areas of secondary hazel scrub in Ireland. Today this scrub is largely confined to the limestones of western Ireland, and we think of Ireland as a country of grassland. But this Ireland, the Emerald Isle of the poet, probably only took shape some 350 years ago, and before that it was for long a country of hazel scrub, merging in some places into secondary woodland or remnants of original forest, and opening out in others into patches of agricultural land.

But if the tillage areas in Neolithic times were small, the cattle could have browsed in the hazel scrubs, as we see them do in the Burren today. And beef was the chief element in the Neolithic meat diet. Our first record of domestic animals is from Ringneill Quay in Down, where the sea as it rose to its maximum level washed away a Neolithic site, and scattered its flints, bones and charcoal; the charcoal had a C-14 age of 5380 years BP. Domestic ox, domestic pig and possibly sheep or goat were identified. Dalkey Island, at 5300 BP, produced domestic ox, domestic sheep (though the possibility of goat cannot be ruled out) and pig (it was not possible to say whether domestic or wild); the absence of red deer should be noted. Other animals certainly eaten were various fish and birds, and possibly eaten were bear and grey seal. Bones of domestic dogs were also recorded.

In a paper published in 1954 Ó Ríordáin described seven sites on Knockadoon, an island in Lough Gur. All the sites were mainly Neolithic, but some had continued in use until the opening of the Bronze Age. All seven sites yielded ox bones in abundance, five yielded some bones of pig (either wild or domestic) and red deer, four yielded sheep (or goat), and two yielded horse. Bear occurred on two sites, and it is thus clear that the bear must have survived at least until this time in Ireland. Dog (or wolf) occurred on three sites.

We can thus picture the beginning of a slow change in the lowland landscape. There would have been some small tillage-patches, but the bulk of the effort went into breaking the forest canopy, and thus encouraging the growth of saplings and bushes, which together with rough grasses, would have provided fodder for the growing herds of cattle. When the tillage-patch was exhausted, the group would move on, and the forest would relatively quickly re-establish itself in secondary woodland in a pattern barely distinguishable from the virgin state. In the regrowth, all traces of house and stockades would be swallowed up, and the next round of clearance would ensure that nothing was left for the future archaeologist. This I feel is the main reason we know so little of the habitation-sites not only of the Neolithic, but also of the Bronze Age. As long as forest regeneration was capable of swallowing up the houses and stockades that had stood in woodland clearings, then evidence of former habitation had little chance of survival; it is only after AD 300 when woodland had shrunk in extent, and timber was no longer so freely available for building, that habitation-sites begin to survive. The natural limestone terraces and light soils around Lough Gur on the one hand attracted continuous settlement, and on the other discouraged regeneration of heavy woodland, and there some record of the Neolithic habitations has survived.

The relative scarcity of remains of red deer is remarkable. Today in many countries venison is prized as a delicacy, and it seems curious that Neolithic man should have turned his back on this animal as a source of meat. Many of the records are of worked antler rather than meat bones. This is all the more curious, because, as we have seen, man's interference with the woodlands must have greatly increased the number of deer.

To obtain adequate food a Mesolithic family would have to wander over a wide area, and so there was an upward limit to the size to which family communities could grow, and there were few operations, other than driving flocks of wildfowl or shoals of fish towards traps or nets, in which more than a limited number of hunters could profitably combine.

Farming produced much more food from a smaller area, and at certain times of the year quite large groups of people could work together with much greater efficiency than smaller groups, and so the successful Neolithic communities tended to expand in size. As they did so, two things became apparent, first that at certain times of the year there was a considerable amount of spare adult labour, and second that if this was to be employed in an organized fashion, qualities of leadership had to be still further developed. The heavy work of transforming woodland into tillage-plots and grassy strips, clearing away large stones and building them into walls, building houses and stockades, and butchering, was obviously for adult men, but the weeding and bird-scaring of crops, and the milking, butter-making, spinning and weaving, and the guarding of stock could be largely carried out by older people, women and children.

Like all primitive folk they will have seen their surroundings as peopled, not only by the living community, but also by potentially beneficial deities who had to be propitiated, by hostile demons who had to be avoided or exorcized, and by the spirits of the former members of the community. The first farmers who reached Ireland obviously believed in the continuity of the community after death, and after cremating the body, they would deposit the burned bones in a communal tomb. This belief and practice were common to all the early farming communities along the western seaboard of Europe from Spain to Scandinavia, and must have had its origin farther to the east, probably on the shores of the Mediterranean Sea.

The essential element in a communal tomb was an accessible chamber, protected by a mound of earth or stones, and from this basic formula a very great variety of tomb-types developed. The chamber was built of tree trunks or large stones, and as the latter are much more durable, by far the majority of surviving chambers are stone-built, and hence the term *megalithic tomb*.

Radiocarbon dating suggests that the first type to appear in Ireland was the *Court-grave*, dated at Ballymacdermot, Co. Armagh, to 4800 years ago. The typical Court-grave has an elongated cairn of small stones, delimited by a kerb of upright stones or dry-stone walling; the cairn is about 30 m long. Recessed into the broader end of the cairn there is a court of roughly oval, circular or semi-circular shape, which gives its name to the tomb-type. The burial chamber opens from the inner end of the court, and consists of a gallery of two, three or four chambers. The gallery walls are of great upright stones, and the roof stones are supported on one or more tiers of slabs, called *corbels*, which are laid overlapping inwards upon the uprights of the chamber walls. The remains of more than thirty individuals in one chamber have been recorded, and unburned as well as cremated burials have been found. In addition to being given a resting-place in a communal grave, the dead were provided with necessities for the afterlife as these tombs yield polished stone

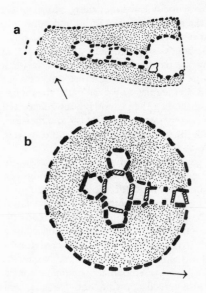
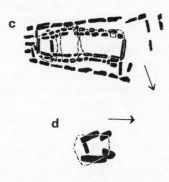

Types of megalithic tomb found in Ireland: **a**, court-grave, Browndod, Co. Antrim; **b**, passage-grave, Carrowkeel (K), Co. Sligo; **c**, gallery-grave, Labbacallee, Co. Cork; **d**, dolmen, Kilfeaghan, Co. Down.

axes, arrowheads, scrapers and pottery vessels (see figure on p. 120).

Over 300 Court-graves are known in Ireland, mainly north of the central lowlands. Their distribution is a scattered one, and suggests that they are the tombs of a rather spread-out ranching community. Estyn Evans sees their builders coming up the Irish Sea to a landfall in eastern Ulster; Ruaidhrí de Valéra pictures them as coming from atlantic France by a western route, by-passing the south of Ireland, and landing around Sligo and Killala Bays.

In England the closest relative of the Court-grave is the Long-barrow, which centres on the Severn Valley, and the two types are similar in many details of form and content. From the south of England a coastal movement up the east side of the Irish Sea would first reach the Severn basin, and if continued on would ultimately bring Ireland clearly into sight and tempt a crossing into eastern Ulster.

But the Wicklow Mountains can be seen from the top of the Lleyn Peninsula on a clear day, and in summer the cumulus clouds over the mountains could be seen from sea-level, and these early navigators would have been aware of the significance of cumulus clouds over the horizon. In good weather a direct passage could be made to the Leinster coast.

This was certainly the route taken by another important group of tomb builders who favoured a round mound delimited by a circular kerb of horizontal stones, in which they set a passage lined with tall stones and a lintel roof, the *Passage-grave*. At its inner end the passage typically expanded into a chamber, which could have a variety of shapes, and often had side- and end-chambers; the roof of the chamber was usually formed by a fine corbelled vault. The stones of the passage and chamber, and also of the kerb around the mound, are often richly decorated with incised abstract designs, ultimately derived from Iberia. Cremation was the general rule but unburned bones are also present. Some tombs which had not been opened since Neolithic times were crammed with cremated human bones, sometimes to a depth of 1 m in the chamber and completely filling the passage. Hundreds of burials can be inferred. Unburned bone pins, lying among cremated bone, suggest that the burned bones may have been placed in leather or woven bags, the mouth of the bag closed by the bone pin, and the bag then carried in and deposited in the tomb. Round-bottomed coarse pottery decorated by stabs and incision, hammer shaped pendants, stone balls like children's marbles, and a wide assortment of beads are commonly found in these tombs.

Almost 300 of this type of grave, generally known as Passage-graves, are known in Ireland, chiefly in groups or cemeteries sited on hills or ridges in eastern Ireland, but sending out limited numbers into Court-grave country in Sligo and Antrim. They reach their highest development in the Boyne valley at Newgrange (dated by radiocarbon to 4500 years ago), Dowth and Knowth. The recent excavations being carried out at Knowth by George Eogan have attracted especial attention because two, and not one, chambered tombs arranged at opposite sides of the great mound have been discovered (see figure on p. 129). One of the tombs has especial resemblances to similar tombs in Brittany, not only in its design but also in its decoration, and it would seem that there must be some fairly direct connections. (Pl. 16)

If we look again at the figure on p. 94, we see the peninsulas of southern Ireland, southern Wales, Cornwall and Brittany, where evidence of an old phase of earth movement, which I have called Armorican, can still be clearly traced. But these areas are united by more than a common experience of geological upheaval. The rocks that were disturbed were of similar lithology, and the subsequent history of erosion and of positioning in relation to sea-level appears to have been much the same in all four areas. Today the promontories run westwards towards the Atlantic Ocean, and the water that at once both separates and unites them is taking on the name of the Celtic Sea.

Whenever there was migration up the western fringe of Europe, whether of plants, animals, men or ideas, the similar environments of the Armorican lands induced similarities in the invaders. These similarities appear over and over again; they certainly appeared when the Passage-grave builders were moving into north-west Europe, because such tombs are found throughout the area, and in Brittany go back beyond 5500 years BP.

The great mound at Knowth, with its ring of decorated kerbstones, was surrounded by smaller satellite tombs, one of which dates back to 4850 years BP. The satellites are of various design; some contain central chambers with side-chambers; others have only a simple passage without chamber. At Townleyhall some miles away Dr Eogan had earlier excavated a simple passage without chamber, sometimes awkwardly called an *Undifferentiated Passage-grave*, meaning, I suppose, that the passage has to serve the function of both passage and chamber, and the Townleyhall tomb had been erected over the site of a Neolithic house, from which both carbonized wood and cereals were recovered. The charcoal had a radiocarbon age of 4680 years ago, and the cereals were presumably of like age. At the time of the excavation the field surrounding the tomb was carrying a cereal crop, and it gave one an uncanny sense of continuity in the Irish landscape to realize that the same field had perhaps been performing the same function for some 4500 years.

Undifferentiated Passage-graves also occur in Waterford and in the Scilly Islands, and it may well be that there were early crossings from the Scilly Islands to Waterford, across the waters of the Celtic Sea.

We have also very simple megalithic tombs, the *Dolmens* (p. 125), consisting today of no more than some erect stones supporting a capstone. Originally the whole structure was probably protected by a mound or cairn, but these have disappeared, as have also any contents of the grave, by which we might hope to date it. Some dolmens are probably early in the megalithic tradition; others may be quite late.

Though I have taken the date of 5500 years ago as marking the establishment of Neolithic farming in Ireland, our earliest record, from charcoal associated with Neolithic pottery at Ballynagilly, Co. Tyrone, dates from 5700 years ago, a time at which the earliest Passage-graves were beginning to be erected in Brittany. In Ireland the Court-grave goes back to 4800 years ago, and simple Passage-graves were appearing at Knowth at the same time. Newgrange itself was built 4500 years ago. What did the Irish landscape look like after 1000 years of farming attacks? The farming communities had come on a long way in that millennium, from the time when the first few family parties struggled ashore, to the position where a wealthy and sophisticated group could expend capital and man-power on the erection of large and complicated monuments.

That Newgrange, Knowth and Dowth are large monuments is a matter for simple observation; we are just beginning to realize how complicated they are. If asked a few years ago, 'How were they built?', we would probably have said, 'Well, first of all you laid out the surrounding kerb, and set people to work heaping up the mound inside it with whatever materials came to hand; at the same time others were erecting the passage and chamber, and building ramps of earth – which were subsequently engulfed in the mound – to enable the large stones used to be drawn up into position.'

Today, thanks to the work of Brian O'Kelly at Newgrange, and George Eogan at Knowth, we can see that the actual work was much more complicated. O'Kelly now considers that at Newgrange both the passage and corbelled vault of the chamber were built as free-standing structures, and subsequently buried by mound material; the junction between the lintelled passage and the corbelled chamber is an especially neat point of construction. The roof of the first part of the passage has a second false roof above it, and through the gap between the two roofs, rays of sunlight can shine up the passage and into the chamber at dawn around the time of the winter solstice, and thus the layout of the passage must have been very carefully aligned. The flagstones roofing the passage abut against one another, and had nothing more been done, water could have leaked down into the passage between their ends. Two things were in fact done; soil containing charcoal debris was used to caulk the gaps (and it was this charcoal that gave the radiocarbon date); and to make assurance doubly sure, gutters were cut in the upper surface of the slabs, so that any percolating water was discharged laterally beyond the sides of the passage.

And the mound, both at Newgrange and at Knowth, is not just a heap of randomly dumped material, but a carefully organized structure. Although the bulk of the mound at Newgrange is of water-rolled cobbles, presumably drawn from the glacial outwash gravels of the vicinity, there are also layers of sods, thickest at the perimeter, and thinning out towards the centre. The sods appear to have come from poor pastures, which may have developed on former tillage-plots or fields. The margin of the mound above the kerb was supported by a revetting-wall, which was further embellished in the vicinity of the entrance. Here there were large numbers of oval granite boulders about 25 cm long, of a type of rock that probably occurs in the Mourne Mountains. Such boulders are not common in the local glacial gravels, and must have been carefully collected somewhere, probably between Newgrange and the Mourne Mountains. There were also large quantities of vein quartz, which must also have been specially assembled on the site; there are veins of quartz in the local slaty rocks, and such material could perhaps have been obtained in the vicinity. After very considerable study of the way these materials were lying in their collapsed positions, Professor O'Kelly came to the conclusion that these materials had been decoratively arranged on the wall-face in the vicinity of the entrance. During the recent work that has been carried out by the Office of Public Works at Newgrange, the granite and the quartz have again been put up on the wall-face. While it cannot be claimed that the present arrangement necessarily resembles the original arrangement in any way, it does serve to impress on us still further that for the users of the grave the entrance area had a special significance, a fact already apparent from the splendid quality of the decorative design on the great stone that lies across the entrance.

Dr Eogan has discovered two megalithic tombs in the mound at Knowth, and here again, though the quantities were trivial compared with Newgrange, there were the same granite boulders and the same pieces of vein quartz in the vicinity of the entrances to both the tombs. The mound structure is even more complicated at Knowth than at Newgrange. The knoll on which the mound lies is of black Carboniferous shales, and the mound is built up of layers of shale, layers of water-rolled cobbles, and layers of sods. Just as in building procedures for large modern structures, there must have been both architects and quantity surveyors employed, the architects to design the tombs and the mound, and the quantity surveyors to see that the necessary materials were available in the right amounts when they were called for. (Pl. 17)

What sort of social organization lies behind this ability to erect, probably in a relatively short space of time, three enormous and complicated tombs, separated by distances of less than one mile, and what can have been the landscape that produced the wealth to support the social organization? I think we must reject the concept of simple peasant groups assembling together at such times as the yearly cycle of agricultural activities made it possible to do so, and erecting the tombs by direct labour. There must have

PLATE 15 *Above*, Derryadd raised-bog, nr. Lanesborough, Co. Longford, now being developed mechanically. Here the intact bog-surface (left) formerly showed many open pools. The ribbon of fen that once separated the dome of the bog from the mineral soil of the drumlin island has been damaged by local peat-cutting, but the broad band of pale vegetation between the fields and the bog indicates its former position. The island is now treeless, but the prefix *Derry* in the name of the bog, shows that the region was once covered by oakwoods. *Below*, raised-bog, nr. Woodford, Co. Galway. Hummocks of *Sphagnum imbricatum*, covered by *Calluna vulgaris* (ling), rise from a carpet-like surface of *S. pulchrum*, which is without open pools. Lichens and flowering-heads of *Eriophorum angustifolium* can be seen.

PLATE 16 *Above*, the great Passage-grave mound with its surrounding kerb-stones at Knowth, Co. Meath. Smaller satellite tombs with surrounding kerbs lie nearby; these too would have had mounds, and two reconstructed mounds can be seen at top right. A black circle in the lower right-hand sector covers a reconstructed souterrain; from here a passage in which were found coins struck in Winchester about AD 950 leads down the side of the mound. Scattered masonry blocks on the top of the mound come from an Anglo-Norman building. *Below*, The Mound of the Hostages, Hill of Tara, Co. Meath. The partly exposed mound of stones contained an undisturbed Passage-grave, built about 4000 years ago. A rind of earth was later laid over the original mound, and burials in Cinerary Urns were inserted in this about 3500 years ago. The hostages would be of a much later date.

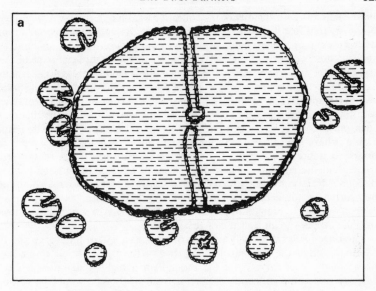

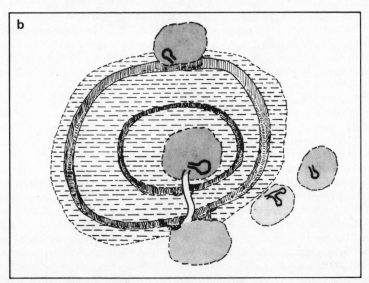

Knowth, Co. Meath: **a**, diagram to illustrate megalithic activities, showing the mound surrounded by a kerb, the passage-graves concealed within it, and the associated satellite-tombs; **b**, diagram to illustrate later activities, extending perhaps from AD 300 to AD 1000, showing the concentric ditches dug around the flanks of the mound, and the occupation-areas with their souterrains.

been chieftains with custody of the collective wealth of a community and with authority to direct the work of the labour force. In modern industrial nations a great deal of wealth and labour is expended on the manufacture of sophisticated weapons of such terrible power that even those who make them trust that they will never be used. Yet when one is made there is no alternative but to make another one, or else much of the economic structure of the nation would collapse. It has recently been argued that the pyramids of Egypt reflect a similar position; the whole economy became geared to the construction of such public works, and when one was completed another had to be begun. Could it have been the same in the Boyne valley? Was the driving force the desire to impress or the need for a large mausoleum? Each of the great tombs had the capacity to hold the cremated remains of thousands of individuals. If the community was of such a size as to make three such mausolea necessary, its numbers must have been very large indeed, and the area it farmed must have been enormous. We need no longer be amazed by the way that the output of elm pollen was reduced.

The ridge of *Brugh na Boinne* lies between the valleys of the Boyne and the Mattock, and on the ridge each mound is set on the top of a knoll. It may have been ritually necessary to set the mound on a high point, in which case whether one could or could not see it from a distance would be without significance. But in the case of the Passage-graves in the Wicklow Mountains, they are not set on the highest point of the relatively flat dome-like tops, but rather a little way down the slope at the level at which they were most widely visible, always provided that the view was not blocked by lowland forest. I think we may take it that the Boyne tombs were placed on their knolls in order to make them more visible from a distance, and this must imply a very considerable forest clearance in the surrounding area.

If we stand on the top of Newgrange and look about us in every direction, we overlook a basin of about twenty square miles before rising ground cuts off our view. If we imagine this basin as completely cleared of trees, everyone working within it could either see the mounds, or feel that he ought to be able to see them, and could perhaps have a sense of devotion or commitment to them. What size of Neolithic population could this basin support? I picture the typical farm family as consisting of one grandparent, two parents, and three children aged 14, 8 and 2; there would thus be four able-bodied persons, an 8-year-old child, capable of tending stock and scaring birds, and an infant. I allow each such family a 60-acre farm, as I reckon the yields would have been far less than those of today, even though the type of farming used was essentially gardening rather than farming. The basin would thus have held some 200 farms with a total population of 1200 persons, a number that is in the same order as today's population. During a two-month spring lull in farm operations, each farm could have spared two able-bodied persons for other duties. The chieftain could therefore hope to call up 400 able-bodied persons for a two-month period to build tombs or do other work. Carrying earth and other materials would have been an important task. If I am given a leather sack and the scapula of a cow, and directed to a gravel pit 400 m from the construction-site – as could have been the case at Newgrange – how

many sacks will I fill and carry during a day? I should reckon not more than
ten, and each day should therefore bring 4000 sacks, and each working-season
240,000 sacks of material to the site. Newgrange must contain about one
million such sackfuls, and so four working-seasons would have been spent on
assembling the material. When we remember that not all the materials came
from near at hand, that stone had to be quarried, dressed, transported,
decorated and erected, and that the layering of the mound had to be arranged,
we can add at least one more working-season. So we can possibly envisage
that twenty square miles, if free of trees and all closely farmed, could support
the building over a five-year period of such a tomb as Newgrange. What
would the cost be today? Twenty-four thousand five-day weeks are involved,
and this at current rates for agricultural labourers represents a bill for £600,000.
While I should be the first to agree that all the figures I have chosen are so
highly speculative as to be almost worthless, nonetheless the point cannot be
avoided that Newgrange represents a very considerable capital investment,
and that a large area of farmland must have been necessary to provide the
capital. Michael Herity has recently discussed this same problem; he reckons
that when the great tombs were being built a population of some 4000 people
based on urban dwellings were carrying out large-scale farming in the Boyne
valley.

Even today some forms of capital investment are imprudent, and it can
only have been imprudent in the extreme for the local farmers to sacrifice the
sods off their fields for the construction of the mounds. The palaeobotanical
examination of the sods tells us that the fields had already passed their prime
at the time they were cut. What can they have been like after the valuable
humus of the sod layer had been removed?

In the foregoing paragraphs I have guessed that all woodland had been
removed frcm this part of the Boyne basin, and therefore there must have
been a pretty substantial output of grass pollen. Yet as already noted such
pollen-diagrams as we have suggest only a very small output of grass pollen as
compared with that of the trees. Area for area, trees produce more pollen
than grass, but it may be that only limited areas in the vicinity of Passage-
grave cemeteries had been so cleared of trees, or alternately that the areas had
still a considerable amount of woodland, and that the community must have
been more widely dispersed in area than I have envisaged.

THE CONTINUING MOVEMENT OF LAND AND SEA

When referring to the archaeological material at Ringneill Quay on Strangford Lough, I said that it had been washed into its present position by the sea.
The sea also damaged the midden at Sutton, Co. Dublin; the midden had
been occupied by Larnian folk in contact with the newly-arrived Neolithic
farmers about 5250 BP. What were the later movements of the land and the
sea? (p. 64.)

As we have seen, when Ireland was severed from Britain, perhaps about
8500 BP, sea-level was rising eustatically, and the north-east corner of Ireland,
which had long been pressed down under the weight of ice, was still rising

isostatically. For how long did these movements continue? The waves built a bar of gravels and silts across the mouth of Glendun, which opens into the North Channel in north-east Antrim, and here at Cushendun, where isostatic movement must have been very marked, we have quite a detailed record. About 8500 years ago the rate at which the sea was rising eustatically overtook the rate at which the land was rising isostatically, and an estuarine silt was deposited on freshwater peat. The rising waves then built silts and gravels up to a thickness of 5 metres. At this time Larnian fishermen were living round the bay, and the flint implements they used were incorporated in the deposits as the sea overwhelmed their camp-sites. An upper silt which is now 5 m *above* modern sea-level had an age of about 7700 years; a similar silt of about the same age in Dublin Bay, an area which as far as we know has not been isostatically uplifted, is still 3 m *below* modern sea-level. So it would seem that at Cushendun isostatic uplift of at least 8 m took place after 7700 BP. (Pl. 13)

Sea-level also continued to rise probably at a fluctuating rate, and there is now a volume of evidence that it reached heights of about 4 m *above* its present level about 5000 years ago, just when the Neolithic farmers were becoming established in Ireland. It probably passed up above its present level about 6500 years BP, because a 'submerged forest' near Bray, Co. Wicklow, discovered by Praeger many years ago, which lies at low spring-tide level, has a radiocarbon age of 6750 years BP.

Continuing rise in sea-level turned Howth Head, on the north shore of Dublin Bay, into an island, which much later was occupied by Larnian fishermen who had acquired polished stone axes from the incoming Neolithic farmers. One night storm-waves washed away part of their midden, and deposited beach gravel on what was left. Charcoal from a surviving part of the midden, *underneath* the storm beach, had a radiocarbon age of 5250 BP. This storm was the culminating point in sea-level rise; as the waves fell back they left an isthmus of sand and gravel 4 m above modern sea-level, which today links the promontory of Howth to the mainland; shells in the gravels gave a radiocarbon age determination of 4650 years BP. The lowering of sea-level is also marked by abandoned storm-beach ridges banked against the flanks of the isthmus; peat that accumulated between two of the ridges had a radio-carbon age of 3730 years BP.

Strangford Lough, Co. Down, a land-locked arm of the sea occupying a basin from whose floor thousands of drumlins rise, tells the same story. No waves can enter the lough, and the formation of waves within the lough is impeded by the numerous drumlin islands. If we thread our way into sheltered bays behind the drumlins, we can trace marine sands, representing the same eustatic rise of the sea, up to a height of 3·5 m above modern sea-level, but no higher; non-marine organic deposits on top of the sand have an age of 3000 years BP, showing that the sea had dropped again in level.

The archaeological site at Ringneill Quay was on one of the drumlin islands. As at Cushendun the eustatic rise of the sea for a time overtook the isostatic rise of the land and a marine silt was deposited. Continuing isostatic recovery and a lagging sea-level rise then brought the silts for a time above sea-level. But when isostatic uplift had ended the eustatic rise in the sea continued to above its present level. The waves were then able to attack the flanks of the island at a higher level than they can today. A Neolithic site came within reach of the waves, and was washed away, and a bench was cut in the earlier silts at about 2·75 m above modern sea-level. The age of the surviving silt immediately below the bench was 7500 BP. At Dublin to the south silt of the same age lies 3 m below sea-level while at Cushendun to the north it is 5 m above sea-level, so we can see how isostatic depression – and subsequent recovery – was greatest in north-east Ireland.

The Neolithic debris at Ringneill Quay was scattered across the wave-cut bench, and it included flint implements, bones from domestic animals and charcoal, which had a radiocarbon age of 5380 BP, not very different from the age at Sutton. Sand was then deposited on the debris to a height of 3·5 m above modern sea-level, the same height as the sand in the inner channels. A further metre of storm-beach gravel was thrown on top of the sand, and then sea-level started to drop back. A hearth was built on top of the beach, and this was dated to 3700 years BP.

The Ringneill Quay evidence suggests that isostatic uplift ended between 7500 and 5500 BP. We get the same impression at Cushendun. A further 2·5 m of beach bar was built up after 7700 years ago, and then final isostatic uplift lifted the beach bar above the reach of the lagging waves to a height of 8·5 m above modern sea-level. The continuing eustatic rise of the sea could not over-top the beach bar, but it flooded the valley of the Dun River inside the bar, and the river built up a terrace to a height of about 3·5 m above modern sea-level. A piece of wood about 1 m below the surface of the terrace had a C-14 age of 4750 years BP. The terrace does not appear to have been isostatically uplifted, and such movement must have been over before it was formed.

The eustatic fall of the sea from its high level about 5000 BP seems to have been relatively rapid, because several radiocarbon dates from 'submerged forests', now between tide-marks in the south and west of Ireland give radiocarbon dates centred on 4000 BP.

The whole question of 'submerged forests' is a complicated one, and urgently requires detailed research. When from its eustatic high above modern sea-level about 5000 years ago, the sea fell again, swamps and woodlands, and man himself, followed its retreating shores below modern high-tide level, and there must have been a further later eustatic rise which flooded the trees and the archaeological sites (see figure on p. 64). So far this later rise has not been satisfactorily dated.

There is the further difficulty that we have two generations of 'submerged forest', the trees that were drowned by the sea as it rose from its glacial minimum to its 5000 years ago maximum, and those that were drowned when it rose again from a later minimum. Without the guidance of pollen-counts and radiocarbon datings, the two can easily be confused. For example, we have *old* 'submerged forests' near Bray, Co. Wicklow – as we have already seen – at 6750 BP and at Roddansport, Co. Down at 7650 BP, and we have *young* 'submerged forests' at Ballycotton, Co. Cork, 4100 BP, and at Spiddal, Co. Galway, 3730 BP.

We have further problems if we ask ourselves what caused the ocean level

to drop back eustatically after being 4 m above its present level. A growth of
the Antarctic ice-sheets would appear to be necessary, yet palaeoclimatologists
tell us that there is no evidence that the Antarctic ice either expanded or
shrank at the time we have been discussing. Geophysicists also say that the
crust of the earth is unstable, and that some areas sink, while others rise. If
an area that included north-west Europe first subsided, and then rose again,
relative sea-level would change in that area in a manner that might be confused with eustatic movements.

A RECORD OF WOODLAND INTERFERENCE, FROM NEOLITHIC TIMES TO THE PRESENT DAY

Some twenty years ago Hilda Parkes and I made a boring 8 m deep in a
raised-bog near Littleton in Co. Tipperary, and she made detailed pollen-
counts of the samples taken. The pollen-diagram showed that the bog held a
continuous record from the Woodgrange Interstadial 12,000 years ago until
almost the present day, and the bog was subsequently chosen as the type-site
for the current warm stage, which is thus in Ireland called the Littletonian
Warm Stage. The bog lies in a fertile area, and its *Sphagnum*-peats provided
a splendid record of the waxing and waning of agricultural activities in the
vicinity of the bog.

With the coming of C-14 dating, we were anxious to give more precision
to the agricultural events recorded at Littleton, and to see to what extent
they could not only be traced throughout Ireland, but also be shown to be
contemporaneous. A research programme was organized, and among the
raised-bogs investigated was Red Bog, Co. Louth, at an altitude of 60 m,
15 km west of Dundalk. The bog had been very much cut away, but this was
all the better for our purpose, because it made it possible for us to collect
vertical columns of *Sphagnum*-peat and bring them back to the laboratory.
There Professor Watts made detailed pollen-counts, and identified the
horizons at which significant changes took place. Slices were then cut from the
column at the critical points, and these were dated in the Trinity College C-14
dating laboratory. Not all the results are yet published, but it does seem that
the major agricultural episodes can be traced throughout Ireland, and are
essentially synchronous.

The diagram (pp. 136-7) shows the percentage values of all pollen taken into
the calculation, with the tree pollens on the left, and the pollens associated
with agriculture on the right. I omitted the pollen produced by the common
plants of the raised-bog surface, the sedges and the heathers, and thus pictured
the bog surface as a sterile area of wet blotting-paper, ever thickening in an
upwards direction, and trapping on its surface successive layers of the rain of
pollen that was carried on to it from the surrounding countryside by the wind.
The division of the diagram into phases, and radiocarbon dates are shown on
the left-hand margin; nominal dates in calendar years are shown on the
right-hand.

The end of the Climax-phase (ILWC) is seen at the base of the diagram,
where pollen of elm falls dramatically in value and pollen of plantain appears.

In the Damage-phase (ILWd$_1$), the values of elm, and later of ash, rise and fall, and grass and plantain make oscillating appearances, as relatively primitive farming attacks the woodlands in a fluctuating fashion; whenever agricultural pressures fall off, the trees can re-establish themselves, at least to some degree.

But at about AD 300 elm and ash are swept away with a thoroughness from which they never recover, and the Destruction-phase (ILWd$_2$), in which more advanced farming ultimately destroys the woodlands, opens here.

About AD 1700 tree planting began, and pollen of pine and beech began to reach the bog surfaces. Unfortunately at the Red Bog the extensive peat-cutting had largely destroyed the bog surface, and only the topmost sample shows traces of these trees, which mark the Expansion-phase (ILWe), with its man-made re-expansion of woodland. This phase was well recorded at the type-site, Littleton Bog.

In the diagram the phases as they are shown at Red Bog have been further sub-divided on a tentative basis. About 3570 BP (say 1600 BC) we see elm fall and grasses begin to be continuously present, but hazel rises in value, suggesting that there was no extensive clearance of hazel scrub at this time. These features probably reflect Early Bronze Age farming. A little higher in the diagram hazel does fall back, the curve for ash becomes continuous, and bracken, plantain and grass are all represented, suggesting a significant increase in forest clearance at this time; these changes may mark the opening of the Bishopsland Period of the Bronze Age at about 1200 BC.

Still a little later in the phase, agriculture is stepped up still further; bracken, plantain and grass reach considerable values, and cereals and a variety of weeds are continuously present; C-14 suggests a date around 700 BC, and this is just the time when the still more wealthy Dowris Period of the Bronze Age was opening. Then the situation goes into reverse; farming ebbs away, and elm and ash expand their pollen output. But this must be the time of the Iron Age in Ireland, and the causes underlying the indicated agricultural decline are not immediately apparent.

This lull comes to an end about AD 300 when there is a devastating clearing-away of the elm and the ash, and a re-appearance of agricultural pollens in still greater force. Here the Destruction-phase (ILWd$_2$) begins. I picture that at this time the continental practice of arming the plough with an iron coulter was becoming known in Ireland, and that tillage became both more easy and more rewarding. As Christianity spread in Ireland, European practices became more and more general, and I have called this phase monastic farming.

Pollen of *Artemisia* (Mugwort) appears about AD 500, and the increase of this weed may be associated with different agricultural practices, perhaps the introduction of the mouldboard-plough.

A feeble return of elm and a weakening of agriculture can be seen about AD 1450, and it is tempting to correlate this with the fall of temperature that is thought to have taken place at this time (see figure on p. 184). At the very end of the phase we see the final clearance of the Irish woodlands, that set in in Tudor times, and see how even the hazel scrub that had for so long dominated the Irish countryside was swept away at this time.

136

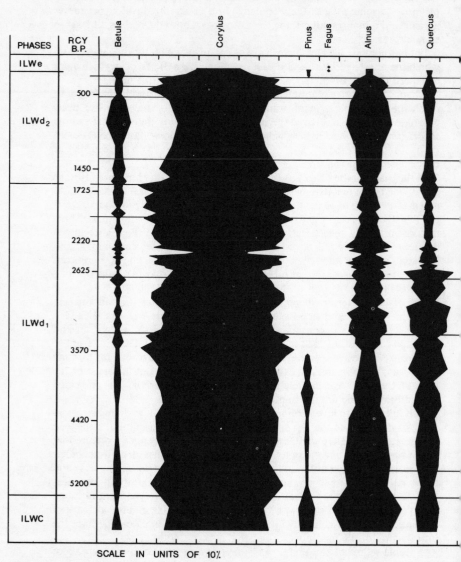

SCALE IN UNITS OF 10%

RED BOG, CO. LOUTH

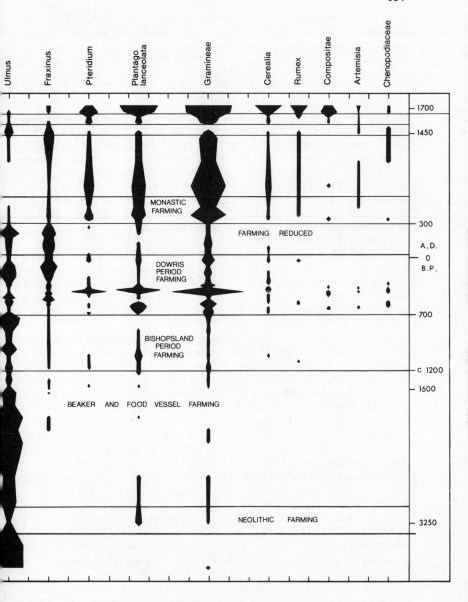

A pollen-diagram from Red Bog, Co. Louth, with a record of vegetational developments through the past 5000 years.

As noted above the top sample, with its traces of pine and beech, probably marks the start of the Expansion-phase (ILWe) when exotic trees began to be planted in large estates.

FURTHER BOG-DEVELOPMENT, BOTH OF RAISED-BOGS AND BLANKET-BOGS

On the lowlands reed-swamp and fen continued to invade and to obliterate open-water, and where raised-bogs had been established, they continued their slow growth both upwards and outwards, building up a *Sphagnum*-peat that was in general highly humified. Hammond's radiocarbon dates from the bogs of the Central Plain enable us to follow the lateral expansion (see figure on p. 109). On the right-hand side of the figure we see that at 5000 BP the *Sphagnum*-community was beginning to develop on top of wood-fen-peat which, as water-logging increased, had been creeping up the sloping surface of the underlying glacial deposit. At the left-hand side of the diagram we see wood-fen-peat beginning to form at a still higher level about the same time. Here after 1000 years had gone by, and about 50 cm of this type of peat had been built up, its surface had become too poor in nutrients to allow this kind of vegetation to continue to grow, and the *Sphagnum*-community moved in, and started to form highly humified peat. Thus throughout the Neolithic period raised-bogs surrounded by a rim of waterlogged fen-woods were invading and engulfing areas of low-lying forest.

When about 4000 BP we move on into the Bronze Age, such bog growth was continuing. The raised-bogs were now creating an obstacle to man's wanderings in the countryside, and trackways were constructed across them at strategic points. Unfortunately the study of, and particularly the radio-carbon dating of, trackways is much less advanced in Ireland than it is in England, where Sir Harry Godwin and others have done detailed work in the Somerset Levels and elsewhere. A trackway in a raised-bog at Corlona in Leitrim was examined by Dr van Zeist, and one of its timbers was dated to 3390 years BP, which places it early in the Bronze Age. It lay in peat of varying composition and humification, but it was not possible to find positive evidence that the bog surface had got wetter (and softer) at the time it was constructed.

At Ballyscullion Bog (see figure on p. 109) at about 4200 years BP peat of varying humification, such as that in which the Corlona trackway lay, began to form instead of the peat of uniformly high humification that had preceded it, and a similar change at Fallahogy Bog was dated to about 4450 years BP. Corresponding changes can be seen in other raised-bogs, and it is not impossible that this more rapid growth was due to a climatic deterioration – an increase in wetness or a decrease in temperature, or both.

At about the same time profound changes were taking place on the uplands, which had the end-result that over thousands and thousands of hectares that had formerly had a relatively well-drained soil, which carried woodland up to a height of at least 600 m, and had in many areas been extensively cultivated by early farmers, the soils first degraded to peaty podzols, and then became buried below thick layers of peat. Upland peat had certainly started to form

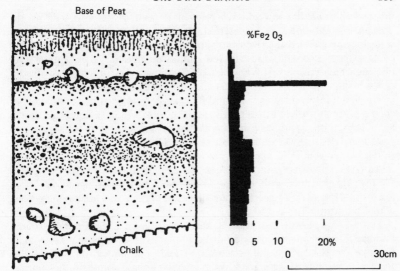

Base of Peat

%Fe₂O₃ — rendered as $\%Fe_2O_3$

0 5 10   20%

0   30cm

Double soil-profile below peat at Goodland, Co. Antrim: the graph on the right shows modest accumulation of iron in the enriched B-horizon of the primary forest soil, and also the much greater quantity of iron in the 'iron-pan' B-horizon of the podzol soil that formed later.

before 4000 BP, and its invasion of new areas appears to have continued at least into the Early Christian period.

This changeover from mineral soil to peat can be well demonstrated at Goodland, Co. Antrim, where at an altitude of about 250 m the bedrock is chalk. About 1 m of sandy glacial material rested on the chalk, and when first deposited this material must have had some content of calcium carbonate; today all trace of calcium carbonate has been removed by long-continued leaching. Early Littletonian woodlands developed in the area, and as the soil formed under forest there was some modest movement of iron downwards, so that a layer about 50 cm below the surface became enriched in iron, giving rise to a brown podzolic soil. About 5000 years ago Neolithic farmers arrived in the area, killed off the trees, and proceeded to scratch the surface of the ground, initiating as they did so a new cycle of soil formation; Early Bronze Age folk continued the farming activities. Then, either due to the continued disturbance of the ground encouraging leaching, or due to a deterioration in climate, podzolization took place, and a layer of iron pan formed about 30 cm below the surface. Waterlogging of the soil followed, as the pan blocked the downward movement of water, and by 4150 BP the wetter parts of the area had been smothered by invading rushes (*Juncus*). The sward of rushes gradually built up a thin layer of amorphous vegetable debris or peat, crowded with *Juncus* seeds, and the soil became a peaty podzol. (Pl. 24)

The surface of this peat was very low in inorganic nutrients, and it was invaded, just as the lowland fen-peats had been earlier invaded, by the *Sphagnum*-community, which started to form a highly humified peat. As waterlogging enabled the rushes to spread, so the formation of peaty podzol could expand also, and gradually the ground became buried beneath a layer of peat which covered it like a blanket, initiating the formation of the so-called blanket-bog, which is now so widespread in Ireland (see map on p. 112).

The locations at which the ground first became sufficiently waterlogged to enable peaty podzol and then peat to start to form will have depended on the local topography, and so, just as with the raised-bogs, peat formation will have expanded outwards from initial foci. There was no point in time at which peat started to form everywhere, and at different points the basal peaty podzols may be of very different ages. Alan Smith and his Belfast colleagues are investigating this problem, and they have found basal layers varying in age from 4150 to 2500 BP. The rate of accumulation was at first very slow, with 1 cm forming in c. 140 years.

There is no reason why still younger basal layers should not be found, because if the blanket-bogs had not been interfered with by man, it is quite possible that they might still be thickening and expanding at the present day. But for thousands of years man has grazed his animals on them, has burned the vegetation to stimulate young growth, and has cut the peat for fuel, or dug it away to reclaim agricultural land. We can show that some of them have built their thickness up by 10 cm during the last 250 years, but we have no record of how their margins have behaved.

We can say 'thousands of years' because of the work that is being done by Ruaidhrí de Valéra, Michael Herity and Seamus Caulfield in north-west Mayo, where blanket-bog has a very wide extent at the present day. In early Little-tonian time forest development in this area seems to have paralleled that in the rest of the country, and a pine-stump at Bellonaboy, rooted in mineral soil, and with a radiocarbon age of 7100 years, goes back to the time when the climax woodlands were developing.

Neolithic man appears to have been established in the Behy area by 4500 years ago. Here an impressive Court-grave on the shoulder of a hill at 180 m dominates a system of large drystone field-walls, which enclose areas about five to seven hectares in extent; within one of the enclosures there is an occupation area surrounded by a circular drystone wall; all these archaeo-logical features are now deeply buried by blanket-bog. Charcoal from the occupation-area had an age of 4450 years BP; the base of the peat around the Court-grave, which like the other features was sitting on mineral soil, had an age of 3900 years BP. There had been some slip from the drystone wall around the tomb before it was buried by peat. The large size of the enclosures suggests that they were used in the management of large numbers of cattle and other stock that belonged to a group of ranchers sufficiently well organized to erect long stretches of heavy walls. (Pl. 18)

Similar walls, also sitting on mineral soil, appear in the Belderg valley, and here Seamus Caulfield has revealed a very complex series of features, all again buried by blanket-bog. Neolithic pottery and flint implements are found on the mineral soil, and there must have been some forest clearance.

Blanket-bog peat then started to form, but after no more than a thin layer had been laid down, its surface was invaded by secondary woodland, with large trees of both oak and pine. A pine-stump, whose roots were clearly separated from the mineral soil by a thin layer of peat, had an age of 4300 BP, and a similar oak had an age of 3850 BP. At Bellonaboy (already referred to) a pine-stump sitting on 20 cm of basal peat had an age of 4350 BP. Here we have confirmation of the slow rate of accumulation of the basal peat. These tree-datings add to the amazement of the modern visitor to this now bleak and treeless area, who has to recognize that not only was it clothed in high virgin forests 7000 years ago, but that after those woods had been damaged by Neolithic man, climate was still good enough 4000 years ago for secondary woodland of tall well-grown pines and oaks to re-establish itself.

Three thousand, two hundred years ago, when Ireland had moved on into the Bronze Age, man returned to Belderg, where blanket-bog was now developed on an extensive scale, though the peat perhaps was not as yet very thick. There is a vein of copper ore in a nearby cliff, and this may have been the lure that brought man back to a site that was by now much less attractive from the agricultural point of view. A house, 10 m in diameter with a drystone wall and post-holes, produced saddle querns and rubbers; a charred block of wood within the house had an age of 3150 years BP. Nearby there were further stone walls; these started on mineral soil but continued on out into the blanket-bog which surrounded the site; here the wall rested on peat. Oak-stakes built into the wall extended down into the peat, and when the wall ended a line of stakes continued into the bog; the stakes had a radiocarbon age of 3200 BP.

The whole site had been subsequently deeply buried by peat, and this had protected the most remarkable features of the site, criss-crossing dark bands in the subsoil, interpreted as plough-marks, or marks of an ard, the more primitive fore-runner of the true plough (see p. 158), and cultivation-ridges of the type still used in western Ireland today, and generally known as 'lazy-beds'. If the modern title is taken to imply lack of energy and enterprise on the part of the farmer who employs this system, it is a complete misnomer, because the building up of drier ridges separated by trenches to drain off the surface water gives an efficient method of cultivating soils with poor natural drainage.

The field-evidence suggests that the house is younger than the cultivation-ridges, and therefore the age of the latter may lie between the Neolithic occupation of the site, starting perhaps at 4500 BP, and the building of the house about 3200 years ago. Whichever end of the range we favour, it is clear that this cultivation method is of high antiquity in Ireland. What of the plough-marks?

There is no doubt that in the past many such marks have gone unnoticed by excavators, and today they are being keenly searched for. The English *Long-barrow* is a collective tomb ultimately of the same ancestry as the Irish Court-grave, and Seamus Caulfield can point to the evidence from the South Street Long-barrow at Avebury, Wilts. Here there were criss-crossing grooves, claimed to be ard-marks, in the subsoil below the mound which covered the tomb; charcoal in the soil overlying the marks had an age of

4750 years BP. By a remarkable chance another set of younger ard-marks were discovered nearby overlying the filled-in ditch of the tomb, and associated with Bronze Age material, dated to 3950 years BP. Thus both South Street and Belderg offer the same type of evidence for the use of the ard in the British Isles as early as the third millennium BC. There is also evidence of early use in northern Europe.

Ploughing-implements originated in the alluvial soils of the Middle East, which were free from tree-roots and from stones. As the plough followed the farmers into north-west Europe, it came first to the forest and its tough tree-roots. In New Zealand today it is reckoned that it takes thirty years for the wood of a tree-root to lose its strength. And beyond the forest-edge it came to the glacial deposits, with their random content of stones and boulders of all sizes. In soils containing tree-roots and rocks, the use of the plough lost much of its attraction.

Even today in Belderg the spade and the cultivation-ridge are preferred to the plough and the furrow, and Caulfield has shown that the cultivation-ridge has a long history there. The ard might have had some success on the stone-free chalky soils of Wiltshire, but the life of a wooden plough in the stony fields of Mayo would have been short. It may be that the marks at Belderg are those of a spade, rather than an ard.

Nearby at Ballyglass a Court-grave had been built on the site of a large rectangular wooden house, and there can be no doubt that this area, which today is so desolate and so lacking in human inhabitants, had considerable settlement in Neolithic time.

If we picture that the 'climatic optimum' was a time of relatively continental climate with warmer summers and fewer rain-days, then we can envisage any subsequent 'deterioration' as involving falling temperatures, more rain-days, and lower evaporation-rates generally. Where raised-bogs already existed their rate of upward growth will have been speeded up, and the soils generally will have become loaded with an increased content of water; raised-bogs will have expanded still further laterally, and the formation of blanket-bog will have been encouraged.

There is some evidence, as we have seen, that between 4500 and 4200 years ago the type of peat being formed in the raised-bogs began to change, a peat that was of uniformly high humification giving way to a peat of varying humification. In south-west Ireland a pine-stump rooted in mineral soil and buried by blanket-bog on the slopes of Carrantoohill at 250 m had an age of 4600 years BP; in east Ireland a pine-stump in like position on the slopes of Kippure at 730 m had an age of 4200 years BP; in north-east Ireland blanket-peat started to form at 4150 years BP; in west Ireland tree-stumps on thin blanket-peat at Belderg had an age of 4300 BP. All this evidence adds up to suggest that climate did alter in the centuries preceding 4000 BP, and that the change enabled the raised-bogs to grow more quickly, and blanket-bogs to start to form throughout the country. As these bogs spread, they gradually covered great areas of country that had been farmed by the Neolithic peoples.

It is tempting to think that there was a deterioration of climate which led inevitably to the development of blanket-bog wherever a critical threshold was passed, and that the part that man played was only a secondary one, in that his agricultural activities had made the soil particularly susceptible to podzolization and waterlogging. It would be nice to know whether man had abandoned the former farm areas after exhausting the soil before peat had started to form, or whether he was as it were forcibly driven out, when the soil became waterlogged to the point that it was impossible to cultivate it. Whatever happened, the upland soils changed drastically as agricultural areas gave way to blanket-bog, and we have to recognize that when work still to be done enables us to draw a map of the soils of Neolithic Ireland, it will differ very substantially both from the sketch-map of the first Irish soils (see map on p. 91), and from the map of Irish soils today (see map on p. 187). As far as prehistoric man was concerned, great areas of agricultural land on the uplands in the east and at low levels in the west must have been abandoned, while farming continued in other areas. If we take two limestone areas both intensively occupied in Neolithic and Early Bronze Age times and lying in the same longitude but at different elevations, we can see this exemplified. The low hills (alt. 120 m) around Lough Gur in Limerick were not buried by peat; the outlines of the Neolithic houses there can still be seen above ground, the sod layer is full of prehistoric pottery, and agriculture still goes on: the higher hills (alt. 250 m) at Carrowkeel in Sligo are covered by peat which has built up to a depth of 250 cm, and partly buries the cairns of the Passage-grave cemetery. Today men cut the peat for fuel, and sheep graze on the blanket-bog, but that is all. People must have moved from the higher land to the lowlands, but the archaeological story is not yet able to tell us whether the refugees endeavoured to take farmland by force from those already occupying the better land, or whether they contented themselves by clearing further woodland and scrub.

Today blanket-bog is extensively developed wherever annual rainfall in excess of 1250 mm per annum waterlogs the ground (see map on p. 112). Thus in much of the west of Ireland the blanket-bog continues down to sea-level, giving great stretches of country buried by peat, which is interrupted only where slopes are steep; below much of the peat there is, as we have seen, a layer of tree-stumps to indicate the former extent of forest. Away from the west coast rainfall only rises to 1250 mm on higher ground, and the blanket-bog is confined to hill-tops and higher slopes.

The blanket-bog areas give an impression of dreary uniformity, covered by a sheet of bog vegetation, pierced only by occasional rocky outcrops or lakes. But the underlying substratum has its own minor relief, rising into elevations and sinking into hollows. In many of the hollows sediment had accumulated since the opening of the Littletonian Warm Stage, and this was the case at Emlaghlea, Co. Kerry, which was examined by Professor Jessen during his programme of work in Ireland. Part of Jessen's section is reproduced as figure c, p. 109, and the early peat which was a wood-fen peat can be seen at the base of the right-hand end of the section.

The fen surface in its final stages seems to have become relatively dry, because pine and birch were able to grow freely on it. Up to this point the formation of the peat had been controlled by surface water and by ground water, and the ridge of higher ground to the left had been bare of peat and perhaps under cultivation. Then some change took place and the oligotrophic plants of the bog community which need to be nourished only by rainwater invaded the whole area, and began to bury it below blanket-bog. At Slieve Gallion, Co. Tyrone, a similar change was dated to 4165 years BP.

Today we tend to draw an arbitrary distinction between raised-bog on the one hand and blanket-bog on the other, but the plants of which both are composed are essentially the same, though the proportions they occupy in the various communities are rather different. Typical raised-bog is found where the topography of the ground can bring about waterlogging of the ground, even though the rainfall is below 1250 mm *per annum* (and can be as low as 750 mm *p.a.*). The additional water is provided, either by groundwater filling a closed basin, or by drainage water being concentrated by a slope. Fen vegetation flourishes, and the raised-bog plants come in as soon as the fen-peat has blanketed off the soil nutrients. The raised-bog is thus always surrounded by a rim of fen where the necessary waterlogging of the ground is taking place. If the lateral advance of the fen is slow, then lateral growth of the raised-bog must be slow. But there is no corresponding limitation on upward growth, and the bog centre thus grows upwards into a domed form, with its plant cover dominated by *Sphagnum*.

In the blanket-bog regions with rainfall above 1250 mm, the ground is of necessity waterlogged, except on steep rocky slopes, and the ombrogenous vegetation can establish itself everywhere. Neither lateral nor upward growth is restricted, and peat forms a layer of relatively uniform thickness. There are some *Sphagnum* hummocks, and there can also be pools, but on the whole the low-growing *Sphagna* are largely concealed by the taller cotton-grass (*Eriophorum vaginatum*), purple moor-grass (*Molinia caerulea*), bog-rush (*Schoenus nigricans*) and white beak-sedge (*Rhynchospora alba*). Among the heathers *Calluna vulgaris* and *Erica tetralix* are widely distributed, while in the west of the country some of the rarer heathers find their last refuge on the blanket-peat. (Pl. 19)

Peat formed in this way is seen at Emlaghlea (see figure on p. 109), where the top of the bog is formed of almost 2 m of blanket-bog peat. The peat was dominated by remains of *Molinia* and fibres of both species of cotton-grass, *angustifolium* as well as *vaginatum*, and twigs of *Calluna* and *Myrica gale* were also common. The bog-myrtle, *Myrica*, is widely distributed on the western blanket-bogs, and it alone of the bog plants can supplement its nitrogen intake by means of symbiotic nitrogen-capturing bacteria living in nodules on its roots, in just the way that clovers and other legumes do; it has a rather less fortunate distinction in that its pollen is very like that of hazel, and must often be confused with it in pollen-counts from such peats.

The human population was not the only population to be affected by the expansion of blanket-bog; plants and animals had also to adjust themselves. Today the country between Roundstone and Clifden carries a lake-studded area of blanket-bog with relict stations for rare heathers, *Erica mackaiana* and *E. erigena*, with St Dabeoc's Heath (*Daboecia cantabrica*) growing on rocky outcrops protruding through the bog. At the end of the last glaciation this was an area of ice-scoured rock with innumerable ponds in the hollows. In

PLATE 17 *Above*, cutting to show the complex construction of the mound at Knowth, Co. Meath. The lowest layer is of field sods, the second is of small stones, and the third is of black shale, the local rock. Similar layering is repeated in the mound. *Left*, the reconstructed cooking-site (*fulacht fian*) at Ballyvourney, Co. Cork, showing the water-filled pit in which heated stones were placed; within the hut a bench-like structure perhaps supported a butcher's block.

PLATE 18 *Above*, section showing blanket-bog overlying the partly collapsed wall of a cairn which contained a Court-grave at Behy, Co. Mayo. *Below*, section showing blanket-bog overlying standing stones and a stone cairn of Bronze Age date at Beaghmore, Co. Tyrone. The site covers a considerable area.

the early Littletonian the area was wooded, and the ponds gradually filled with mud and fen-peat, containing seeds and pollen from the surrounding area. Professor Jessen did a lot of work here, and was able to show that when the mud was forming the surrounding countryside was wooded, and that *E. mackiaiana* was growing in the woods in the same way that it grows in its main centre, north-west Spain, today. It seems almost incredible that this plant, which was presumably already struggling for existence at the limit of its distribution, should have been able to make the drastic change in habitat from shaded forest floor to open blanket-bog, and still survive as it does – just – in Ireland today.

THE BRONZE AGE

Beaker Prospectors and Settlers
4000 to 3250 BP (2050–1300 BC)

Recent years have seen a tremendous upsurge in the intensive prospecting of the Irish countryside for economic deposits of metallic ores, and in several cases the search has been rewarded by massive discoveries. There is no doubt that massive alterations of the landscape will follow. The discoveries have been brought about by the use of sophisticated geochemical and geophysical techniques, whose application in the field has been made all the more easy by the fact that Ireland today is virtually treeless, which is a considerable aid to the transport of equipment and the carrying out of precision surveying.

Today's surveyors are the lineal descendants of the first prospectors who probably reached Ireland about 4000 years ago, bringing trifling quantities of

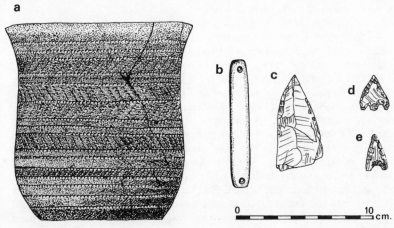

Some typical Beaker objects: **a**, beaker, Dalkey Island, Co. Dublin; **b**, wrist-bracer, stone, Carrowkeel, Co. Sligo (found below 2.5m of blanket-bog peat); **c**, pointed knife, flint, Dalkey Island, Co. Dublin; **d**, barbed and tanged arrowhead, flint, Dalkey Island, Co. Dublin; **e**, hollow-based arrowhead, flint, Dalkey Island, Co. Dublin.

metal with them and hungry for more. It was these people who carried Ireland forward into the Early Bronze Age. They also brought sophisticated vessels of thin walled and highly decorated pottery, pictured as used for drinking and so called Beakers, and these Beaker folk seem to have had a wave-like expansion throughout north-west Europe, just as their Neolithic predecessors had. Some of the Neolithic folk were Ireland's first geologists, and had groped their way through dense woodland to find the all too rare exposures of rock suitable for manufacture into axes. It was in the same woodlands that the Beaker folk had to search, and even though the copper compounds in the superficial layers of the deposits would have occurred as brightly coloured carbonates, green *malachite* and blue *azurite*, nevertheless overhung as they would have been by ferns and mosses, they required some finding.

And find ores the Beaker people did, gold in Co. Wicklow and copper in Co. Cork. Tin eluded them, but for this they cannot be blamed as even to the present day Ireland has not produced any significant quantities of tin. Before long they were fabricating and exporting collars and earrings of gold, and were casting daggers, axes and halberds of copper in flat stone moulds, both for use at home and for export. But beyond their beakers, their jewellery and their weapons, we know very little about their way of life. It is thought that they were accomplished archers, because barbed and tanged flint arrowheads and wrist-guards are commonly associated with them.

At Newgrange after there had been some considerable collapse of the perimeter of the mound, pits were dug and Beaker debris was deposited in them; the accompanying charcoal has an age of 4050–3885 years BP. At Monknewtown, about two miles north of Newgrange, charcoal associated with large quantities of Beaker pottery in an occupation-site had an age of 3810 years BP. The north of Ireland has also produced Beaker material dated between 4000 and 3800 years BP.

The Beaker people seem to have maintained the tradition of communal burial in megalithic tombs, as their pottery is found in a type of *Gallery-grave* which is most common in the west and south of Ireland, and seems to have originated in Brittany. These tombs are essentially a narrow lintelled gallery, often with a double enclosing wall, set in a short oval or circular cairn; the gallery often lies along an east–west axis (see figure on p. 125). Also south-west in their distribution, and also pointing towards Brittany and beyond, are abstract designs inscribed on outcrops of living rock, which seem to have their home in Galicia in Spain. We can perhaps picture roving prospectors from Spain pushing quickly up the west coast of France until in Brittany, the outpost of Armorica, they found rocks and rock structures that reminded them of home, and suggested possibilities of mineral wealth. From here the next leg brought them across the Celtic Sea to Cornwall and its all-important tin, and on to the south of Ireland, where copper and gold awaited them. And when we think of the isolated finds that brought them their wealth, we must also think of the thousands of barren square miles that they prospected in order to make those finds.

Methods of mining changed little from the first prehistoric winning of ore until the Industrial Revolution, and to find a primitive mine-working is no proof that it must be of high antiquity. Mount Gabriel, near Skibbereen in

Co. Cork, is irregularly impregnated with copper ores, and its flanks have many small holes quarried into them, and lying across the mouths of the holes are heaps of broken stone and charcoal; the charcoal has been given a C-14 age of 3450 years, and these mines could well have been operated by Beaker folk. In the holes, on the tip-heaps and trailing up the slope of the hill there can be found rounded beach cobbles, both broken and intact, often with abraded ends showing that they had been used in pounding. We can thus picture the early miners, after they had located a suitable outcrop of ore, first lighting a fire against it to expand the rock, and then throwing on water to shrink and shatter it. The stone mauls, some of which were grooved to give a better purchase for a wicker handle, were then used both to free the shattered rock, and to pound the fragments still further, so that the ore-rich pieces could be collected for smelting. If the richness of the ore made it worth following back into the rock, gradually a tunnel developed, and the diameters of the tunnels or holes in the hillside suggest that elaborate staging was not used, as they are about the size that would be excavated by a man standing on the ground, and using a handled hammer. The miners could only go a limited distance into the hillside, because beyond a certain point ventilation would become difficult, and seepage of water from the tunnel walls would make it difficult to apply heat effectively to them. Since the mines were abandoned, peat has formed both on the hillside and on the tip-heaps.

We know very little about their agricultural practices, although at Bally-nagilly, a site with a well-marked Beaker phase, there was evidence of forest clearance around 3850 BP. It is not impossible that it was Beaker folk who set up the cultivation-ridges at Beldberg, although their characteristic pottery has not been found on the site. Deposits of copper are available, there is a Gallery-grave on a nearby hillside, and the ridges were probably in use before 3250 years BP. But the pollen-diagrams in general give little indication of their presence, and the scale of disturbance that they created in the woodlands must have been of the same order as that produced by their Neolithic pre-decessors. Louise van Wijngaarden-Bakker has produced a very interesting analysis of the animal bones at the Newgrange Beaker site, and the following table is based on her work.

	Bone-fragments %	Minimum number of individuals %
DOMESTIC ANIMALS		
Cattle	57	37
Pig	31	30
Sheep/Goat	5	12
Horse	2	6
Dog	4	12
GAME ANIMALS		
Red Deer	1	3
	100	100

Hare, wild cat, goshawk and water-rail were also identified. We see, as always, the dominance of cattle, with the pig in second place.

The Individual Grave and the Food Vessel
3750 to 3150 BP (1800–1200 BC)

Rather later than the first finds of Beaker material, and perhaps about 3750 BP, we begin to find skeletons which had been inhumed, often in a crouched position, in a simple box or cist of stone slabs, sunk into the ground, often into glacial sands and gravels. Here we see the rejection of communal burial, and a different concept of afterlife, because the remains are often accompanied by a pottery vessel, and sometimes by a weapon as well. Thus we all too easily leap to the conclusion that the vessel must have contained provisions for the next world, and call it a Food Vessel.

So-called Food Vessels are generally of heavier texture and rougher ornamentation than the lightly walled and delicately ornamented Beakers. They have two main forms, one with a rounded base or bowl-form, and the other with a more flower-pot form and flat base, the vase-form. The bowl-form may represent a native development from an amalgamation of earlier Irish pottery forms, but the vase-form is thought to have affinities with Britain.

The call for cremation seems to have been very strong in the prehistoric world, and this rite gradually re-established itself in Ireland, though the remains continued to be deposited individually. To protect the cremated debris a larger pottery vessel, the Cinerary Urn, decorated with cordons, rosettes and zig-zags in bands of applied clay, was evolved, probably with its origins in the vase-form Food Vessel. The cremated remains were placed in the urn, which was then buried in an inverted position in a cist or pit. Sometimes a mound was then thrown up over the burial, or the burial was inserted in a pre-existing mound.

There is no doubt that the abandoned megalithic tombs must have been a source of fascination to these Bronze Age people, just as they are to us today. They have been used over and over again, either as burial places, or as convenient fireplaces, or, as in the case of Professor de Valéra's excavation at Behy, as a site for an illicit still. As a result they may contain charcoal of all ages, and often produce bizarre results when efforts are made to date them by the C-14 method. Sometimes they were substantially altered before being used again as a burial site.

The Mound of the Hostages at Tara started its career as a Passage-grave, built of stone about 4000 years ago, and parts of the chamber still contained the original cremated debris. Other parts had been cleaned out by Food Vessel people, who had deposited uncremated bodies in crouched positions, accompanied by food vessels, a bronze awl and conical V-perforated buttons of jet and stone. Users of Cinerary Urns then laid down a rind of clay about 1 m thick on top of the cairn of stone, and inserted their burials into the clay. Most were single cremations in inverted urns, sometimes accompanied by food vessels and weapons. One burial was accompanied by a magnificent stone battle-axe and a bronze dagger, both severely burned, probably in the funeral pyre. One unburned body, that of a youth about 14–15 years of age, had been inhumed in a flexed position with an elaborate and very valuable

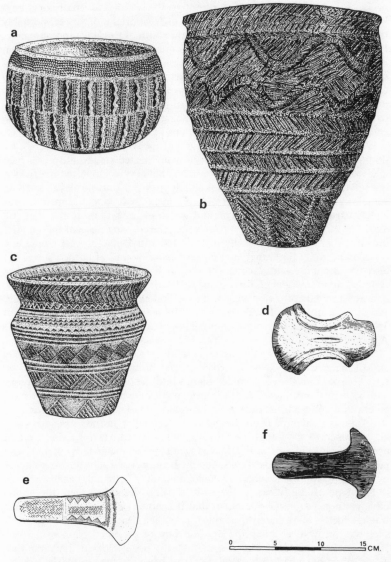

Some typical Food Vessel objects and one Cinerary Urn: **a**, bowl-form vessel, Mount Stewart, Co. Down; **b**, Cinerary Urn, Burgage Mor, Co. Wicklow; **c**, vase-form vessel, Ballon Co. Carlow; **d**, battle-axe, stone, Bann Valley; **e**, flat decorated axe, bronze, Scrabo Hill, Co. Down; **f**, flanged axe, bronze, no locality.

necklace around the neck. He was perhaps the son of a chieftain, or a boy-king. The beads were of bronze, perhaps of Irish origin, of amber, probably from Scandinavia, of jet, probably from the south of England, and of *faience*. Faience is made by fusing blue glass and quartz grains, and moulding them into the required form; its production is a considerable technological achievement, and many people think that its manufacture was carried out in the eastern Mediterranean; some think it was made in Britain also. But wherever it was made it was at all times prized, and its occurrence at Tara adds emphasis to the value of the necklace, which demonstrates by its varied elements the wide range of Ireland's trading connections at this time. (Pl. 16)

While on the whole we know very little of the way of life of the times, we do have some glimpses. Cooking by throwing heated stones into water held in a wooden trough in the ground, or in an animal skin supported by sticks is one of the oldest methods of cooking; it survived into medieval times in Ireland, and is still practised in New Guinea. In Ireland the method was widely used during the Iron Age, and the heaps of burned stones that still mark the former sites are called *fulacht fian*, the cooking-place of the wandering warriors. Professor O'Kelly investigated some sites in west Cork, and revealed not only the trough and its associated mound of burned stone, but also hearths, huts and various fittings; in his usual thorough manner he rounded his excavation off by cooking and eating meat processed in this way, and was amazed at the efficiency of the method and the tastiness of the result. Wood from one trough was dated to 3710 years BP and from a second to 3500 BP, and so the method of cooking goes back to this stage of the Bronze Age. (Pl. 17)

Some of the wood bore the marks of small axes or adzes, and a *fulacht fian* at Millstreet, Co. Cork, produced a flanged bronze axe of this period. At Ballyvourney O'Kelly reassembled planks into the oak trees from which they had been cut, and showed that the carpenters were able to deal with trunks 50 cm in diameter from trees over 100 years old. The woods used for construction, the charcoal from the fires, and the pollen in the associated peat, all combined to show that the area was still wooded when the sites were in use. This is an acid area, with Old Red Sandstone as the underlying rock, and peaty podzols as the modern soils, and the Bronze Age woods were dominated by oak, pine and birch, with only small amounts of elm and hazel.

This type of site is nearly always in a damp situation, where the water-table is almost at surface level, so that if a hole is dug it quickly fills with water, which is immediately available for cooking. One of Professor O'Kelly's sites was on what is today the dry alluvium of the flood plain of a river, 50 m back from the water's edge, and Professor O'Kelly pictured that water would have had to have been carried from the river to fill the trough.

This immediately raises another question, which has so far been entirely neglected in Irish geomorphological studies, namely – What is the age of the flood-plains of the Irish rivers? We look idly at these features today, and imagine they have always been there – but have they? Man has been interfering with them for centuries, by building roads and bridges across them, by erecting weirs and mill-races for water-power, and by deepening and narrowing their channels in an effort to drain the surrounding agricultural land.

Perhaps at the time that the Ballyvourney cooking-site was in use the Sullane river was still building up its flood-plain, and the water-table may have been higher, high enough to fill the cooking-pit on the flood-plain. At the southern tip of the Blackstairs Mountain range near Ballinvegga in Wexford a shallow basin is drained by a stream which runs north-westwards to join the Barrow. The stream has an extensive flood-plain which is now being drained artificially, and the walls of the drainage-cut show about 150 cm of sands, gravels and silts resting on glacial deposits. The deposits of the terrace are crowded with drifted vegetable material, ranging from oak trunks to hazel nuts. An oak trunk at the base of the deposit was given a radiocarbon age of 3825 years BP, or in other words it *could* have been growing at the time that people in Cork were cutting down oaks to construct *fulacht fian* – and *fulacht fian* are quite common in Wexford. Could it be that there was extensive forest clearance in the valley by Bronze Age farmers, that the run-off regime of the stream was changed when there were no longer trees to retard water flow, and that the flood-plain as we see it today is the result of forest clearance 4000 years ago?

A very extensive drainage scheme is going on over the whole catchment-area of the River Boyne at present. Scariff Bridge, about four miles south-west of Trim, was built across the flood-plain in medieval times. There was a drainage-scheme in the nineteenth century, a channel was cut down into the flood-plain, and a big arch was inserted into the older bridge. Now with modern earth-moving machinery a much more ambitious scheme is under way, and the channel is being further deepened. Again about 2 m of terrace material rest on glacial deposits, and muds, bones and driftwood lie in what were former channels across the accumulating terrace. A piece of driftwood at the base of the terrace was given a radiocarbon age of 1680 years BP (AD 280). This was a time at which the clearance of woodland was being resumed in Ireland, and it is not impossible that the Boyne flood-plain, though its date is very different from that at Ballinvegga, may also owe its origin to a change in river regime consequent on forest clearance. The bones include those of red deer and cat. Discussing the history of the cat in Ireland Louise van Wijn-gaarden-Bakker considers that the domestic cat, which reached England in Roman times, probably was introduced into Ireland during the first centuries AD. The cat remains at Scariff Bridge may therefore be from a domesticated animal. There is considerable argument as to whether the true wild cat was ever native in Ireland, as it still is in Scotland.

The increased prosperity of the Bishopsland Period
3150 to 2650 BP (1200 – 700 BC)

Around 1200 BC immense economic changes were taking place in Europe, and it was not long before these changes affected Ireland. Rich ore deposits were now being worked in central Europe, and this area was beginning to outstrip the eastern Mediterranean in wealth and in technical achievement. Gold ornaments, of technically advanced manufacture, found both singly and

The Irish Landscape

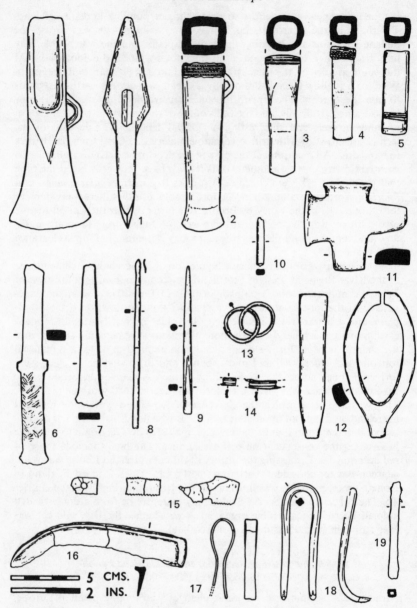

Bishopsland hoard, mainly of bronze tools: **1**, palstave; **2**, socketed axehead; **3, 4**, socketed hammerheads; **5**, light hammer or punch; **6, 7**, chisels; **8, 9, 10**, gravers; **11**, anvil; **12**, slotted anvil; **13**, rings; **14**, bracelet fragment; **15**, saw; **16**, sickle; **17**, tweezers; **18**, flesh-hook; **19**, hollow bar.

in hoards, indicate corresponding prosperity in Ireland. But the most interesting, though not the most opulent, evidence of these new influences is the
hoard of bronze tools and implements that was discovered at Bishopsland,
Co. Kildare. When the rock-walls of the Poulaphuca meltwater channel were
being scraped down to remove loose debris, so that the end of a dam for a
hydroelectric scheme could be bonded firmly to solid rock, a shower of
bronze implements was released from some cache where they had been hidden
for about three thousand years.

The hoard obviously belonged to a travelling smith. He had socketed
hammers, two anvils, a punch, a graver, chisels and a saw; one of the anvils
(12) was slotted so that sheet metal could be held in it, while it was being
embossed or engraved. The only old-fashioned item is the *palstave*, or axe
with flanges and a stop-ridge for hafting (1), which could have been cast in a
simple two-piece stone mould. In sharp contrast is the socketed axe (2),
which first appeared in northern Germany, and from there overflowed into
England and Ireland; the axe has a basal loop, and when the axe was being
secured to its handle, string would be passed through the loop, and then
wound round the base of the axe and the end of the haft, to bind the two
firmly together. If we look closely at the base of the axe, we seem to see a
decorated rim, but this is in fact a replica in bronze of remains of such binding
string. This shows that the axe was manufactured by copying a pre-existing
axe by a complicated moulding-process, involving taking a cast of the original,
and that when the cast was taken, the original axe still had remnants of string
wound around its socket. One of the hammers (4) shows the same feature.
The use of such a complicated process is one of the technical advances that
marks the period.

The flesh-hook (18) and the sickle (16) have a special interest for us. The
flesh-hook exemplifies the importance of meat in the Irish diet, and the sickle,
which stems from Europe, is the oldest example of this implement so far
found in Ireland.

Contrasting the period of the Bishopsland hoard with the earlier periods of
the Bronze Age in Ireland George Eogan says, 'the difference is glaring, so
much so that hand-in-hand with the development noticeable in the ornaments
and implements must go a development in society, a society not only rich in
artistic and technological talents, but, indeed, a society with altered attitudes
and habits'. Dr Eogan considers that increased exploitation of the country's
natural resources was to a great extent responsible for the new wealth in
Ireland, which was thus able to keep pace with the general European advances
of the times.

Unfortunately except for the ornaments and the implements, which are
widely distributed in the northern two-thirds of the country, we have very little
other evidence of these developments. The gold was presumably won from
the river gravels of Co. Wicklow, but as these rivers are flash-flood streams,
rising rapidly in level when there are rainstorms in the hills, and dropping
again equally quickly, simple gravel workings would have been quickly
obliterated by later floods. The copper continued to come from surface
exposures, but these early workings will have largely vanished also. The

development of steam power made the draining and pumping of water from mines immeasurably easier, and the bigger and deeper working of mineral deposits in the nineteenth century has removed most of the evidence for working in prehistoric times.

But a society, like an army, marches on its stomach, and the rise in the standard of living, and presumably in population numbers also, must have brought a greatly increased demand for agricultural products. The Red Bog pollen-diagram (see p. 137) has a radiocarbon date at 3570 BP (say 1600 BC), and a little higher we see clear indications of extended agriculture. Elm remains at a low level, ash pollen becomes uninterruptedly present – though at a low level – as field margins now offered an ecological niche not previously available, hazel shows a substantial fall as secondary scrub is cleared away, and bracken and plantain join the grasses in the record. It is not unreasonable to think that here we see the more intensive agriculture of the Bishopsland Period. At Ballynagilly extensive woodland clearance was recorded at 1200 BC and at Gortcorbies agricultural activity was greatly intensified at 1075 BC. Jon Pilcher has made a detailed study of the peat at an altitude of 430 m on the slopes of Slieve Gallion, Co. Tyrone. As at Emlaghlea, the lower peat was a reedswamp peat, rich in wood in its upper part. About 4165 years BP (2250 BC) this type of peat was supplanted by blanket-bog peat, and at three levels in the blanket-bog peat there are signs of increased agricultural activity. The first is around 1500 BC, when cereal pollen is present and oak shows a fall; this may indicate some Food Vessel activity in the region. The second is around 1300 BC, where plantain rises to a maximum and oak is again reduced; the third is around 900 BC, where plantain again reaches a higher level. The second and third episodes could be associated with the Bishopsland Period. Pilcher notes that overall there is a fall in oak and a rise in hazel, which may be a cumulative effect of forest clearance and the production of regenerating scrub.

Barry Raftery is engaged on an important excavation at Rathgall, a hill-top site in Co. Wicklow. Complicated structures and numerous finds indicate a long story of occupation on the hill. A large V-shaped ditch seems to be one of the earliest features, and some of its fill was given a radiocarbon date of 1000 BC, which would place it in the Bishopsland Period, a date which is also hinted at by the discovery of clay mould fragments for socketed implements with rope mouldings round the sockets. We have seen that such implements are present in the Bishopsland hoard.

Still greater wealth in the Dowris Period
2650 to 2150 BP (700–200 BC)

In the diagram from Red Bog (p. 137) a C-14 date of 2625 years BP (say 675 BC) corresponds with a marked increase in agricultural activity. Above this level grasses and plantain expand substantially, and bracken is almost continuously present. Cereal pollen is present, and pollen of weeds appear intermittently. Elm woods and hazel thickets were cleared away, and a little later the attack spread into the oak woods.

This date approximates closely with 700 BC, the date that George Eogan has reckoned for the opening of his Dowris Period of the Bronze Age in Ireland, when there were still wider contacts with northern Europe, west-central Europe, Iberia and the eastern Mediterranean, and a further marked increase in wealth, indicated by the numerous finds of gold ornaments and of caches or hoards of bronze implements. In the later Bronze Age northern Europe relied principally on two areas for its supplies of copper, the Carpathians and the Alps. In the eighth century BC the Carpathian area was thrown into chaos by barbarian invaders from the east, and in consequence its output of copper was drastically reduced. Northern Europe then turned to Ireland as an alternative source, and this trade brought not only further prosperity, but still more innovations, to Ireland. Some of them could perhaps have been done without; the whole style of warfare was changed; hitherto the warriors had poked at one another with rapiers or halberds; now they cut at one another with slashing swords, while protecting themselves with shields, made of bronze, leather or wood, depending on social or economic status. Feasts were provided with buckets and cauldrons, and musical interludes were given by trumpets. Gold ornaments became still more numerous, and were accompanied by ornaments of imported Scandinavian amber. The horse was utilized, and provided with elaborate trappings. Wheeled carts appear. Hoards of bronze and gold were deposited, perhaps for safety, perhaps as sacrificial offerings: the hoards are widely distributed throughout Ireland.

Our interest is more particularly with the impact these Dowris folk had on the landscape. What tools did they use, where did they live, how did they farm? The chief tools of the Dowris Period (p. 156) are the knives, both socketed and tanged, with straight and curved blades, the chisels, both socketed and tanged, and the socketed gouges, all of which made a very much higher standard of wood-working possible. Socketed sickles also appear, and these, combined with the saddle-querns and the steady presence of cereal pollen in the diagram, indicate a more intensive system of agriculture. Pottery, of which there is no record in the Bishopsland Period, reappears as flat-bottomed bucket-shaped vessels of poor quality.

Four settlement sites are known, the hill-top site at Rathgall, which continued in use, and three crannogs, or man-made structures in lakes, where the lake waters had a twofold effect – they not only gave protection to the site when it was occupied, but if wet conditions persisted after the site had been abandoned then there was a good possibility that the organic debris left behind by the crannog-dwellers would be preserved.

At Rathgall a socketed bronze gouge, coarse pottery, clay moulds for casting swords and several radiocarbon dates ranging from 600 to 250 BC make it clear that the occupation continued on into the Dowris Period. In addition to saddle-querns a small mass of carbonized crushed cereal grains was found; the mass must represent either a loaf, or porridge, or brewers' grains; the first probability is perhaps the most likely; the radiocarbon age was 540 BC, which would place the material firmly in the Dowris Period.

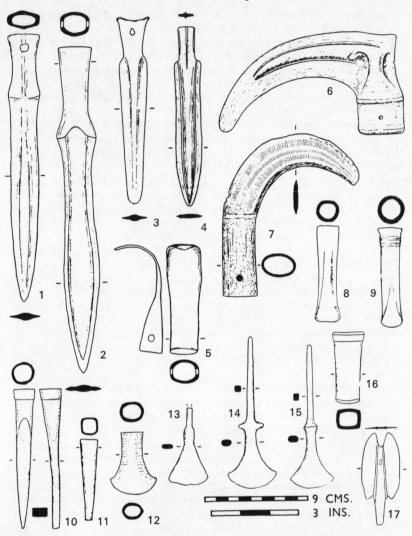

Bronze tools of the Dowris Period of the Bronze Age: **1, 2, 3, 4**, socketed and tanged knives; **5**, curved socketed knife; **6, 7**, socketed sickles; **8, 9**, socketed gouges; **10, 11, 12**, socketed chisels; **13, 14, 15**, tanged chisels; **16**, socketed hammerhead; **17**, razor.

Knocknalappa, Co. Clare, is the simplest of the crannogs. In a shallow part of Rossroe Lake an oval area, 40 m long and 20 m across, was surrounded by a ring of hazel stakes. Peat and stones were then laid inside the ring of stakes, and charcoal and archaeological objects were apparently carried in from some other site with the peat, as there was no evidence that the crannog itself had ever been occupied for any significant length of time. A count of 43 pieces of charcoal gave the following result – hawthorn 18, hazel 15, oak 4, alder 2, willow (or poplar) 2, ash 1, holly 1 – and this count strongly suggests that the gatherers of firewood had immediate access to secondary scrub which had not been long established, and was still rich in hawthorn and hazel. Carpenters could get other material because a wooden structure showed a rather different count – oak 5, willow (or poplar) 4, ash 2, hazel 1, alder 1. Animal bones were dominated by ox, and sheep (or goat), pig and horse were also found. A layer of lake-mud rested on the crannog, and Dr Raftery thought that this had been artificially deposited, but as at the second site, Ballinderry, Co. Offaly, lake level appears to have risen after the crannog had been abandoned, and a layer of mud had been deposited naturally on top of the crannog, it is not impossible that the same thing happened at Knocknalappa.

At Ballinderry the settlement seems to have been on a low gravel island in a lake, and in places brushwood and rings of piles extended the occupation-site out into the lake-edge. The lake subsequently rose in level and deposited muds on the former settlement; later in Early Christian times a much larger crannog was built at the same spot on top of the earlier settlement.

On the site there were a number of circular wicker huts between 1 and 2 m in diameter, and it is possible that these were used as granaries. There was also an elaborate wooden foundation about 12 m square of parallel rows of oak planks about 1·5 m apart joined at the ends by cross beams; each plank had a row of squarish holes to carry an upright post about 6 cm in diameter. It suggests an aisled hall of some type, though the aisles might have been inconveniently narrow. One saddle-quern and some rubbing-stones were found. An unusual feature was the abundance of red deer bones, but some of them may be the remains of animals which had died naturally in and around the lake, and were not necessarily killed by the crannog-dwellers. Of the other bones about three-quarters were of ox, one-tenth were pig, and the remainder sheep and horse. The bulk of the charcoal was of alder, ash, hazel and willow, and hawthorn and yew were represented in the pieces of worked wood found.

At Rathtinaun in Lough Gara a small settlement site had been constructed in the shallow water of a swamp, by laying down a ring of wooden piles, and building up the enclosed area with brushwood and peat. Evidence of occupation was scanty, but there were a number of hearths surrounded by clay-plastered wicker-baskets; pieces of the baskets were dated by radiocarbon to about 150 BC. There must have been a kiln for drying grain which became overheated on at least one occasion, with the result that the contents became completely carbonized, and were dumped over the edge of the crannog into the lake. Naked barley provided the bulk of the material, but Hans Helbaek also identified small amounts of hulled barley and of wheat; other food plants were various species of *Polygonum* (Knotgrass) and *Chenopodium* (Goosefoot), blackberries and raspberries (*Rubus* spp.), with in addition flax (*Linum usitatissimum*) and a large variety of weeds.

How did the Dowris people farm? As we have seen the Red Bog diagram (see p. 137) shows a dramatic upward spurt of agricultural activity about

700 BC. It is very probable that this expansion is due to the introduction of some form of plough. At this time ox-drawn ard-ploughs were being used in Scandinavia, and finds of amber beads in Ireland prove that there must have been trading connections with the north. Similar ards found in Danish bogs range in radiocarbon age from 900 to 350 BC, and an ard in Scotland was dated to 400 BC. If the ard-plough was being used in Scotland at this time it will certainly have been in use in Ireland also. (Pl. 20)

The type of plough or *ard* used was, of course, very simple compared with the modern plough. It had not got either a *coulter*, a vertical knife-like blade to cut the roots in the soil, nor a *mouldboard* to turn the surface layer over, and so create ridges and furrows. It was a device for drawing a pointed oak rod, the *share*, across a field immediately below the surface of the ground. As it moved across the field the share would push the soil it was penetrating upwards and forwards, while at the same time some of the upper soil was falling down into the cavity left by the share as it moved along. In this way not only was the soil loosened, but some lower material, richer in nutrients than the already cultivated earth above it, was brought nearer the surface, where it was more accessible to plant roots. The wear on the share was, of course, very heavy, and in modern experiments the share had to be replaced, or resharpened, six times in the course of ploughing one acre. In the experiments the ard, because it had not got a coulter, was not able to break up old grassland, and the sod had to be chopped up with spades or hoes before the ard could be used. A second ploughing at right angles was necessary to break up the whole of the ground, and the fields would thus tend to have a square outline.

It seems quite legitimate to picture that cereal-growing in ploughed fields made a substantial contribution to the rise in the standard of living that took place during the Dowris Period in Ireland. However, such a standard depended on the fertility of the soil, and could not be maintained unless the fertility remained high also.

POSSIBLE CLIMATIC DETERIORATION *c.* 2550 BP (600 BC)

Forty years ago it was axiomatic to think that there had been a marked climatic deterioration in western Europe at about 600 BC (2550 BP), and that at about that time all the raised-bogs of the region had increased their rate of growth, as a new type of relatively unhumified *Sphagnum*-peat started to form. Intensive efforts were made to identify in the raised-bogs a well-marked *Grenz*, or horizon of change, which would have well-humified peat below and fresher peat above. Today it is realized that the changing shape of the bog as it continues to grow can have an influence on its hydrology, and on the type of peat that will be forming at any point on its surface at any moment of time; changes in humification might be purely of local significance. Nonetheless if there were regional climatic changes these should be reflected in bog structure, as deteriorations of climate would probably induce more rapid accumulation of peat.

At Red Bog the uniformly highly humified peat in the lower layers of the bog had given way to a moderately humified peat with lenses of fresh *Sphagnum* by the time of the opening of the Dowris Period at 2625 BP. At Littleton Bog a prominent layer of fresh *Sphagnum*-peat separated a more highly humified peat below from a less highly humified peat above, just at the level where the opening of the Dowris Period agriculture was recorded in the pollen-diagram. At Fallahogy Bog a marked change in humification which could be traced laterally for some distance was dated at several points to about 2500 years BP (550 BC).

When he was working in Ireland Professor Jessen formed the opinion that at all the sites of Bronze Age finds that he visited, objects of Late Bronze Age type were found in fresh *Sphagnum*-peat above the *Grenz*, while older objects occurred below it. If we substitute 'Dowris Period' for 'Late Bronze Age', and recognize that the development of the *Grenz* may vary considerably from bog to bog, and from one part of one bog to another part of the same bog, then Professor Jessen's view remains essentially correct.

The blanket-bogs also show in general a more highly humified peat below and a fresher peat above, but so far no sustained attempts have been made either to date the change, or to see if it is consistent in level from one bog to another.

If there was a climatic deterioration, did it bring about a general rise in water-tables and a rise in lake-levels? The Dowris Period lakeside site at Ballinderry was flooded by water and buried by lake-mud, and it is not impossible that the same happened at Knocknalappa. The site at Rathtinaun was only revealed when a big drainage scheme lowered the waters of Lough Gara. But because throughout this period the raised-bogs were expanding and blocking up natural drainage-outlets, it is difficult to say how much of the flooding is due to a general rise in water-table brought about by climatic deterioration, and how much to the damming-up effect of continuing bog-growth.

Here we have another of the apparent paradoxes that are constantly arising as we try to picture the development of the Irish landscape. On the one hand we are told that there is widespread evidence throughout northern Europe for a deterioration of climate about 600 BC (2550 BP); yet this is about the time that our pollen-diagrams tell us that agriculture was expanding vigorously, and archaeological finds indicate that the standard of living was rising. We face another version of the same problem in the next section.

THE DIMINUTION OF AGRICULTURE IN THE PAGAN IRON AGE
2150 to 1650 BP (200 BC – AD 300)

If we look at the section of the Red Bog diagram (see p. 137) that follows after the burst of agricultural activity that marked the opening of the Dowris Period, we see a gradual fading away of evidence of agriculture. The weeds of cultivation disappear first, followed by cereals and bracken, while grass and plantain fall in value. On the other side hazel rises first, followed by rises in ash, elm and oak. And then with dramatic suddenness, the situation is reversed. At 1725 radiocarbon years BP (AD 225) grass, plantain and bracken rise sharply, accompanied by the reappearance of cereals and the weeds of cultivation. Elm and ash fall back from relatively high values, and hazel falls markedly.

And this is not a phenomenon unique to Co. Louth. It can also be seen in diagrams from Limerick, Tipperary, Meath, Antrim and Tyrone. The renewal of agriculture has been dated at several points, and in general the dates centre around AD 300. Unfortunately we have as yet no date for the point at which the previous decline becomes clearly apparent, and, rightly or wrongly, for our present purposes I have taken it to occur at about the time Iron Age influences began to reach the country about 200 BC (2150 BP).

We must therefore ask ourselves 'What was going on in Ireland at this time, and what was happening to the landscape?' First iron objects and a knowledge of ironworking were beginning to spread. We are not concerned here with fashion. We do not want to know when it was that designs fashionable in Iron Age Europe first began to be copied in bronze in Ireland, or when it was that glass beads began to be imported, in addition to amber beads. What we want to know is when did the properties that for many purposes make iron superior to bronze come to be widely recognized in Ireland, and when was the first iron object fabricated in Ireland.

We must retrace our steps to the crannog site at Rathtinaun in Lough Gara. Here as at Ballinderry there were two stages of occupation separated by a period of desertion, caused in the opinion of the excavator, Dr Raftery, 'by a sudden and unexpected rise in the level of the water'. For the earlier stage there are a cluster of radiocarbon dates ranging from 300 to 200 BC; for the later stage there are two dates 150 BC and AD 320. The earlier stage produced typical Dowris material in bronze, gold and pottery; the later stage produced similar bronze and pottery, with in addition an iron pin, an iron fork and an iron axe-head with a shaft-hole, clumsily forged out of three pieces of metal; here surely we have the arrival of iron in Ireland.

Second we see the earliest examples of the small isolated homestead surrounded by a bank and ditch of earth or stone, the *rath* or ring-fort. In a rath at Feerwore, Co. Galway, Dr Raftery found another forged iron socketed axe-head and other items, which suggest that the rath may be of the same age as the Lough Gara site. Dr Raftery had been attracted to the rath at Feerwore because it was in its immediate vicinity that the famous Turoe Stone, decorated in abstract curvelinear style, originally stood. This impressive monument is fashioned from a glacial erratic of Galway granite, and must weigh several tons; it cannot therefore have been carried into Ireland by boat from distant parts, but must have been smoothed and decorated nearby, perhaps in the first century BC. Its designs, in *la Tène* style, stem from Celtic Europe, and such designs also occur in Ireland on numerous portable objects – sword-scabbards, spear-butts, horse-trappings, gold ornaments – which again have prototypes in Europe.

Should we picture bands of invading warriors, displaced by the Roman conquest from Britain and Gaul, plundering their way through the Irish countryside, and bringing about a collapse of an organized society and its pattern of agriculture? But there would be little point in capturing Ireland, if

PLATE 19 *Above*, Blanket-bog, Connemara, Co. Galway. Peat-cuttings are seen in the foreground. *Below*, blanket-bog vegetation, nr. Roundstone, Co. Galway. Bog-pools with bog-bean (*Menyanthes trifoliata*) can be seen, and on the right there is a prominent hummock of *Sphagnum imbricatum*, with cotton-grass (*Eripohorum angustifolium*) and heather (*Erica tetralix*).

PLATE 20 *Above*, Bronze Age ard-plough. *Centre*, medieval coulter-plough; the boy should be walking backwards in front of the team; the man sowing has nothing to do with the plough. *Below*, medieval mouldboard-plough.

the assets of the country were destroyed in the process. The Romans clearly recognized that if an area was to be worth conquering it had to be capable, not only of maintaining a Roman garrison, but also of providing a surplus for the imperial exchequer. It is perhaps relevant at this point to recall that the Romans dismissed Ireland as not worthy of invasion.

It may be that the invading Celtic warriors reorganized the social structure, placing themselves at the top as an aristocratic élite, with the native population forming subject tribes. The tribal chief and his entourage would install themselves in a hill-fort, which they would occupy as a palace in times of peace, but all the tribesmen and their cattle could be accommodated within its defences in times of danger. This is the picture that Warner would draw of the hill-fort at Clogher, Co. Tyrone, probably built not long before the opening of the Christian Era. Here a roughly rectangular area about 4 acres in extent was protected by a bank, created from the upcast from a ditch immediately outside, and downhill from it.

The fort at Clogher is a relatively small structure. In England the disturbed times of the Iron Age brought about the erection of very large hill-top and promontory forts; did the same happen in Ireland? The Hill of Tara carries an enormous enclosure, Ráth na Ríogh, but the ditch lies *inside* the bank – the opposite of what one would expect in defences – and as we have seen the so-called Mound of the Hostages, which lies within it, was first built as a Neolithic Passage-grave; in England the bank is outside the ditch in many Neolithic monuments. On the hill but outside the enclosure there is the Rath of the Synods – first excavated one hundred years ago by British Israelites looking for the Ark of the Covenant. Re-examination by Sean Ó Ríordáin revealed concentric ditches and post-holes for wooden structures; the inhabitants were in touch with the Roman world in Britain and Gaul, and finds of a seal, a lock, glass and pottery showed that the occupation of the site extended from the first to the third centuries AD. In addition to enamelling, iron-smelting was being carried on, and here we must be firmly in the Iron Age. The site threw no light on contemporary agriculture. (Pl. 21)

The large hill-top enclosure with the ditch inside the bank, and evidence of Neolithic occupation, such as we have seen at Tara, is repeated at the Navan Fort near Armagh, and Knockaulin in Kildare. Both sites also produced inner ditches and post-holes. The Navan Fort had been occupied in Dowris times as was shown by both typical objects and appropriate radiocarbon dates; glass beads and fragments of iron were also found. A great conflagration seems to have put an end to the occupation of the site about 265 BC. Knockaulin produced glass beads, coarse pottery, and a sword of la Tène type that would have been at home in the second century BC.

We cannot be certain if the Iron Age occupiers regarded these sites as primarily defensive. Freestone Hill in Kilkenny was a hill-fort, where a bank with an external ditch enclosed an area of about five acres. No structures were found, and it was thought that the site had perhaps only been occupied for about one hundred years; a find of a Roman copper coin of Constantine struck about AD 340, and in mint condition, suggested a mid-fourth-century date for the occupation; some iron objects were found. There was no evidence of agriculture; the report says, 'Neither quernstones, plough-shares, coulters, billhooks, sickles or any other implement for tilling the soil came to light'. By far the majority of the animal bones were ox; pig was frequent and next in quantity; sheep were in small quantity, and there was one goat horn-core; horse was present in small numbers; there were a few remains of dog. Antlers of red deer had been turned into simple pick-axes. Freestone Hill is one of the very few Irish sites where molluscs have been studied, and as a result we have a useful landscape picture. The earth at the base of the ditch contained snail-shells, and here Arthur Stelfox identified seventeen different forms. He considered that they were types characteristic of a fairly dry woodland. 'I do not mean trees, but what we call scrub. I would suggest that the sides of the hill (below the ditch at any rate) were covered with patches of hazel (*Corylus*) scrub, giving plenty of shade under the bushes, but with open areas between patches of scrub.' Freestone Hill is an outlying limestone hill on the slopes of Castlecomer Plateau; today these slopes are in many places still carrying hazel scrub of the type envisaged by Stelfox.

From these vague glimpses we can perhaps draw two conclusions; first that warriors with lavishly decorated weapons and jewellery came into Ireland from Celtic Europe in the centuries immediately preceding the birth of Christ, and second that there were contacts with the Roman world both in Gaul and Britain. Why should the pollen-diagrams tell us that this was a time of marked agricultural decline? I believe they reflect the culmination of a long-continuing and widespread exhaustion of the soil, rather than a drastic social upheaval brought about by military conquest. Areas of primary fertility, i.e. where the parent materials of the soils were rich in basic nutrients and had a texture that meant that soil drainage was good, had by this time had that fertility progressively depleted by cropping which had been in operation for some three thousand years.

For the first two thousand years the net loss of fertility was probably small. The Neolithic farmers scratched the surface of the soil, and quickly drew down the nutrient supplies available; but they then moved on, and woodland reoccupied the site; the deep roots of the trees could penetrate far below the level of Neolithic disturbance and draw on nutrients farther down in the soil; when they shed their leaves and other debris on to the soil surface, the contained nutrients restored the fertility of the upper layers. But as the population grew during the Bronze Age the agricultural pressure on the good soils increased, and the intervening periods when the soil lay fallow under secondary woodland shortened, and the rate of loss of fertility must have steepened.

When 'Welfare States' became established in the western world after World War II, poverty was very widely reduced, and the average *per capita* consumption of staple foods increased. We can be sure that much the same happened when the wider European contacts that marked the opening of the Bishopsland Period about 1200 BC materially increased the wealth of Ireland, and more and more nutrients must have been drawn from the soil. Increasingly sophisticated technical skills were largely responsible for the increase in wealth, and as technique becomes more complicated it also becomes less mobile. For an increasing proportion of the population the practice of changing one's residence, as the local soils became exhausted, will have become more and more difficult.

And we must remember that until the opening of the Dowris Period about 700 BC when – in my opinion, though I may well be wrong – the ard first came into use in Ireland, all cultivation was done with a mattock, a spade or a digging-stick, and that these implements could not reach down deeply into the soil. Only a very thin superficial layer was turned over, but this happened again and again, and in Ireland's wet climate, leaching of nutrient from this loose layer will have been severe, and it will have grown progressively sour and acid. This still happens even with the modern deep plough, but today's farmer rectifies the acid condition by adding calcium carbonate, in the form of ground limestone, to the soil.

At first sight the introduction of the ard might have seemed the panacea for all soil evils. On average the share of the ard did penetrate more deeply – else we should have no 'plough-marks' to discover – and it did lift some lower soil materials, still relatively rich in nutrient, nearer to the surface where crop-roots could draw on them. But the all-wooden ard must have been very vulnerable to collision with stones, and women, children and old folk will have been kept busy collecting stones from what we can now call fields, and depositing them in heaps or building them into walls. Heaps of field-stones, buried by peat, have been found both in Antrim and in Mayo. This further factor, that the ard was more successful in stone-free fields than in rough open ground, will have tended to 'fix' farming operations still more firmly in certain localities, and restrict them from wandering in search of less exhausted soils. As population rose, 'empty' land to move on to must have become increasingly difficult to find.

It may well be that the ard, which in the short term appeared to be such a boon, turned out in the long run to be a disaster. In the beginning the ard did bring new nutrient material to the surface, but only from the still very limited depth to which it could reach; it probably created a good 'tilth' more easily than the spade, and for a time all went well. But the more finely divided the tilth became, the more easily nutrient could be lost from it by leaching, and a very acid surface layer created. If the climate did deteriorate around 600 BC, leaching may have become still more severe.

Today between Newbridge and Kildare we have The Curragh, a great expanse of gravelly glacial deposits, chiefly occupied by a racecourse and a military barracks. The modern soil is a grey-brown podzolic and as its name implies leaching is carrying surface materials down to lower levels. Where the modern farmer owns his fields, he counteracts this by adding farmyard manure and other fertilizers to the fields, and the grey-brown podzolic then gives him one of the best soils in Ireland. But in recent times much of the Curragh was held in common and used as a sheep-walk; as it belonged to everyone, no one fertilized it. Thus in certain areas the soil went undisturbed and neglected for long periods, with the result that although the parent material was calcareous, continued leaching combined with over-grazing removed all the calcium carbonate from the surface layers, which became acid and low in nutrients. As a result, ling (*Calluna vulgaris*), a member of the heather family, which can survive on a low supply of nutrient, invaded the area, and covered parts of it with a heath vegetation. We have already seen *Calluna* growing on bog-surfaces, where the nutrient supply is also low.

It may well be that as the Dowris Period progressed large areas of agricultural land, through over-cultivation with the ard, and increased leaching due to climatic deterioration, became depleted of nutrient. Grasses could no longer thrive, and the fields degenerated into heath. If this happened the output of pollen of grass and its associated weeds into the air would be reduced, and the output of pollen of the heather family (ericaceous pollen) would be increased. Unfortunately, as I have already explained, most of the pollen-diagrams in this book are based on samples from bogs, and as their purpose is to illustrate changes in the vegetation of the surrounding countryside, and not the development of the bog, the pollens arising from plants growing on the bog-surface itself have been omitted from them. Thus if heaths surrounding the bog started to produce ericaceous pollen in addition to that developed by the bog vegetation, this is not revealed by the diagrams. This further illustrates the weakness of the 'relative' type of pollen-count. Suppose we are making counts of 'trees' on the one hand, and 'grasses' on the other: if the supply of grass pollen to the air is reduced by heath taking over former grassland (and we do not take into consideration the extra ericaceous pollen produced), then the quantity of 'tree' pollen in our counts will rise, even though the tree cover may not have expanded significantly. But this does not vitiate our argument that if pollen and spores of grasses and its associated weeds, plaintain and bracken, fall drastically in value, agriculture must have been reduced, and that if they bound up again, agriculture has returned in force.

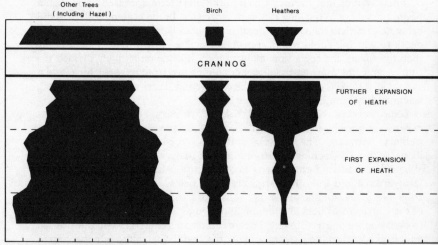

A schematic pollen-diagram to show development of heath vegetation at Lagore, Co. Meath.

PLATE 21 *Above*, Hill of Tara, Co. Meath. On the left are two conjoined raths in an enclosure (with later cultivation-ridges) surrounded by a ditch with external bank, all older than the 6th century AD. The ditch swerves to avoid the older Mound of the Hostages (see Pl. 16). To the right is the disturbed Rath of the Synods, dating to the 1st to 3rd centuries AD. In the right margin is the uphill end of a ceremonial approach avenue, the so-called Banqueting Hall. Above it there are more rath-like structures. *Below*, nr. Shrule, Co. Mayo. This hill-top caher, with a drystone wall, lies almost on limestone bedrock. Part of its interior was cleared relatively recently, but bushes are re-invading it. The clearance revealed older cultivation-ridges; some are still buried by heavy scrub.

PLATE 22 *Above*, Craggaunowen, Co. Clare. In a museum project, John Hunt has built this modern version of a crannog, based on information derived from excavations. *Below*, Lislough, Co. Armagh. We see poorly drained drumlin country, with rushes (*Juncus*) in the fields, and lakes, fens and cut-away bogs on the lower ground. In the centre, a crannog, overgrown by bushes, stands in a lake; below left, a splendid rath crowns a drumlin.

Let us see what a pollen-diagram from a lake, as opposed to one from a bog, can tell us. Near Dunshaughlin in Co. Meath there is an extensive lake-basin surrounded by calcareous glacial deposits; today the local soil is a grey-brown podzolic. A large crannog in the basin, Lagore Crannog, was excavated by Hugh Hencken, and shown to have been built not later than AD 650. The crannog was built on lake-mud, and there was a further thin deposit of mud on top of the margins of the crannog. The muds below the crannog produced a piece of Neolithic pottery and a bronze spearhead, and their contained pollen indicated long-continued farming activity in the country around the lake. We cannot put absolute dates on the diagram, but it begins in the later part of the Bronze Age.

At the base we see low values for birch, and very low values for heathers. A townland about one mile away carries the name 'Red Bog', and the name suggests that a raised-bog, now completely cut away, may have formerly existed there, and the bog-surface may have been the source for the very few heather pollen that were then reaching the lake. A little higher in the diagram, values for both birch and heather rise. Birch as well as heather is a plant of dry acid soils, and here we see the heath community invade the exhausted fields as their surface layers become increasingly acid. Higher again the ericaceous pollen rises still further in value, and by now there must have been extensive heaths growing on the acid surface of the over-leached grey-brown podzolic soils around the lake.

If such developments were widespread in Ireland, agriculture will have been very much reduced. In the primitive cultivation-plots of earlier times the soil fertility had never been so seriously reduced; the forest-trees could regenerate in the plots, and their deep roots could draw fertility to the surface once more. But the soil of the heaths had become too infertile for forest-trees to re-establish themselves, and the heaths, once established, tended to be self-perpetuating. The farming of the Dowris Period that had opened with a bang with the introduction of the ard, may have ended with a whimper as infertile heaths extended widely.

The crannog, which served as a palace for the local kings, was then built in the lake; in the course of excavation it produced many iron tools and implements, including a share and a coulter for a true plough, and these finds make it clear that the crannog-dwellers had moved on into a new agricultural world. With their new ploughs they were able to rip up the heaths, and bring up subsoil from a deeper level, and so restore fertility to the area. Thus we are not surprised that in the mud which rests on the crannog values for heathers have shrunk drastically, and birch has also fallen in value.

5

The Rise and Fall of Population, AD 300 to 1900

FARMING WITH THE COULTER-PLOUGH, AD 300 TO 600

As we have seen, at a date that radiocarbon tells us must lie at about AD 300, there was a dramatic expansion in agriculture (see diagram on p. 137). Grasses, plantain and bracken increase in value, and pollen of cereals and docks are continually present. Part of these rises may depend on the bringing back of land that had degenerated to heath into agricultural production once more, but the final disappearance at this level in the diagrams of pollen of elm and ash suggests that extensive areas of secondary woodland were being cleared away. Here the Destruction-phase (ILWd₂) of the woodlands opens. It seems reasonable to assume that new farming practices are being introduced, that agricultural output is rising, and that the population is increasing. Agricultural land is still more in demand.

By AD 300 the principle of mounting a vertical iron knife or *coulter* on the frame of the plough so that it would cut through matted roots as it was drawn along, and so open up the way for the *share* (which was itself fitted with an iron shoe to protect it), was well known in Roman Britain, and from there must have spread into Ireland, because we now know that there were contacts between the two areas. The simple ard could not deal with matted roots, which had to be given a preliminary cutting with a spade blade. The coulter speeded up the rate of ploughing, but as the plough had as yet no *mouldboard* to turn the cut sod upside down, cross-ploughing must still have been necessary. (Pl. 20)

But we must not think that the day the first Irish farmer saw a coulter-plough at work, all Irish farmers immediately adopted its use. Shortage of capital combined with innate conservatism, probably combined to make the spread of the use of the new plough a very slow one. History repeated itself at the beginning of the nineteenth century when all-metal ploughs, which were more efficient and required fewer animals to draw them, were beginning to become available; many contemporary writers deplored the way farmers clung to their locally built wooden ploughs, and could not be persuaded to change.

Perhaps as important as the appearance of the plough was the coming into general use of iron implements for a wide range of operations. In addition to the plough share and coulter, the crannog at Lagore produced axes, bill-hooks, a hammer, an adze, a spokeshave, saws, chisels, gouges and awls. As befitted a royal seat, the Lagore crannog was a very big one, about 40 m in diameter, and surrounded by three wooden palisades. Oak was the

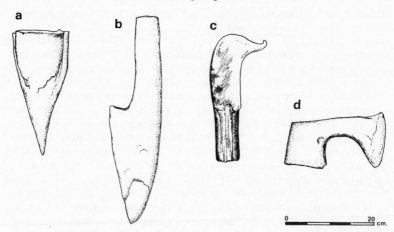

Iron implements from Lagore Crannog, Co. Meath: **a**, plough-share; **b**, plough-coulter; **c**, billhook; **d**, axe.

principal wood, hazel was second and ash third, with small quantities of poplar, yew, elm, holly, hawthorn, birch, cherry and dogwood. Not a single piece of pine was found, and alder was only used in small pieces of carpentry. The brushwood fill also contained sods from the surrounding fields, straw, and – in harmony with what we have seen from the pollen-diagram (see p. 164) – pieces of peat and twigs of heathers. Most of the timber came from secondary woodland and scrub, but there were occasional large oak timbers, including part of a dug-out boat, that must have come from a tree not less than 1 m in diameter.

The concept of the *crannog*, an artificial island protected by a natural moat of lake-water, is a simple one, and some small crannogs may go back to the Bronze Age, but the large crannog seems only to have developed when iron tools became generally available. The crannog continued in use until the seventeenth century AD. About 250 are known, but this number pales into insignificance when compared with the number of the other type of simply fortified circular site, the *rath* and the *cashel*, which is estimated to lie between 30,000 and 40,000. (Pl. 22)

Like the crannog, the rath may go back to the Bronze Age; there certainly were a few in the Pagan Iron Age, but the majority seem to have sprung up in Early Christian times, and some continued in use until the seventeenth century. Radiocarbon datings of raths are still all too few, but they seem mainly to lie between the fourth and the eighth centuries AD.

The rath is the fundamental structure of this early period of advanced farming, and if we could understand its organization, we would understand much of the social life and the landscape of the time. The word *rath* is cognate with 'digging', and the simplest type of this structure is a circular bank of earth about 20 m in diameter, the earth being obtained from a ditch which encircles the bank on the outside. When in use the bank was supported by timber palisades or stone revetments. More important raths may have up to three banks and ditches, and an overall diameter of 125 m. In regions where suitable stone is available the earthen bank is replaced by a wall of stone, and the structure is known as a *cashel*. If the walls are impressive and the structure is large, it is often called a *dun* or a *caher*. (Pl. 21)

In an earlier chapter I deduced that the paucity of remains of Bronze Age occupation-sites implied that they and their surrounding stockade had been constructed of wood, and that the sites had been completely obliterated when the area in which they lay had first been reclothed by secondary wood-land, and later recleared for further agricultural use. The corollary of this is twofold: first, after the secondary woodlands had melted away in the face of advanced agricultural practices, there was no longer an unlimited supply of heavy timber for the building of stockades, and banks of earth and stone had to take their places, and second that if the banks were overgrown by secondary woodland, their stout construction meant they could survive further clearance.

We can perhaps picture the simple type of rath as the homestead of the lowest rank of 'free' farmer, who might have had (as we shall see later – p. 180) about seventy statute acres (thirty hectares) of good land, or 'home farm', together with rights elsewhere to pasture, timber and peat. How does this match up with the density of raths in the countryside? Not all the raths whose banks have survived will have been in use at the same time, and we may thus arrive at too dense a spacing; once built, many will have an extended occupation; others will be abandoned and will be ploughed out. If we go to Co. Cavan, where raths are common, though not unusually so, and take 6″ Ordnance Survey map No. 21 we can count 59 raths in the 15,000 acres covered by the map, or about 1 rath to 250 acres. We can pick out one square mile (640 acres) which holds 6 raths, or about 1 rath to 100 acres. Such a density is compatible with the size of farm we have envisaged, and more important it signifies that if the land is well cleared of trees the raths will be intervisible from one another, and this was absolutely vital in a countryside where cattle-raiding was a constant occupation. We can almost picture a group of raths as forming a type of extended village.

Raths are sometimes called *ring-forts*, but they are not forts, if we mean by that a strong-point capable of resisting siege for some time. Raths almost never have a well, and the bank and ditch would have offered little difficulty to a determined attack. But they could offer short-term protection to live-stock, and they were intervisible. I picture that all the raths of a vicinity would belong to the same clan. If cattle-raiders from other groups came into the locality, each clansman would drive his stock into his own rath, and then hurry off to assist in the defence of whatever rath was first attacked, and if possible drive off the raiders. Modern strategists would call it defence in depth; it was almost inevitable that the first rath to be attacked would be pillaged, but then the counter-attack would come, and it would have a good chance of success.

That the defenders of the raths did not expect the attacks to be prolonged is shown by the presence of underground passages and chambers, known as *souterrains*; a Limerick example was dated to the eighth century. The passages often have constrictions and obstacles to compel slow movement, and so place an intruder who forced an entry at the mercy of a defender already inside. Presumably the women and children, taking the family valuables with them, will have hidden in the souterrain at the first threat of attack, but they could not have remained there for long, even if smoke was not used to force them out. Such a type of refuge can only have been devised on the assumption that the raider, if he did temporarily overrun the rath, would only be there briefly before he was forced out by a counter-attack. The temperature of the souterrain would have been below that of the outside air, and would also have been relatively constant, and in time of peace it would have provided a useful storehouse for dairy products and other foods.

Within the rath there was an open green space, the *lis*, where livestock could be penned in time of emergency, and there were also houses and small farm buildings. Who lived in the houses? Perhaps only the farmer and the members of his immediate family, while the servants lived in huts propped against the inside of the bank, or squatted in the ditch outside the rath. Unfortunately in early Irish society the lower orders, who probably formed the largest part of the population, had no legal status, and therefore no legal existence, and the laws are silent about them. But there were serfs who were tied to their masters and owned neither land nor stock, there were slaves and there were prisoners of war, and it is as yet quite impossible to say what part they played in the social structure.

Thus we have the problem – did only one important family reside inside the rath, in relatively solid houses of which we can hope to find some trace by excavation, or were these houses surrounded by other flimsier huts of which all traces have vanished? If there were a group of dwellings, then here we have a type of settlement which has a long history in Ireland, and has been given the name of *clachan* by Estyn Evans. Several workers have drawn attention to the fact that it is possible to find elaborate systems of souterrains without any associated rath, and have suggested that such souterrains may have been the refuge point for a hut village which has completely vanished.

The farmer himself was a member of a clan group, and as such was linked to the head of the clan in a relationship of mutual obligation; the chieftain gave legal decisions and organized military forces; the clansmen submitted to his adjudication, did service in his army, and provided food and hospitality at regulated times. The chieftain had surplus land, stock and equipment. The farmer could rent land, paying with stock and services, and he could get stock and equipment on a hire-purchase system. While the chieftain enjoyed special lands that went with his office, essentially the land was held in common by the full members of the clan, and no individual could alienate land from the clan.

The rath and the lands surrounding it at first sight suggest an independent farm on today's pattern, but there was the important difference that today when the farmer dies the whole farm generally passes to a single chosen heir, usually *in primogeniture* to the eldest son, but in early Ireland the use of the land had to be apportioned *in severalty* over all the immediate kin, with the result that there was extensive sub-division and constant rearrangement of holdings. Neighbouring raths of the same clan group probably co-operated with one another, and there may well have been interlocking holdings.

The advanced agriculture made possible by the coulter-plough must have increased output, and caused the population to grow. This in turn created a demand for still more farmland, and the ability 'to clear plains', and thus

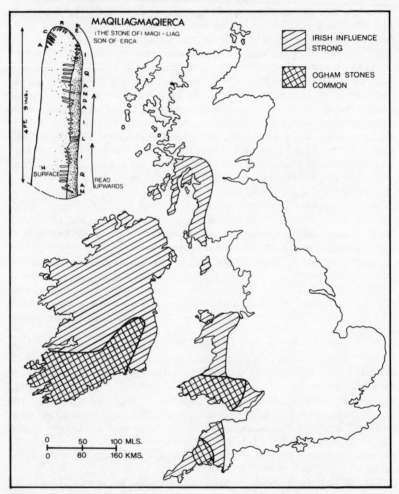

Typical ogham-stone, and distribution-map to show areas where such stones are common, and also areas in western Britain into which there was migration from Ireland in the 4th century AD.

provide more land, became an attribute of heroes. Place-names containing the words *rath, lis, dun, caher* and *cashel* are both common and widespread in Ireland, and probably in quite a short time all the land from which a living could be wrested was occupied.

It is not easy to understand why western Britain, with its much closer contacts with the Roman world, should not have undergone a similar growth in population, and why there was empty land there, but emigrants from Ireland were able to cross the Irish Sea and settle down. Writing had now reached Ireland, but with a clumsy cipher version of the Latin alphabet, and standing-stones with simple *Ogham* inscriptions became common in the south of the country. From here in the later part of the fourth century Irish emigrants carried this type of monument into Wales and Cornwall, and perhaps the rath and the souterrain also, the latter reappearing as the *fogou* of Cornwall. There was also a movement from the north of Ireland into Scotland and the Isle of Man.

In turn at the opening of the fifth century Christianity began to reach Ireland from western Britain and from Gaul, and when the Irish church later began to be moulded in monastic rather than diocesan form, the Irish students went to St David's in Wales and to Whithorn in Scotland. Already by the opening of the sixth century there was trading contact with the Continent, and oil and wine in Mediterranean jars were being exchanged for wolfhounds. By contemporary standards Ireland was probably a fairly prosperous and well-inhabited country, even though she still lacked towns and an established coinage.

The kin-group rather than the individual was dominant, authority was diffused rather than centralized, and occasional hostings of clans served the purpose of cities, parliaments and law-courts. The larger monasteries, such as those at Derry and Clonard, may have served as local centres of population, but the figures of the Annals, which number the inhabitants of these 'monastic cities' in thousands, are probably greatly exaggerated. Finances were catered for by loans in kind, barter, services, and an elaborate hire-purchase system, and the lack of coinage did not give rise to special difficulties.

There were at least the elements of a road system. The wheeled cart had come in in the Iron Age, and the heroes of the sagas were driven to battle in light carriages, extravagantly described as chariots. Roads capable of carrying such vehicles must have had some foundation, and there were also unsurfaced droving-roads, cattle-tracks and pathways. *Slige*, a general word for road, implies 'felling' or 'cutting-down', and suggests the cutting of a way through forest. *Toghers*, tracks made across wet ground and bogs by throwing down timber and brushwood, continued to be made.

FARMING WITH THE MOULDBOARD-PLOUGH, AD 600 TO 1150

The next advance in agriculture was the addition of a sloping board, the *mouldboard*, to the plough. The leading edge of the board inserted itself into the vertical cut made by the coulter, and as the plough moved forward the wedge-like action of the sloping board turned the sod over, so that it fell upside down into the gutter or furrow that had been created by the plough in its previous trip along the field. Once the plough was on the move it was desirable to keep it going as long as possible, so as to reduce the number of times the clumsy plough-team would have to be turned around. This was the origin of the *furlong*, the length along which the team of oxen or horses could be made to cut a furrow, without having to stop for a rest. Cross-ploughing was no longer necessary, and long narrow fields replaced the earlier small square ones. (Pl. 20)

Such fields appear in Anglo-Saxon England, and it must be from this source that the mouldboard-plough reached Ireland. The pagan Anglo-Saxons had arrived in England about AD 450, and their conversion to Christianity, in which missionaries from Ireland played an important part, took place around AD 600. From then on the church in Ireland was in close contact with the church in Britain, and groups of churchmen kept coming and going between the two countries. The monasteries, with their emphasis on vegetable diets, will have exchanged farming information.

Although study of the origin of fields and field-systems is still in its infancy in Ireland, the field cannot be ignored in any examination of the Irish landscape. In proportion to its length, the circumference of the circle encloses the largest area, and hence all primitive enclosures are circular in shape. But for dividing and enclosing an area, the square is the most practical, and at Brideswell, Co. Roscommon, we can see both modern and ancient enclosed fields of this shape. For spade cultivation the size of the field is immaterial, and may be dictated by the number of stones encountered, for the easiest way to get rid of these is to build them into long rows, which automatically become walls. With the ard where cross-ploughing is necessary, the square is a convenient shape, and its size will again depend on the distance the team can draw the ard without pausing for a rest. In general these fields will be small, and will probably be held in single ownership. Small enclosed fields of this type go back at least to the Bronze Age in Ireland. (Pl. 23)

The mouldboard-plough gives rise to elongated plots, and it requires a much greater length of fence to enclose a rectangle rather than a square of equal area. In a district of limited size where the soil is essentially uniform, and the weather is the same, all vegetative processes will proceed simultaneously, and all crops will ripen at the same time. Under such circumstances communal operations in a single large enclosure, or *common-field*, will make much more sense than individual operations in narrow fields with uneconomic fences. In many cases different farmers will have contributed one or more beasts to the plough-team, and the width of the strip that the team could plough in one day became the fundamental land-unit.

But though the operations will have been conducted in common, the various land-units in the common-field will have been private property. Inheritance in severalty meant constant further sub-division of land-holdings, and plots were frequently exchanged so as to maintain a fair distribution of the better and the poorer land. A complex mosaic of differently owned small plots must have developed.

Beyond the common-field was the permanent pasture, probably held in

PLATE 23 *Above*, Brideswell, Co. Roscommon. Here there is thin soil on limestone. Within modern square walled fields we see similar older enclosures and cultivation-ridges, now being invaded by scrub. The smaller enclosures may have been worked with spades; the walls both protect a space and provide a dump for field-stones. *Below*, Ballyduagh, Co. Tipperary. The ruined 17th century house is on the site of a moated manor house of a deserted medieval village. Ruins of its church lie in the tree-enclosed graveyard. At top centre there are foundations of cottages. Banks and ditches surround wet, rushy fields. It is tempting to think that the area was drier in Anglo-Norman times.

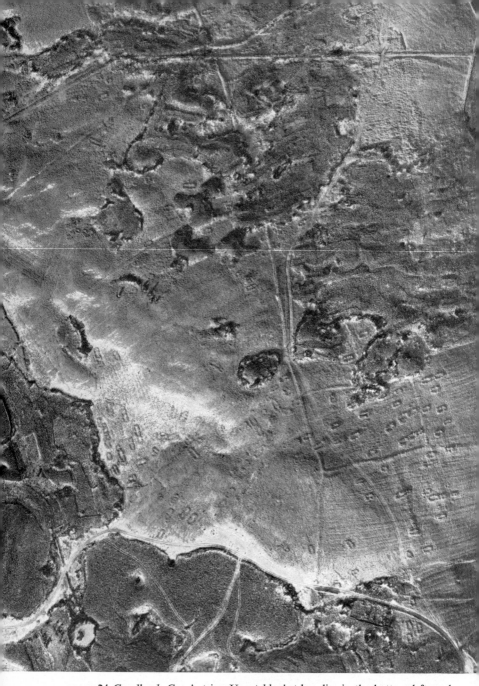

PLATE 24 Goodland, Co. Antrim. Uncut blanket-bog lies in the bottom left, and there are smaller outlying patches of bog. At the bottom the bog buries Neolithic and Beaker material. Slightly right of centre a field bank can be seen where the peat has been cut away, and it runs north, occasionally still buried by peat. At lower right, right of the bank, fields with plough furrows made after AD 600 by a mouldboard-plough can be seen. The cut-away area shows the foundations of many huts, some of which sit on abandoned field-banks; they probably belong to the 15th/16th centuries, when the area was under grass, and was used for summer-grazing in the practice of *booleying*.

common but with varying rights, not defined by area, but by the number of head of stock that different members were entitled to put on it. If the group flourished, more of the pasture would be taken into the common-field; in adverse times, the common-field would shrink. At higher levels were the hill-grazings, 'the unenclosed above all', to which the booleying herds would be driven in the summer.

Weeds have always been a problem for agriculture, and it is well known that different agricultural practices each bring their own suite of weeds in train. The inversion of the sod by the mouldboard-plough buried the weed seeds that were lying on the surface deeper in the soil, and in this position some of them found it impossible to germinate. As a result some weeds were greatly reduced by this practice; at the same time the changed practice may not have affected other weeds, and *Artemisia* or mugwort may have been enabled to become relatively more common by the introduction of the mouldboard-plough. This plant puts down a deep vertical branching root-stock, and as long as ploughing was relatively shallow, and parts of the root stock could survive, it was a very serious weed of cultivation. In Ireland pollen of *Artemisia* first becomes common in the diagrams at about AD 600, and it is tempting to see in this rise a reflection of the introduction of the mouldboard-plough. At Red Bog (see diagram on p. 137) the appearance of *Artemisia* was dated to AD 500.

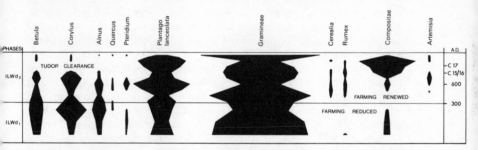

A pollen-diagram from blanket-bog at Goodland, Co. Antrim, to illustrate change in land-use on the drier soils in the immediate vicinity of the bog.

We have already referred to the site at Goodland, Co. Antrim, where blanket-bog expanded into areas that had been cultivated in Neolithic and Beaker time. Though many pollen-counts have been made in the peat here, and there has been considerable archaeological investigation, detailed radio-carbon dating is lacking, and what follows contains a considerable element of speculation. Peat growth was at first extremely slow, but in the diagram a feeble expansion in hazel, and a reduction in the amount of grass pollen, can be seen to indicate the reduction in agricultural activity that took place at the end of the Damage-phase (ILWd$_1$). The opening of the Destruction-phase of advanced agriculture (Phase ILWd$_2$) at AD 300 is then seen as the tree pollens fall away, while grasses expand, and cereals and dock make their appearance.

A little higher grasses fall back, plantain rises and bracken, *Artemisia* and other composites appear about AD 600. Though they were not seen at the point from which the pollen samples were taken, at other points at about this level in the peat stones occurred in irregular layers and heaps, and these were interpreted as stones collected from the neighbouring fields and thrown out on the bog-surface to lessen the risk of damage to the plough. Some pottery sherds and a wooden knife handle were associated with the stones, and these would have been at home in an Early Christian or Early Medieval context. The fields themselves can be seen nearby, and they still carry furrows characteristic of those produced by mouldboard-ploughs. That these fields are early is certified by the fact that in the fifteenth and sixteenth centuries huts were built in the area, and these were placed indiscriminately on the now abandoned fields, and the banks which separated them. (Pl. 24)

It seems not unreasonable to assume that about AD 600 farmers, equipped with mouldboard-ploughs, and practising a system of tillage that encouraged *Artemisia*, occupied the Goodland area. This land-use gave way to very different operations in the fifteenth and sixteenth centuries; fragments of a jug of this age were thrown out on the bog-surface, and this level is also indicated in the diagram, which is now dominated by pollen of grass and composites. Calcareous grassland infested by thistles is indicated, and the area was probably used for the summer pasturing of cattle, whose booleying attendants built and occupied the flimsy huts whose remains are dotted over the area. There is then the final clearing away of all tree growth following on the plantation of Ulster in the early seventeenth century, and perhaps a minor phase of tillage, before the uppermost sample shows the establishment of the modern grasslands.

We have seen that the earth bank of the rath might be replaced by a wall of dry stone masonry to form a cashel. Cashels of larger than average size and strength, often surrounded by concentric walls, called cahers, also occur, and one of these at Cahercommaun in Co. Clare was excavated by Hugh Hencken. The central space was about 30 m in diameter, and protected by a wall about 7 m thick and still standing to a height of 3 m, though doubtless originally considerably higher. The central space showed the remains of several small structures and several souterrains, but there was no sign of any important residence. The caher stood on the cliffed edge of a ravine, and so the surrounding walls were D-shaped; there was an inner wall 70 m in diameter, and an outer wall 100 m in diameter. Radial walls divided up the space between the walls, and there were also minor structures here, but some of these were probably not of any great antiquity. The entrance passage led through all three walls, but there were no defensive structures associated with it. Finds of weapons were few; there were some querns, and evidence of iron-working. Over 95% of the bones were of ox, with small quantities of sheep, goat, pig, horse and red deer. Though the sea is 15 km away, shells of edible molluscs were found. The charcoals in order of frequency were hazel, yew, ash, hawthorn, blackthorn, willow and elm. These obviously come from secondary woodland and scrub; the limestones of Clare today provide the refuge of the last native Irish elms, and it is of interest that even in Clare it was almost extinct one thousand years ago. The frequency of yew, and the absence of oak, on the limestone should be noted. The occupation of the site was thought to centre on AD 800; there was little evidence of domestic structures, and it may have served chiefly as a cattle compound for the stocks of a wealthy king.

Much the same type of structure appears to have been adopted by the larger monasteries, because the monastic site at Nendrum in Strangford Lough was essentially similar in layout. It may be, of course, that the monastery took over a pre-existing structure, but when the site was excavated it provided no evidence for occupation earlier than the beginning of the eighth century. At Nendrum the inner cashel had been largely destroyed by later alterations, and the space between the outer walls was occupied by the workshops and scriptorium of the monastery.

AD 800 saw the arrival of yet another series of influences in Ireland, those from the Viking world of northern Europe. For the first fifty years the Vikings contented themselves with raiding, especially monasteries that were within easy reach of the sea-coast. The larger monasteries were the nearest thing to a town that Ireland could offer, and were certainly worth plundering; a monastery that could command a work of art like the Book of Kells or the Ardagh Chalice was obviously generally wealthy in its own right, while its strongly built church provided not only a place of sanctuary, but also a safe-deposit for the store-chests of the local population. At times the Viking raiders would be in need of food supplies and also weapons and tools to replace what had been used or lost on their marauding cruises, just as much as gold and jewels, and the church with its stores of weapons, tools, clothes and food was the obvious source of supply.

After AD 850 the Vikings began to set up trading-ports in suitable harbours, and to settle into the country in the vicinity of these first towns in Ireland. The Viking nature was as turbulent and quarrelsome as that of the Irish themselves, and before long different groups were engaged in internecine struggles and in fluctuating alliances with warring Irish groups. By the tenth century Dublin city was the focal point, with an area of settlement – Fingal – to the north and west, and outlying dependencies in Carlingford and Strangford Loughs, and there were the trading-towns of Wexford, Limerick, Waterford and Cork. Coinage was introduced to facilitate the import-export trade. In addition to everyday dealings, luxury goods were also handled, as an account of the pillaging of Limerick refers to special saddles and silk cloths, as well as gold, silver and jewellery. Viking knowledge of ships and shipping spread to the Irish, and soon there were fleets, both legitimate and piratical, on the coastal and inland waters.

A thirteenth-century account speaks of wealthy Norse farmers owning large numbers of cattle in Wexford, but by and large the impact of the Vikings on the landscape was probably small, and the modest native farm-steads, protected by a bank and ditch and provided with souterrains, continued in operation. This is well exemplified at Lough Gur, where a typical cashel, with associated houses both inside and outside it, on a rocky knoll known as *Carrig Aille*, produced a hoard of Viking silver of tenth-century date. Cattle provided 90% of the bones, sheep and pig accounted for the rest, except for trifling amounts of horse and red deer; there were also bones of dogs, cats and domestic fowl. Hunting on the lake was indicated by fish-bones, and bones of ducks, geese and swans. There were numerous rotary querns, and carbonized seeds of flax and its associated weed, corn spurrey (*Spergula arvensis*) were also found. The presence of flax is perhaps a further indication of Viking contacts. There was also evidence of the working of iron and of bronze.

Similar continuity was demonstrated at Knowth, where the great prehistoric mound had been reoccupied, probably in the course of the expansion of population that set in about AD 300 (see figure on p. 129). Two large ditches were dug, one around the base of the mound, and the other around the top, and some inhumed burials date from this phase of activity. The ditches were later allowed to silt up, and houses with souterrains were built on and in the fill. The entrances to the large tombs were discovered, and the intruders entered the tombs, and scratched their Irish names on its stones. The passages were incorporated into the souterrain system, doubtless accompanied by the belief that magical giant souterrains had been provided by propitiated gods. These giant souterrains may well have served as local storehouses, just as the churches did, and as such attracted the attention of the Vikings. The Vikings certainly took their boats up the Boyne, and the Annals tell us that in AD 860 the 'cave' of Knowth was searched by the Vikings, who returned again in AD 934, when they attacked and plundered it. The general finds suggested an occupation until at least AD 1000, and this was confirmed by the discovery in one of the souterrains of two Anglo-Saxon pennies of late tenth-century date. Bones of ox, horse, pig and sheep were found, and there were several stones from rotary querns. There was also some iron slag.

By the year AD 1000 the feudal system was well established in western Europe, and the Norman victory at Hastings in AD 1066 established it in England. By AD 1100 an embryonic feudal system was beginning to develop in Ireland also. Chieftains were becoming more powerful, and the kingship of all-Ireland was beginning to be established, although the complicated system of succession in severalty resulted in constant instability. European ideas of strategy began to be appreciated, and strong-points or castles, inter-communicating by roads and bridges on land, and by fleets of boats on the water, began to develop. Although all owed allegiance to a chieftain or king, some farmers were independent and self-sufficient, while others though independent borrowed stock, seeds and implements from their overlord. Below this level were the landless tenants, who though they had some stock and equipment, had to rent their land for goods or services rendered to their lord. There was also a large understratum (still with slaves among them) without either land or property, without any security and subject to constant exploitation.

A LITERARY REFLECTION OF THE EIGHTH-CENTURY LANDSCAPE

Some years ago Kenneth Jackson published a short book entitled *The oldest Irish tradition; a window on the Iron Age*, in which he tried to glimpse the

PLATE 25 *Above*, Connemara, Co. Galway. An isolated farm, established in rocky terrain by clearing stones into field-walls, and bringing in sand and seaweed. The round fields were worked with spades; we see potatoes in cultivation-ridges, and a patch of oats. *Below*, Kilshannig, Co. Kerry. Old glacial deposits, smoothed out by more recent frost-action, lie on solid rock (compare with Pl. 6). Man has spread sea-sand over the area to replace a poor soil with a fertile one. On the right we see cultivation in unfenced strips.

PLATE 26 *Above*, Cahir, Co. Tipperary. This early 17th century engraving shows a landscape free of trees, except on the lower slopes of the Galty Mountains. The fields are enclosed by banks, walls and wattle fences; within some fields parallel lines suggest cultivation-ridges. The walls of the castle, like those of a tower-house, are pierced only by very small windows. *Below*, nr. Castlepollard, Co. Westmeath. By the mid-18th century the large-windowed mansion, with its planted trees and its formal gardens, has replaced the fortified castle and the tower-house. The adjoining land has been surveyed, and laid out in regular fields; further away there is uncleared scrub. Cultivation-ridges are prominent everywhere.

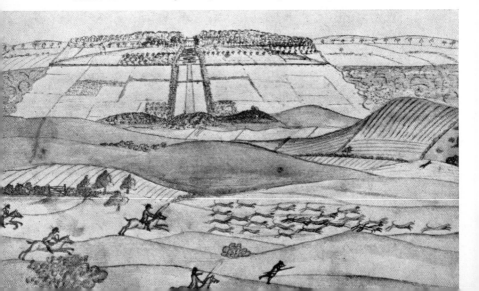

heroic society of the Pagan Iron Age through the sagas which were perhaps first committed to writing in the eighth century AD. The same material and the early Irish laws also contain a wealth of information about the countryside and the farmers of the time. Unfortunately the early law-makers had a taste for detail and for symmetry, and very often the picture is what we would get from a distorting-mirror, rather than from a window. Nevertheless an attempt to peer back into the past is well worth making.

i Trees, bushes and other plants

One legal tract codifies all the penalties for unlawfully interfering with trees and bushes, and the fines range from the forfeit of two milch-cows for cutting down a valuable tree to the loss of a sheep for destroying a bush. The severity of the fines indicates the value that timber had reached through scarcity. There are four categories of importance:

Noble trees	Commoner trees	Lower ranks	Bushes
Oak	Alder	Blackthorn	Bracken
Hazel	Willow	Elder	Bog-myrtle
Holly	Hawthorn	Spindle	Gorse
Yew	Rowan	Whitebeam	Blackberry
Ash	Birch	Arbutus	Heather
Pine	Elm	Poplar	Broom
Apple	Cherry (?)	Juniper (?)	Rose (?)

Some of the rankings seem odd to our modern eyes, and Fergus Kelly, who has been working on the lists, thinks that the compiler took into account (a) size of tree, (b) quality of its timber, and (c) other uses, particularly of the fruit. If we look at the lists, it is curious to see pine in the first rank, while elm and alder are relegated to the second. The disappearance of pine – for today it is thought that all the pines we have in Ireland have been reintroduced from Scotland, after the native stock had become extinct – seems to have been a gradual one. It had disappeared from north-east Ireland by 2000 BC, but seems to have survived in the south-west till about AD 200. Whenever bog-surfaces became relatively dry, pine could invade them, and some stunted trees were still growing on midland raised-bogs at AD 300. But it is not easy to see that well-grown pine trees could have been common enough at the time the law was codified for them to merit such a high place on the list. Fossil pine-wood, or *bog-deal*, was available in large quantities in many bogs, and was used as timber in later times, but the fines clearly envisage living trees. (Pl. 31)

Elm can only be put down to the second rank because of the extent to which it had been cleared away. As we have seen it made a considerable recovery in the centuries preceding AD 300, but with the vigorous renewal of agriculture at that time it was largely swept away. Elm leaves, bark and wood were all valued by early peoples, and if it had been still common in the countryside, it would have had a higher place in the list. Alder on the other hand was probably still fairly common, but its wood was not used in timber structures; it was used for small objects, shields, containers and dishes. Yew wood, though difficult to work, was prized for high-grade carpentry, and masters in yew-carving had a special social rank.

Oak and hazel head the list, and we have seen how wood and charcoal of these trees occur over and over again on archaeological sites. Oak wins out on all three of Kelly's criteria. It could be a very large tree, its wood was used in carpentry and its bark in tanning, and its acorns were a valuable food for pigs. Hazel, though smaller in size, and in one sense a pest because of the ease with which it invaded abandoned fields, was valued for its coppiced stems for wattle-work and for its nuts.

We can perhaps form some impression of a countryside in which woods of alder and willow were still common on wetter ground. There were some oak-woods, but large and well-grown trees were beginning to command a premium; well-grown hollies (especially valuable for cart-shafts) and yews were also becoming rare. Ash, though probably well-distributed in hedgerows and secondary woodland, was in demand for general carpentry and for handles. Secondary hazel scrub would have been widespread. Pine was rare but much sought for, while elm had become so uncommon that it had rather dropped out of sight.

Elder would have been growing round houses and on ruined sites, and any neglected fences would have had hawthorn and blackthorn, and probably many of the other bushes as well. Just as today, the birch and the rowan, the heather, the gorse and the broom would have been growing on rocky hillsides.

ii Classification of land

There were three grades of land, and if land was to rate as first class, it had to be level, capable of growing a wide range of crops, and free from weeds. Madder (*Rubia tinctorum*) is among the crops listed, but there may be some error in translation here, because madder, an important plant in dyeing, is not known in Ireland today, and only survives in Britain as a casual. In Ireland this plant would have been on the limit of its range, and is not likely to have produced much dye. Weediness was measured by turning a horse on to the land, and if it collected briars, thorns, burdocks or thistles on its legs the land was lowered in value. Land that was potentially first class might be partly or wholly encumbered with trees.

Uncultivable land also had three grades – which probably indicates a love for tripartite divisions, as much as an eye for soil quality. Rough land is 'land of ferny plains and untouched land', and this may well be badly drained land in valley bottoms, land that is still largely uncultivated today. Very rough land is the upland, 'heathery mountain with furze on it'. This type of land is still abundant today, but nowadays in the absence of the wolf it carries flocks of unattended hill sheep: in Iron Age Ireland a shepherd would have had to stay with the sheep at all times to protect them, and this was work for slaves, as we know from St Patrick's account of his life. (Pl. 20, below)

'Black land' is probably the modern peaty gley or peaty podzol, with a thin layer of decomposing humus, not deep enough to be described as bog, resting on waterlogged mineral soil.

If the land had development value, its worth – just as today – was raised accordingly. The bonus points might be accessibility by road or track, access to mountain-grazing, the sea-shore or water, a site for a water-mill, mining-rights, or woodland.

iii Fields and fences

Where wood was scarce and the soil was clayey, banks and ditches surrounded the fields, just as they surrounded the raths themselves. In stony areas walls of at least three courses of stone were substituted; the stones were often quarried with the aid of a crowbar. Where coppiced oak and hazel stems were available, fences of closely placed stakes interwoven with at least three bands of lighter stems were used. The erection of such fences was regarded as heavy and menial work, and it was below the dignity of a nobleman to use a hammer, bill-hook or maul, all of which were necessary in such fencing. The top of the fence received a band of blackthorn twigs, which served the purpose of modern barbed wire, or 'thorny wire' as it is still known in the Irish country-side. After the corn had been harvested temporary fences were put up around the plots, and the stock of several farmers might be turned into the plots; this practice was probably primarily intended to manure the land for the next year's crop, rather than to provide grazing on the stubble. There were elaborate rules for the maintenance of common fences, and if stock trespassed, appropriate damages had to be paid.

iv Farming practices

Some farmers had to render food to their chieftains, and the food-lists give some indication of the farm produce of the day; but the lists only show the aristocratic foods that had to be offered to the chieftain and his retinue, and give no indication of what common folk ate; they name calves, sheep, pigs, pork, milk, cream, butter, other dairy products, kiln-dried wheat, loaves, malt and herbs.

It is very difficult to attempt to assess the size of the farms. This is due to the fact that the basic standard of the measurement of wealth was a female slave – a *cumal* – and this measure, like many modern currencies, apparently 'floated', so that it is hard to define its value at any time. It was perhaps about 35 acres of land. We are given lists of the stock possessed by farmers of different grades, but the law-makers were so anxious to get everything neat and tidy that each farmer is credited with equal numbers of cattle, sheep and pigs, and there never has been a system of husbandry that carried stock in such proportions.

	EIGHTH CENTURY		TODAY
	Laws	*Excavation Finds*	*Modern Stocks*
Cattle	33%	80%	50%
Sheep	33%	10%	35%
Pigs	33%	10%	15%

The table makes a comparison between the figure of the Laws, excavation results, and the modern population.

If we put various hints together, it would seem reasonable to say that a *cumal* was about 35 statute acres, and two such units or about 70 acres were the minimum required if one was to establish a position as an independent farmer. According to the figures in the Laws, a 'strong' farmer would have ten times as much, say 700 acres, and these figures are not impossible if we remember that both stock and yields would be less than today's equivalents. In the first English 'Plantation', farm sizes (in acres larger than statute acres) ranged from 25 to 500 acres.

The 'strong' farmer was fully equipped. His house was 30 feet long, with an annexe 20 feet long, and he had a sheep-fold, a calf-pen, and a pig-sty. For tillage he had a complete ploughing outfit with all its accessories, a barn, a drying-kiln and a share in a mill. He sowed sixteen sacks of grain each year, and if we say that this was at the rate of two sacks per acre, he would only have eight acres under grain each year, which seems a very small proportion of 700 acres. On the other hand excavation results, with their overwhelming quantities of animal bones, and only a very occasional plough-share or quern, do suggest that stock-raising rather than tillage was the main occupation.

Cereal grains were used as units of measurement, and in particular for measuring the size of wounds. Binchy and O'Loan have endeavoured to identify the various grains referred to in medical tracts, and suggest that two varieties of wheat, barley, rye, oats, peas and beans are all referred to. For the word *ruadan* which Kuno Meyer translated as 'buckwheat' – still eaten in central Europe today – Binchy and O'Loan prefer 'red wheat'. Buckwheat (*Fagopyrum esculentum*) is a member of the Polygonaceae, which also includes the knotgrasses (various species of *Polygonum*); knotgrass seeds are brown in colour. As knotgrass (or meld) formed part of the diet of the famous Danish Iron Age Tollund Man, whose remarkably well preserved body was found in a bog, and was also much eaten in medieval Dublin, I think it very likely that *ruadan* refers to Polygonaceae in general, and that these were grown as a deliberate crop, and not just gleaned off the fallows. Flax was grown for its oil and its fibres, and woad (*Isatis tinctorum*) was a source of blue dye.

Where the land was level, it would be tilled with a plough drawn by four oxen, but we do not know at what rate the plough would work, nor how many times the land was tilled in the course of a season. Grasses were allowed to flower and wither in the meadows, which were subsequently grazed by stock, as the scythe and the practice of hay-making were unknown. Some land will have been lying fallow. There will also have been fenced pasture, and on the 'strong farmer's' land this was big enough to maintain his flock of sheep, without the necessity of moving them on elsewhere. He would also have had grazing-rights on the uncultivable land, which was held in common by the clan to which he was affiliated. He brewed his own beer from his own barley, and the making of malt was a very important task. If there was a bog in the vicinity, he would have a peat-bank, from which to draw fuel.

The small farmer on 70 acres was not so fully equipped. He only expected to plough three acres, and for this it would have been extravagant to maintain full ploughing equipment; he presumably combined with three neighbours, as he was required to provide a quarter part, namely an ox, a plough-share, a goad and a halter. This rule, combined with other references, shows that the plough-team was made up of four oxen.

By modern standards the cattle were small in size. Their chief importance was as a source of dairy products, and the meat and the hides were a by-line. The young stock was slaughtered in the autumn, and only the bulls and the milch-cows were retained. Young male stock were castrated, and carcass quality, based on the proportion of fat to lean meat, was taken into account. Calving took place in the spring, and when the early summer flush of milk was on, the cows were driven up to mountain pastures, accompanied by herdsmen and women who lived in temporary huts, in the practice known as *booleying*. What to do with the annual flood of milk must always have been a problem. Milk itself was drunk in various forms, was solidified into curds, and was churned into butter. The technique of fermenting milk to make cheese – in the strict sense of the word – does not seem to have been known, and to this day Irish people are not great cheese eaters. Some of the surplus butter was buried in bogs, where cool, anaerobic and relatively sterile conditions slowed up the developments by which it became rancid.

The sheep were also small, and were valued chiefly for their wool. The pigs were much leaner and more rangy than the modern pig, in keeping with their more active lives in which ranging for acorns (mast) was important (p. 190). There are many references in the Annals to years in which mast was plentiful, and to years in which mast was lacking. Bacon was graded as to fat and lean, and a sow was expected to rear a litter of nine, a standard with which the modern farmer would be well satisfied.

v Gardening

Many monastic rules laid emphasis on vegetables rather than meat in the communal diet, and gardens were a feature of the monasteries rather than the lay farms. Cabbages, onions, leeks and celery were principally grown, and there were orchards with apples and damsons.

As I have said our mirror is sometimes clearly distorting, but from it we can form an impression of a countryside in which all the good land is parcelled out in an orderly fashion, and is being worked to a standard of which no modern farmer would need to feel ashamed. There may be battles and raidings, but the basic pattern of life will be resumed when these die away. Beyond the good land there is poorer land, and there the members of the clan will have commonage rights. Expansion can only come either from extension of the good land by the further clearance of trees and bushes, which once gone will have little opportunity to return, or by improved tillage practices which will increase the yield of the land.

FURTHER CHANGES IN SEA-LEVEL

We have seen that about 5000 years ago sea-level stood about 4 m above its present level. The sea then fell back from that level, and as it did so both natural vegetation and human activities followed its retreating shores to levels apparently below those of today (see map on p. 64). Sea-level subsequently recovered to its present height, but when we try to date these movements, we immediately run into difficulties. Most of our field evidence lies between tide-marks in bays and estuaries, and there are sceptics who say that the accumulation or removal of sand-dunes or beach-bars could explain the drowning or revealing of 'submerged forests' and archaeological sites, without any change in sea-level one way or the other. But the evidence is widespread, and local factors cannot be responsible in every case.

'Young', i.e. post-5000 BP, 'submerged forests' are common round the Irish coasts, and for some of these, ranging from Galway to Wexford, we now have radiocarbon dates lying between 4775 and 3730 years BP. At many places along the west coast of Ireland blanket-bog, which formerly extended down below modern sea-level, now lies exposed to modern waves, which are cutting cliffs in its seaward margin. So far we have not been able to fix the point in time at which they were invaded by the sea, but the sea must have been at a lower level when the blanket-bogs were growing.

We have five 'drowned' archaeological sites, but so far it has not been possible to date their submergence – if such has occurred – with any precision; the submergence ought obviously to be younger than the youngest site. At Rostellan in Cork Harbour a simple megalithic tomb stands on the foreshore in such a position that it is almost covered by the sea at high tide; such a tomb, if genuine, might have been built about 4000 years ago; in Brittany some megalithic tombs of the same order of age are similarly partially sub-merged at high tide. On the south shore of Clew Bay near Killadangan several stone monuments – standing-stones, a stone circle, and a small cairn contain-ing a tomb – are now surrounded by salt-marsh, which is submerged at high spring tides; the relation of the site to sea-level must have been different when the monuments were being erected. The site recalls that at Beaghmore, Co. Tyrone, where rather similar monuments are now buried by blanket-bog; these monuments were perhaps erected about 4000 or 3500 years ago. At Darrynane Bay, Co. Kerry, an Ogham stone stands on the foreshore, sur-rounded at high tide. At Ardmore in Co. Waterford marine erosion exposed for a short time what appeared to be the remains of a crannog; there was a double ring of large oak piles, wattle-work of hazel, charcoal, wooden vessels and animal bones; the structure rested on peat, and was submerged at high tide; such crannogs perhaps fall between the seventh and the ninth centuries AD. At the inner end of Crookhaven Bay in Co. Cork a line of high slab-like stones, probably part of a field boundary, is almost completely submerged at high tide; drowned walls are also described in the Isles of Scilly. (Pl. 18)

If we dare to venture on the most tentative of conclusions, we can say that the sea may have been below its present level 4000 years ago, and did not regain that level before 1000 years ago.

ANGLO-NORMAN FARMING AND ITS DECAY, AD 1150–1550

The feudal world wanted wealth and military power, and the land had to be the main source of wealth. Subsistence farming on indifferent land was no longer good enough, intensive farming of high quality land had to produce a handsome cash surplus. The great monastic orders were the first to bring this world to Ireland, and of these the Cistercians, with their emphasis on agriculture, had the greatest impact on the Irish countryside. The Cistercians depended wholly on the land for their income, and developed a system for selling their farm produce – cattle, horses and wool – which did much to promote commerce in western Europe. Mellifont was consecrated in 1157, and within a few years daughter houses had sprung up in many parts of Ireland.

The second impact, the military one, began in 1169, and soon great areas of the best agricultural land had been won, a task that was made the easier by the internecine strife that had been raging on a scale that was high, even by Irish standards. 'There has been fighting in all provinces, endless campaigns, cattle-raids, burnings, atrocities – Ireland lies like a trembling sod.'

What did Ireland look like to the invaders? We are fortunate that a Welsh travel correspondent, Giraldus Cambrensis, came to Ireland about 1185, and if we try to see Ireland through his twelfth-century eyes, and not through our twentieth-century ones, we can get some vivid impressions. To adjust our vision we must remember first that he was a cleric, accustomed to the sermonizing of his day, and apt to burst into theological excursions at any time; second, that with his contemporaries he believed all too literally in hell and its torments, and saw the world as populated with monstrous beasts, lying in wait both for the just and the unjust; and third that he was a propagandist, always ready to flatter his betters, and to exalt the Welsh and denigrate the Irish.

Giraldus certainly was an acute observer; he gives a word-picture of an illuminated manuscript that has never been bettered; in natural history he gives a clear description of a dipper, which he thought to be a variety of kingfisher. He refers to raths and cahers, and reports that the Irish 'have no use for castles. Woods are their forts and swamps their ditches' – a comment that was to reappear in many subsequent dispatches from Ireland.

His report tells us that 'Ireland is the most temperate of all countries. Snow is seldom, and lasts only for a short time. There is such a plentiful supply of rain, such an ever-present overhanging of clouds and fog, that summer scarcely gives three consecutive days of really fine weather. Winds are moderate and not too strong. The winds from the west-north-west, north and east bring cold. The north-west and west winds are prevalent, and are more frequent and stronger than other winds. They bend (in the opposite direction) almost all the trees in the west that are placed in an elevated position, or uproot them.

Ireland is a country of uneven surface and rather mountainous. The soil is soft and watery, and even at the tops of high and steep mountains there are pools and swamps. The land is sandy rather than rocky. There are many

woods and marshes; here and there there are some fine plains but in comparison with the woods they are indeed small. The country enjoys the fresh-
ness and mildness of spring almost all the year round. The grass is green in the
fields in winter just the same as in summer. Consequently, the meadows are
not cut for fodder, and stalls are never built for the beasts.

The land is fruitful and rich in its fertile soil and plentiful harvests. Crops
abound in the fields, flocks on the mountains, wild animals in the woods, it is
rich in honey and milk. Ireland exports cow-hides, sheep-skins and furs.
Much wine is imported. But the island is richer in pastures than in crops, and
in grass rather than grain. The plains are well clothed with grass, and the
haggards [farmyards] are bursting with straw. Only the granaries are without
their wealth. The crops give great promise in the blade, even more in the
straw, but less in the ear. For here the grains of wheat are shrivelled and small,
and can scarcely be separated from the chaff by any winnowing fan. What is
born and comes forth in the spring and is nourished in the summer and
advanced, can scarcely be reaped in the harvest because of the unceasing
rain. For this country more than any other suffers from storms of wind and
rain.'

Giraldus also offers detailed information on fish, amphibians, reptiles,
birds and mammals, but this is so threaded through with medieval folk-lore
that it is difficult to pick out fact from fable. He reports that salmon, trout,
eels and lampreys are common in Irish rivers, but that many others, pike,
perch, roach, chub, dudgeon, minnow, loach and bullheads are absent. Most
of these do occur in Ireland today, but they may well have been introduced
since Giraldus wrote. The Anglo-Normans did introduce the rabbit.

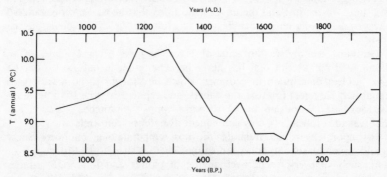

A graph to illustrate fluctuation of mean annual temperature in England, by 50-year
averages, for the past 1000 years (After H. H. Lamb).

What Giraldus has to say about wheat failing to ripen is of particular
interest, because a temperature curve shows he was writing at a time when
mean annual temperature in England – and presumably in Ireland also – was
rising to its thirteenth-century peak. During that peak the Anglo-Normans
certainly grew good wheat crops on the manorial estates they established in

south-east Ireland, but conditions for cereal crops became difficult again when temperature fell again in the late fourteenth century. It is not easy to pinpoint this effect, first because of the consequences of the Bruce invasion early in the century, when the warring armies 'between them left neither wood nor lea nor corn nor crop nor stead nor barn nor church, but fired and burned them all', and second because of the Black Death in the second part of the century, which reduced the population drastically – halving it according to some estimates.

It was thus between AD 1170 and 1350 that Anglo-Norman influence was most clearly stamped on the Irish landscape. At first the lightly-equipped Irish soldiers could offer no resistance to the heavily-armed and well-drilled invaders, who cut through the country smelling out the better lands like well-trained truffle-hounds. The Anglo-Normans were prepared to expend capital on the organization of their manorial farms, and were only interested in land from which they could hope to draw a dividend on their investment. Fertile and well-drained soils were what attracted them.

This was the first occasion on which financial considerations directly impinged on land use in Ireland. In the later periods of the Bronze Age there was a fairly regular scatter of sites throughout the country. It is the same with place-names containing such elements as 'rath' and 'lis', most of which will stem from the early centuries of the Christian Era; these are scattered throughout the country, avoiding only higher ground, especially in western areas. In Ireland for farming at subsistence level there has always been land enough for all, and the Irish in the twelfth century, as at all times, reckoned their wealth in stock, principally in cattle. On the other hand the Anglo-Normans were hungry for commercial land, especially ploughland, and they reckoned their wealth in acres.

The distribution of Anglo-Norman sites is very different, and the pattern of the sites is so closely related to the occurrence of good soils in Ireland today, that it seems reasonable to assume that the soils we know today had developed by the time the Anglo-Normans reached the country. In the map of modern Irish soils (overleaf), we see the immediate contrast between the poorly-drained soils of the north and west (the gleys, peaty gleys and peats – including peaty podzols – shown in dark hues on the map), and the more freely-drained soils of the south and east (brown earths, acid brown earths, brown podzolics, grey-brown podzolics, shown in lighter hues on the map). A continuous line on the map separates the two soil regions.

If we look at a meteorological map (see map **a** on p. 87) that shows numbers of rain-days, a very similar line will divide a region with more than 175 rain-days to the north and west from a region with less than that number to the south and east. In other words in Ireland today the soil will be waterlogged if rain falls on at least half the days in the year.

We can picture this line as the edge of a cloud. If climate deteriorates (and the number of rain-days increases), the cloud-edge will advance to the east and south; if climate improves (and gets drier), the cloud-edge will withdraw north-westwards. Meteorologists tell us that the Anglo-Normans arrived in Ireland during a phase of very favourable climate, but there is nothing about

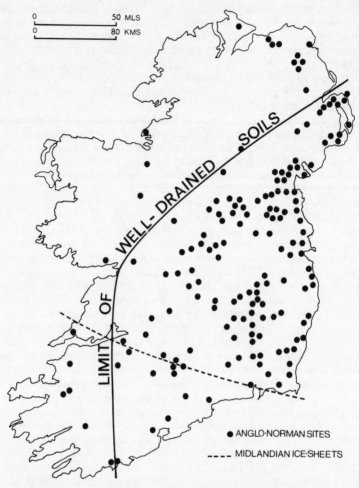

0   50 MLS
0   80 KMS

LIMIT OF WELL-DRAINED SOILS

● ANGLO-NORMAN SITES

---- MIDLANDIAN ICE-SHEETS

The distribution of Anglo-Norman sites in Ireland, and their relationship to areas of well-drained, fertile soils.

the distribution of their sites to suggest to us that better-drained soils then stretched farther to the north-west than they do today.

The parent material of a modern grey-brown podzolic soil has a higher content of calcium carbonate than a brown podzolic, and if we look at the soil map we see that the former are common on the glacial deposits of the last cold stage (the Midlandian), while the brown podzolics are almost entirely confined to the older glacial deposits of Munsterian age in the south of the country. The glacial deposits of Munster have been exposed to atmospheric

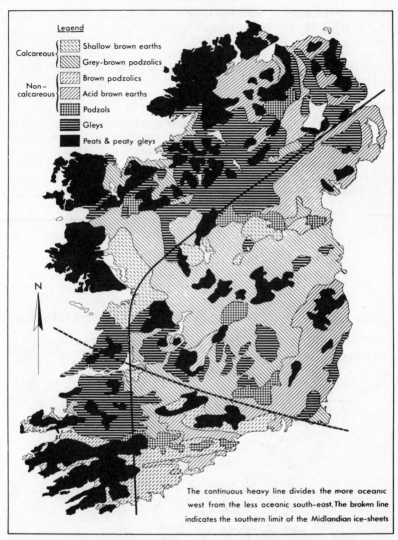

An outline-map to show the distribution of the leading soil-types in Ireland to-day. Poorly-drained soils predominate in the north and west. The more fertile soils, brown earths, acid brown earths and grey-brown podzolics chiefly occur on the glacial deposits of the last cold stage (Midlandian). (an Foras Talúntais).

attack for much longer than those of the Midlands, and we have to ask ourselves if they have passed through a phase when they had a higher content of calcium carbonate, and perhaps had soils related to the grey-brown podzolic, while today through loss of calcium carbonate coupled with loss of clay from the B-horizon the soils have changed from grey-brown podzolics to brown podzolics, losing some of their inherent fertility in the process. At any rate the map of Anglo-Norman sites makes it clear that the settlers found the brown podzolic soils of the south less attractive than the grey-brown podzolics of the midlands, despite the fact that the south had warmer temperatures and a longer growing season. Today the south is regarded as the best farming region in the whole of Ireland.

Wherever they found soils to their taste, or a strategic point worth defending, the Anglo-Normans erected an earthen mote, later replaced by a stone castle in places of especial importance, and proceeded to settle themselves into the surrounding countryside. On the whole, as we have seen, they did not advance beyond a line running from Skibbereen through Galway to Coleraine, and settled most densely in Leinster and east Munster, an area of good land interrupted by only one large island of bad land, the uplands of the Wicklow Mountains, which were to prove a centre from which Irish forces would frequently emerge to harass the farms and towns of the surrounding lowlands.

The probable lay-out of an Anglo-Norman 14th century moated manor at Cloncurry, Co. Kildare. (A. R. Orme, after J. O'Loan and P. J. Tuite).

The basic Anglo-Norman unit was the manor, extending perhaps to 3000 acres, and here the lord would have his home-farm or stead, often protected by a moat, containing his house and his farm-buildings, with its surrounding fields. Radiocarbon has dated a moated house at Kilmagoura, Co. Cork, to

AD 1225. Other large farm units would be given to supporters, linked to the lord by allegiance as well as rent, to rent-paying individual farmers, and to borough communities of burgesses, with land in common, and their own court and other privileges. The holders of these larger units came from outside Ireland. The favourable climate had brought about a population explosion in most of western Europe, and in England, Wales and Flanders there were men anxious to get tenancies of good arable land in return for payments in money, in services and in kind. But the supply of such men was not inexhaustible, and the lord would endeavour to retain the Irish work-force which had originally occupied the lands. Where possible he would reduce their status to that of villeins, who would be his property both in their persons and in their goods. Some got small parcels of land, paying rent but with no security of tenure, others held cottages but no land, and a third group, certainly Irish, the *betaghs*, had land without tenure held mainly by service. As their service-labour was largely communal, they tended to form a compact group, probably living in close association in houses clustered together in a 'clachan'. Even today we can find *Ballybetagh* as a place-name, and it is tempting to think that here we may have a link with the Anglo-Norman betagh villages or hamlets.

In the list of the Bruce devastations we can identify the units of the Norman farm – stead, barn, corn, crop, and lea – and other documents spell out the round of duties of those who owed service. The corn was usually wheat or oats, and the service-tenants had to plough, harrow, sow, weed, scare birds, reap, tie, stook, cart, stack and thrash in the course of their duties. On the lord's land the crops were probably peas, beans and flax, but the poorer folk will also have had meld and goosefoot in their rotation, which will have included periods when the land lay fallow.

It would be nice to think that on the manor in Ireland the normal practice of crop sequence – winter corn, spring crop, fallow – was carried out in neat enclosed fields, but it is more probable that the smaller tenants at least held separated strips scattered through large open common-fields, which cannot have made for efficient working. Such strips have a long history in Ireland and up till 150 years ago farms made up of such scattered strips could still be found; very often the plough furrow took on an arcuate form, and this shape also survives in some modern Irish field-boundaries (see figure **d** on p. 201).

On the leas, if they had been shut up as meadows, the hay had to be made. The tenants had to scythe the grass, spread it, turn it and put it up in cocks, and then carry it to the haggard. It is probable that the scythe made its first appearance in Ireland in Norman times. As well as the meadows, there was 'pasture' and 'herbage', though what the exact difference was is unknown, and here the length of the grazing-period was carefully controlled. In the woods rights to hunting, cutting timber, grazing and the eating of acorns by swine were spelt out in detail; swine had to be ringed to stop them grubbing up the trees. There was usually a rabbit-warren and a dovecote. The lord had a water-mill, and if the tenants wished to grind their corn at home on a hand-mill, a fine had to be paid.

Swine eating acorns. (After Röslin, 1562).

The colonists prospered for a time. Throughout Leinster and east Munster they took the flatlands, the rivers, the coasts and the Norse trading-towns, leaving the hill-country, the woods and the bogs to the Irish. A network of walled towns, castles and roads made the settlers secure and wealthy. Wool and hides were sent in large quantities to France, Flanders and Italy. Woollen cloth, linen and furs were exported, and luxury goods – in food, wine, figs, raisins, walnuts, and in fabrics, satins, silks and cloth of gold – were imported. But the Bruce invasion, the Black Death and the deterioration in climate all combined in the fourteenth century to give the Anglo-Normans blows from which they never really recovered.

Irish resurgence then made life impossible for the open manor and the open village. The lord had to retire into the uncomfortable protection of the tower-house, while the ordinary folk either fled back to Britain, leaving their 'deserted village' behind them, or sought security in the walled towns, which continued to operate – like mini Hong-Kongs – in a countryside that was basically hostile, yet tolerated their existence for the trading-contacts that they brought. To give more shelter to crops, and to make it more difficult to drive cattle off the lands, efforts were made to surround the fields with stone-faced banks and ditches; to encourage timber the banks were to be planted with ash trees. (Pls. 26, 23)

By 1515 the remaining territory under English control, apart from the walled towns, was now sadly shrunken to a coastal strip, which itself had to be protected on its inland side by a bank and ditch – the Pale – which ran from Dundalk through Kells to Kildare, and from there back east across the northern foothills of the Wicklow Mountains to reach the coast south of Dublin at Dalkey. Outside the Pale the remaining landlords of English origin no longer set their lands for money rents, but through share-cropping agreements advanced working-capital to their tenants, demonstrating in this – as in many other ways – their gradual adoption of Irish ways.

THE MARKETS OF MEDIEVAL DUBLIN

In the same way as we formed some impression of eighth-century farming from the law texts relating to agriculture, we may get some sidelight on medieval farming from the refuse that accumulated in and around Dublin city, and has been brought to light by recent excavations. The refuse, dung and other litter, was largely derived from the agricultural produce that reached the city markets. A narrow ridge of higher ground lies parallel with the River Liffey on its south side, and the city was first founded on the eastern tip of the ridge. To the west a route led away along the crest of the ridge, and a market sprang up outside the west gate; the site is still known as the Cornmarket.

As the name implies corn was certainly sold there. There would have been winter wheat for the production of fine white flour; there was also spring wheat, but this was probably heavily contaminated with the black seeds of the corn cockle (*Agrostemma githago*), which are much the same size as the cereal grains. The corn cockle seed was also farinaceous, and for a long time it was quite happily accepted as part of the crop, was ground up along with the wheat, and speckled the flour with fragments of its dark seed coat. But the seed has a high content of saponin, and can be injurious to health; modern seed-cleaning methods separate the grain and the weed, with the result that the corn cockle, formerly very common in Irish fields, has now almost totally disappeared. Barley was sold for baking and for brewing, and oats and rye would probably have been on offer also.

In the city refuse there are large quantities of crushed seeds of *Chenopodium album* (goosefoot), and of various species of *Polygonum* (knotgrass or meld). Though these seeds are not eaten as human food in western Europe today, in prehistoric and in medieval times they formed a large part of the diet of the poorer classes either as bread or gruel, and were almost certainly grown as crops in their own right, and not just gleaned as weeds from the fallow. Buckwheat (*Fagopyrum esculentum*), sometimes known as sarrasin because of its eastern origin, is closely allied to *Polygonum*, and is still widely eaten in eastern Europe. A German traveller in Ireland in 1828 records that buckwheat, potatoes and oats were the crops he saw most frequently, and it is possible that it was still grown in the nineteenth century. Peas and beans would also have been for sale, as well as cabbages and onions.

As in later times dung-carts would have carried their loads out to the surroundings of the city, where they would have been utilized in vegetable-gardens and in orchards. At the right season of the year there would have been stalls offering pears and apples, plums, damsons and sloes, cherries, raspberries and strawberries. Some fruits came from farther afield – black-berries from fieldbanks, and bilberries or fraughans (*Vaccinium myrtillus*) from the slopes of the Dublin hills. Imported luxuries, figs, raisins and walnuts, would also have been on sale.

There were large numbers of dairies and piggeries in the city, and these were a constant source of nuisance. But they were tolerated, and hay and straw, together with bracken for bedding, would also have been on sale. Other stalls would offer rushes and sedges to strew on house floors. Moss served as toilet-paper for the fastidious, and bundles of moss collected on trees around the city were on sale. Butchers' stalls were probably confined to a special area, the Shambles, while the fishmongers would have been found, as the name makes clear, in Fish(sh)amble Street, which still runs down to the river.

THE PLANTATIONS, AD 1550–1700

Before the Tudors came to the throne, the kings of England had been kings of western France as well, and could afford to look on Ireland as a pleasant western annexe. The Tudors faced a potentially malevolent Europe, and malevolence grew as religious differences deepened. To the Tudors Ireland was the 'soft underbelly' of England, and appropriate steps had to be taken to secure the western flank.

What did Ireland look like to the Tudors? In Leinster they could see the well-kept Pale, and beyond the Pale the lands formerly loyal to the Crown but now in the hands of 'English rebels', lords of Anglo-Norman stock who had abandoned their allegiance, and adopted many of the ways of Irish life. In the foreground were the well-wooded Wicklow Mountains, still a stronghold of the 'Irish enemies'. In east Munster there were the fortified towns of Water-ford, Youghal, Cork, Kinsale and a few others, and again the lands of the 'English rebels'. The great valleys of the Blackwater and the Lee were still filled with dense oakwoods. But this view stopped in west Munster, where the soil got poorer and the hills crowded more closely together. It was cut off again at the Shannon basin, where woods and bogs lay on both sides of the ill-defined river channel. If they looked north, Ulster was hidden by the tremendous belt of drumlins that stretched south-west from Strangford Lough to the headwaters of the Erne, and then followed the valley of that river north-west to the sea in Donegal Bay (for location of drumlin belt, see map on p. 60). Dense woods on the drumlin slopes and tops, and lakes, bogs and sluggish streams between them, made this very difficult country for the military man.

What impression of Irish farming and food can we form from the reports of Tudor observers, steeped in prejudice as most of them were? Cattle made the most impact. Milch-cows were prized; 'they will not kill a cow, except it be old and yield no milk'. Milk-products of all kinds continued to be eaten. Booleying was in full force; the people in summer lived 'in booleys, pasturing upon the mountain and waste wild places and removing still to fresh land . . . driving their cattle continually with them and feeding only on their milk and white meats [milk products]'; it was a good thing that 'in this country of

PLATE 27 *Above*, Aran Islands, Co. Galway. The soil for these cultivation-ridges has been made by bringing in sand and seaweed, and spreading them on bare limestone rock. *Below*, Carrownaglogh, Co. Mayo. Cultivation-ridges going back at least to the earlier Bronze Age, are revealed when blanket-bog is cut away.

PLATE 28 *Above*, Lenankeel, Co. Donegal. This small clachan is still viable. Strips of unenclosed common-field are in the background. Note the lack of trees and bushes. *Below*, nr. Manor Kilbride, Co. Wicklow. An abandoned clachan lies beside its cultivation-ridges; the varying shapes and proportions of the ridges show that different crops were being grown in them.

Ireland, where there are great mountains and waste deserts full of grass, that the same should be eaten down and nourish many thousand of cattle'.

The other cattle were readily killed and eaten, and the large quantities of meat eaten without any accompanying bread was a constant source of surprise. Meat was eaten raw, boiled, roast, and used as an ingredient in soup. Blood was drawn, and consumed after mixing with milk, butter, or grains. Mutton, pork, hens and rabbits were also eaten. Venison appeared in pasties.

Wheat and rye were only on the better lands; barley was essentially for brewing and distilling; on poorer land and in the west oats were dominant. The heads of grain were singed, not thrashed; such a practice looked primitive, but considerable judgement was needed to hit on the exact second at which to jerk the grain out of the burning stem. Ploughs were hitched directly to the horses' tails; by modern standards this was a cruel practice, but in days when hanging and quartering, and breaking on the wheel, were matters of everyday routine, definitions of cruelty were rather different; the practice certainly reduced the wear and tear on the plough. Slide-cars were drawn in the same way. People constantly on the move had little use for vegetable gardens, and water-cress and wood-sorrel served as salads.

It was the easy-going wandering life of the Irish pastoralists that particularly irritated the Tudors, who thought that all would be well if the nomadic natives could be anchored on tillage-farms, where a more settled round of duties would tire them out and leave them less time for mischief. Able-bodied men should have more to do than 'follow a few cows grazing . . . for this keeping of cows is of itself a very idle life and a fit nursery for a thief'. If they were exhausted by working in the fields or gardens, they would have less energy for raiding; as it was 'when it is daylight they will go to the poor village . . . burning the house and corn and ransacking of the poor cottages. They will drive all the kine and plow horses, with all other cattle, and drive them away'. To make wandering Irishmen into settled Englishmen was the goal.

The Tudors were business men and they decided they could not afford to take Ireland by a single massive onslaught. They would open up the country by cutting passes through the woods, bridging the rivers, building roads, and keeping the roads open by erecting forts and blockhouses along them. Apart from the good lands in the east and south, and the coasts from Lough Foyle down the Irish Sea and round to Galway Bay, the geography of Ireland was little known, and extensive surveys would be carried out to find out exactly what the country held. Inter-clan wars and risings against English authority would occur from time to time; these would be ruthlessly put down, the 'Irish enemies' killed off or transplanted, and English settlers and English ways brought in in their stead wherever the land was of sufficient quality to support 'the English way of life'. The areas that were ultimately taken were essentially the same areas of good land that had appealed to the Anglo-Normans (see map on p. 186), with in addition the good land in Munster.

The first opportunity came early in the sixteenth century when disturbances in Leix and Offaly, between the Pale and the Shannon, gave the English forces a chance to intervene. Victory was followed by the transformation of the area into King's County and Queen's County; the Irish were dislodged, their chief was pensioned off with 3000 acres, and the rest was parcelled out to settlers from England in lots ranging from 500 to 25 acres. The larger grantees had to pay a rent, perform military duties, manage the local water courses and fords, and supply timber. To prevent their land becoming sub-divided in the Irish manner, the grantees had to undertake to leave it in tail-male to their eldest son.

Lack of adequate survey gave rise to difficulties in division, and efforts were made to improve surveying methods. From such surveys we get glimpses of the landscape. Primary woodland was encountered round Athlone, where the map-maker recorded extensive forests of 'great oaks' in contrast to 'much small woods as crabtree, thorn, hazel, with such like'. In north Kerry some of the woodlands were clearly secondary as they consisted of 'underwood of the age of fifty or sixty years, filled with decayed trees, ash-trees, hazels, sallows, willows, alders, birches, whitethorns and such like'.

The acquisition of Munster came next, and after the Desmond Rising had been crushed in 1585 the areas of brown podzolic soils that had been avoided by the Anglo-Normans were offered to new settlers, for whom about 600,000 acres were made available. Mouths were encouraged to open wide, and blocks of 4000, 6000 and even 12,000 acres were offered, together with blue-print development layouts showing lots ranging from 1000 acres for the

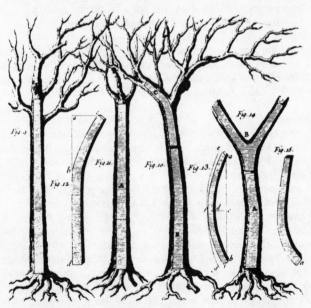

The curved timbers necessary for ship-building had to be selected with great care; the picture illustrates the timber possibilities of variously-shaped oak-trees. (After Duhamel du Monceau, 1764).

demesne to five and a half acres for the cottages. Edmund Spenser got 3000 acres; favourites like Sir Walter Raleigh received 20,000 acres, to whet his appetite for still greater plantations in north America; Richard Boyle, later Earl of Cork, subsequently purchased Raleigh's estate. No nucleus of local government that might grow to a regional authority was provided, though Boyle did what he could. What with difficulties in securing settlers, difficulties in satisfying them when they did arrive, and the partially successful efforts of the original owners to regain the land, Munster in 1600 by no means presented the happy picture of contented English settlers farming enclosed fields on fertile farms protected by natural defences and near to the sea, a river or a town that had been put forward by the prospectuses for the scheme. The comment 'Enclosures are very rare amongst them, and then no better fenced than an old wife's toothless gums . . . as for the arable land it lies almost as much neglected and unmanured [unworked] as the sandy deserts of Arabia' is probably nearer the mark.

But the plantation did throw the woods of Munster at the mercy of the new entrepreneurs, and the commercial exploitation of the forests began in earnest. From the woods a continuous stream of timber flowed out – trunks from good large trees for ships and houses, branches from these trees and

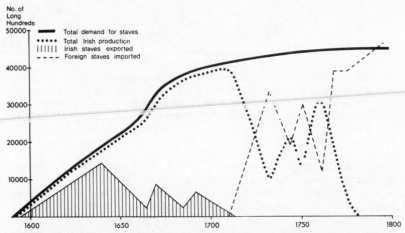

A schematic diagram to suggest the rise and fall in the trade in Irish oak barrel-staves (and, with the fall, the disappearance of the Irish oakwoods). Production (and export) had begun before 1600. By 1615 staves were going to the Mediterranean for wine casks. After 1640 home demand for barrels to cask salt meat for export rose, and the export of staves fell away. When the export of live animals was prohibited in 1665, the demand for staves rose sharply. Until about 1710 the Irish woods could meet the full demand, but in that year staves had to be imported for the first time. From then until about 1765 Ireland could still meet about half the demand, but after 1770 there were no more Irish staves, and all had to be imported. (Based on data in McCracken, *Irish Woods*).

smaller trees for barrel staves, and lop and top and all other wood for charcoal for iron and glass works. It is hard to gauge the amount of large timber that was exported, but we can get some impression of the stave and charcoal trades from the information made available by Eileen McCracken.

For barrel staves I have taken her figures, and tried to cast them in a crude graphical diagram (p. 195); much is conjectural, and for this I take full responsibility. As can be seen the production of staves made tremendous inroads on the oak woods. Throughout the seventeenth century the number of staves produced in Ireland rose steadily, and over-production led to eventual exhaustion of supply. After 1770 all needed staves had to be imported.

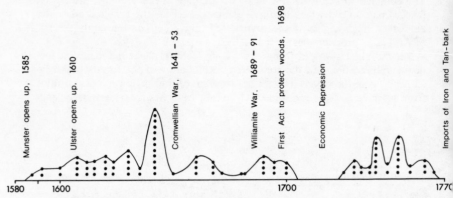

A schematic diagram to show the times at which new charcoal-burning ironworks started to operate in Ireland. Each dot represents the opening of a works. The influence of military and economic events is clearly seen. The sharp decline after 1750 indicates the exhaustion of supplies of charcoal. (Based on data in McCracken, *Irish Woods*).

Mrs McCracken gives the years in which about one hundred charcoal-consuming ironworks started to operate, and again I have plotted these dates in a crudely graphical form. Production started in Munster shortly before 1600, and such was the consumption of woodland that, after no more than one hundred years, parliament in 1698 was compelled to pass the first of a long series of acts both to conserve any remaining stocks, and to encourage the planting of trees.

Between 1593 and 1603 there were nine years of general country-wide war, when an organized Irish army with foreign contingents was defeated by an Elizabethan army, and the independence and isolation of Ulster were brought to an end. Five hundred thousand acres were available for plantation, and this time the mistakes made in Munster were not repeated. Two thousand acres was the upper limit on the blocks offered, and those who accepted had to bring in tenants from Britain, and build defences – a castle and a bawn – to protect their lands, tenants and goods. Roads and bridges were organized,

PLATE 29 *Above*, Cappaghmore, Co. Galway. A successful small farm on low-lying limestone. *Below*, Ballinloghane, Co. Limerick. An unsuccessful 'cabin' high on a sandstone hillside.

PLATE 30 *Above*, Glendalough, Co. Wicklow. In the early 19th century the valley was stripped of timber, as wood for fuel and charcoal for smelting. The monastic buildings stand out like ruined teeth in a bare gum. *Below*, for this similar picture the photographer had to move up from the floor of the valley. Its left-hand slopes now carry secondary oakwood, pines and exotics have been planted on the right, and there is young plantation on the low ground between the two lakes. Only the top of the Round Tower (now restored) and part of one church can be seen.

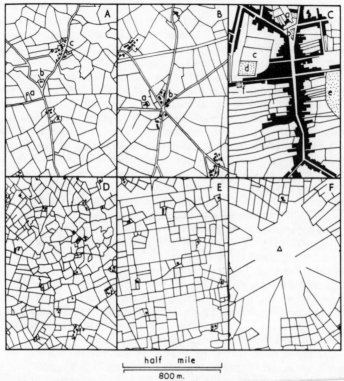

half mile

800 m.

Settlements and fields stemming from the Plantation of Ulster (after Common and Glasscock): A, Clachan: **a**, church house; **b**, church; **c**, clachan; **x**, site of rath. B, Roadside hamlet: **a**, church; **b**, local post office. C, Planned town: **a**, technical institute; **b**, open area; **c**, brickfield; **d**, fairgreen; **e**, demesne; **f**, linen factory. D, Small irregular fields. E, Regular fields with surveyed boundaries. F, Fields laid out to accord with hill slope topography.

towns and villages laid out and with growing commercialism markets, shops and local industries were established. A regular pattern of small enclosed fields for arable farming was established. The Plantation of Ulster was more than the replacement of one group of farmers by another; it was truly an implantation of a different way of life, a difference that has maintained itself to the present day.

Like Leinster, Ulster has its upland areas of poorer soils, the Sperrins and the mountains of Donegal. The displaced natives withdrew to these areas where tillage was still more difficult, and there their nomadic habits became still more pronounced. Excessive sub-division of land as generation succeeded generation, and the constant fear of crops being burned or otherwise destroyed in raids and war, had brought about still further concentration on livestock, which might escape pillage if kept on the move. The seasonal booleying moves to summer pastures had always been strong, and the more drastic practice of *creaghting*, whereby whole communities and their livestock kept more or less constantly on the move, drifting from the protection of one lord to that of another, became more pronounced.

But when peace returned, agricultural output turned quickly upwards. Fish, hides and furs fell back in importance as exports, and cattle, butter and wool took their place. It may be that as the forests of Munster shrank, the numbers of cattle and sheep rose; certainly the ports of Youghal, Cork and Kinsale grew dramatically at this time. The bone content of some fifteenth/sixteenth-century ditches at Newgrange also demonstrated the rise in the importance of sheep at this time; sheep (or goat) provided almost one third of all the bones found in the late medieval ditches, whereas in the prehistoric levels at the same site they only amounted to one twentieth.

The drastic action that had been taken in Ulster was followed by land confiscations in Connaught, and the general hostility to these plantations, as well as to the strong central government in Dublin, provoked a further rising during the English Civil War in 1641. This led to a further general country-wide war, which lasted for twelve years, before it was brutally terminated by Cromwell's victories. Two and a half million acres were involved in the population shifts which followed; the Irish landowners were pushed to the west, to the wet and infertile lands beyond the Shannon; those of English extraction whose loyalties to England were considered sufficiently safe were retained on the best soils in the south-east between the Boyne and the Barrow, and between these two groups a colonial buffer zone with ex-soldiers and new settlers straggled down central Ireland on lands of varying quality.

Once peace returned the country recovered quickly. An upturn in climate was bringing record harvests in Europe; Ireland concentrated on livestock. The markets and fairs that had been initiated in Ulster spread through the country, and with an improving road system cattle easily found their way either to the docks or the slaughterhouse. Sheep went to stock the English sheepwalks. Even when the English market was closed by embargo, alternate overseas markets were readily to hand. Sugar produced by slave labour was now pouring out of the West Indies, and meat was urgently required to feed the population there. Cork and its stockyards became the Chicago of Ireland, and heavily salted beef was crammed into barrels for the West Indian trade. As we have seen, the export trade in barrel staves faded away, as every barrel was needed for the trade. Generally it was a time of some prosperity. Petty reported that the general standard of clothing was equal to that of Europe. Chimneys were appearing in houses. Many people owned a horse. The emphasis on pasture rather than tillage left many people underemployed, and cottage industries, the spinning and weaving of wool and flax, were a source of supplemental income.

The short war that followed, from 1689 to 1691, was not altogether of Ireland's making, but she had to provide campaign fields for the 'Irish' army of James II and the 'English' army of William III. William's victory was followed by the reshuffling of at least one million acres of land, and when that was over only 15 % of the land of Ireland was left in Irish ownership, and the ascendancy of the English landlord was complete.

What did Ireland look like in 1700, one hundred and fifty years after the first plantation? The population had probably doubled, though it is difficult to give exact figures; Petty reckoned the population in 1672 at 1,200,000, and if we think of 1,000,000 in 1550, and 2,000,000 in 1700, at least our order of number will probably be correct (see graph on p. 204). In 1550 people still trusted in stone castles, but these had been made obsolete by gunpowder, and in 1700 confident estate owners were beginning to build houses with large windows, through which they could admire the newly planted exotic trees in their gardens and demesnes. When these new pollens appear in our pollen-counts we bring the Destruction-phase (ILWd$_2$) to an end, and open the Expansion-phase (ILWe), when the slow process of restoring Ireland's woodlands takes its first tentative steps. (Pl. 26)

Though the road system still left a lot to be desired – 'the great rain has made the ways almost impassable, the horse road which is most old causeway being broken up and quite out of repair and the footway in the fields very boggy with abundance of ditches at that time full of water' – the stage coach was beginning to appear. Stock could move easily to market, and from there to the point of export. Banks to facilitate trade were coming into existence. The woods had shrunk out of all recognition, and been replaced by meadows and fields to support the larger population.

The potato was beginning to take its place in the Irish diet. When did the potato appear in Ireland? At an early meeting of the Royal Society in 1662 Robert Boyle spoke in terms that suggested that the potato had already saved thousands from starvation in Ireland; but it may be that he was indicating what the potato could do, rather than what it had already done, because at the same time his gardener was still struggling to produce the few potatoes needed to provide a delicacy in salads rather than an item of everyday diet.

References to the potato in Ireland do not become common until the 1670s, and then they suggest that the potato was still a garden, rather than a field crop. Dunton writes, 'Behind one of these cabins lies the garden, a piece of ground sometimes of half an acre, and in this is the turf-stack, their corn – perhaps two or three hundred sheaves of oats – and as much peas; the rest of the ground is full of those dearly loved potatoes, and a few cabbages which the solitary calf never suffers to come to perfection'. At the end of the century the potato stood poised and ready to revolutionize life in Ireland.

CONSOLIDATION IN THE EIGHTEENTH CENTURY, AD 1700 – 1785

By comparison with the turbulent centuries which had preceded it, the eighteenth century was one of relatively uneventful development. By 1785 the population had doubled once more (see graph on p. 204), and trade had increased tenfold. A vigorous programme of road-building (accompanied by the full establishment of a stage-coach system) and the construction of canals both integrated the country and centred it on its capital, Dublin, to an extent hitherto unknown. The last Irish wolf had been killed.

Unfortunately the now universal landlord-tenant relationship concentrated the new wealth in the hands of the landlords, who erected the palatial houses looking out on well-wooded demesnes that are still such a feature of the Irish landscape. Outside the demesne the lodgings of their tenants remained at their former miserable level. In the earlier part of the century the interposition of a middleman who took large blocks of land on long lease from the landlord, and let it in small blocks on shorter lease at higher rent to the tenant, ensured that such prosperity that escaped the landlord was siphoned off by the middleman, and little or none of it was enjoyed by the tenant. The middleman was not entirely useless, because he sometimes employed his capital in leasing dairy stock to tenants who could not afford their own, and so took them into 'clientship' in a way that had been widespread in early Ireland. In this way he exemplified that power to spring again from a cut-down stock that has typified much of Ireland throughout the ages. (Pl. 26)

The cottage industries based on wool and flax continued to provide valuable supplements to family incomes, and bleach greens became a feature of the Irish countryside. But Ireland was a backward agricultural country caught up in the rapidly-developing British mercantile system, and when that system was shaken either by harvest vagaries or by wars, then the fortunes of Ireland fluctuated also.

The agricultural revolution was slow to reach Ireland. Already in the middle of the sixteenth century farmers in the Netherlands had eliminated the hitherto universal period of fallow. They replaced it with turnips and clover to feed increased numbers of stock, whose larger output of manure was used to fertilize the land for the corn crops. Animal and crop husbandry were now united in one system, capable of very intensive production. The weed problem was solved by the invention of the seed drill in 1700. With the young plants in neat rows, a hoe could be drawn between the rows, and the weeds eliminated while the crop was growing. Ability to survive a hard winter on scanty rations was no longer the criterion by which stock had to be judged; with animal feed assured, it was now possible to breed for production of meat, milk and wool.

Eventually the wind of change did reach Ireland. A Linen Hall was founded in Dublin in 1711 to promote the growth of flax and oversee the weaving and sale of linen. The Royal Dublin Society was founded in 1731, for 'the advancement of agriculture and other branches of industry and for the advancement of science and art'. The society circulated agricultural books, imported implements, and gave premiums for stock-breeding, tree-planting, spinning, weaving and a host of other activities. It did much to stir up an interest in agriculture among the landlords who formed its membership, and in the later part of the century the middlemen withered away, as many landlords took a direct and improving interest in the management of their estates. An improvement was badly needed; each year the Cork stockyards alone slaughtered 300,000 head of cattle, but the cattle were small, averaging only 4–8 cwt against the 10–15 cwt of contemporary English breeds.

If the quality of the cattle population was to be improved, controlled

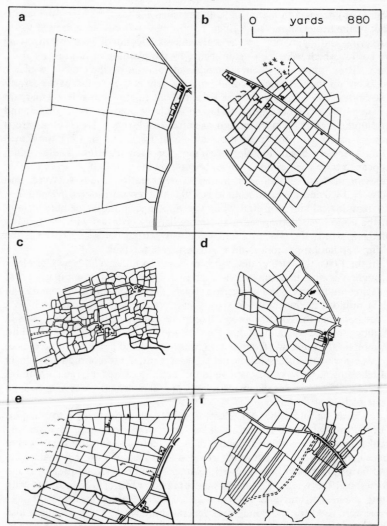

Some Irish field-systems (after Buchanan): **a**, large regular fields, Jordanstown, Co. Meath; **b**, small regular fields, Ballykine Lower, Co. Down; **c**, small irregular fields, Glinsouth, Co. Kerry; **d**, curved strip fields, Nicholastown, Co. Kilkenny; **e**, ladder farms, Foriff, Co. Antrim; **f**, strips in common-fields, with surrounding ring of pasture, Dalkey, Co. Dublin, *c*. AD 1850.

breeding was necessary. Improved pastures and hay and roots for winter fodder made it possible to carry bigger stocks, and here control was also necessary. Hedged fields prevented stock from wandering, controlled the degree of grazing and manuring, and provided shelter, while the ditch at the foot of the hedge improved drainage. Soon the landlords were hard at work, surveying and laying-out new field alignments, digging ditches and throwing up banks, which were then made secure by the planting of hawthorns along them. They 'improved' their tenants' lands as well as their own, in places breaking up the old clachans and building new houses well separated from one another. On flat ground the arrangement might be highly regular, on isolated hills such as drumlins the layout would be adjusted to the slopes, and on sloping ground a ladder pattern was often employed. After 1698 numerous acts of parliament promoted the planting of trees, and in 1735 the Royal Dublin Society began to offer premiums for such planting. These stimuli appear to have been quite effective, because by the year 1800 at least 132,000 acres of plantations had been added to what native woods survived, and between 1800 and the Famine another 210,000 acres were added. We had thus the paradoxical situation that while the landscape in the immediate vicinity of the estates was getting more and more densely crowded with trees, many of them exotic, the general countryside was getting barer and barer as the rising population got more and more desperate for fuel.

In the 1780s the pace of development began to falter. The New Corn laws brought a swing to grain-growing against cattle, and the population was entering on that period of staggering growth that was to bring it from four to eight millions in the course of sixty years. We are very fortunate to have a record of what the country looked like in the immediately preceding years in Arthur Young's account of his *Tour in Ireland* in 1776–9. Like Giraldus Cambrensis, Young was from Britain, was human and not without prejudice; he was not very successful as manager of Lord Kingsborough's estate in Mitchelstown, he was conservative in outlook, he carried a large chip on his shoulder, but from his extensive travels and experiences we can build up a clear picture of the times.

In Cavan he found that Mr Clements had 'been very attentive to bring his farm into neat order respecting fences, throwing down and levelling old banks, making new ditches, double ones six feet wide and five deep, with a large bank between for planting'. He also approved of Lord Farnham, who had farmed in Norfolk, and sowed his turnips and cabbages with a drill and horse-hoed the weeds. The fields were drained, and liberally fertilized with dung, ditch-earth and lime. There was a herd of Lancashire cows, and although oxen were used for ploughing and general draft work, Lord Farnham also bred work-horses. The estate was well planted with Scots Fir, Silver Fir, beech, oak and ash. 'Upon the whole Farnham is one of the finest places I have seen in Ireland.' Outside the demesnes the tree position was different; Co. Galway 'is perfectly free from woods, and even trees, except about gentlemen's houses'. Near the cities the position was worse; at Dunkettle, outside Cork, he reports 'Fuel; a very little coal, the rest supplied by bushes, stolen faggots, etc., as there is no turf in this part of the country.'

He also approved of Mr Oliver, of Castle Oliver, Co. Limerick, but not of his tenants who raised bullocks on farms of up to 500 acres. 'The face of the country is that of desolation; the grounds are over-run with thistles, ragwort, etc. to excess; the fences are mounds of earth, full of gaps; there is no wood, and the general countenance is such, that you must examine into the soil before you will believe that a country, which has so beggarly an appearance, can be so rich and fertile.' At the bottom of the scale we hear 'Great quantities of flax sown by all the poor and little farmers, which is spun in the country, and a good deal of bandle [narrow] cloth made of it. This and pigs are two great articles of profit here; they keep great numbers, yet the poor in this rich tract of country are very badly off. Land is so valuable, that all along as I came from Bruff, their cabins are generally in the road ditch, and numbers of them without the least garden; the potato land being assigned them upon the farm where it suits the master best. The price they pay is very great, from £4 to £5 an acre, with a cabin; and for the grass of a cow 40s. to 45s. They are, if anything, worse off than they were twenty years ago. A cabin, an acre of land, at 40s. and the grass of two cows, are the recompence for the year's labour; but in other places they are paid by an acre of grass for potatoes at £5. Those who do not get milk to their potatoes, eat mustard with them, raising the seed for the purpose. The population of the country increases exceedingly, but mostly on the higher lands; new cabins are building everywhere.' It is clear that in Young's time the potato had become a field, rather than a garden, crop, that it was the principal item of diet for the majority of the population, and that a rapid expansion of that population was making itself felt. What Young could not realize was that that expansion was going to produce a further sub-division of land into tiny potato-patches, and impede the orderly realignment of field boundaries, of which he approved so highly.

The landlords, like Lord de Montalt, at Dundrum, Co. Tipperary, might follow the advice of the Dublin Society and use Warwickshire and Shropshire ploughs, but elsewhere it was different, as at Castletownroche, Co. Cork. 'Four horses and three men to every plough, one to drive, one to hold, and another with a pole, bearing on the beam to keep it in the ground; but they do an acre a day, by means of leaving a great space untouched in the middle of each land, where they begin by lapping the sods to meet.' Such a plough-scene can have changed little since the fourteenth century, though two men are now sharing the job the ploughman alone did then (see Pl. 20, centre). In the stony west everything was done with the spade. 'Upon asking whether they ploughed with horses or oxen, I was told there was not a plough in the whole parish, which was 12 miles long by 7 broad. All the tillage is by the Irish loy; ten men dig an acre a day that has been stirred before. It will take forty men to put in an acre of potatoes in a day.' He appreciated that spade cultivation was not necessarily to be despised as it could give a better return than the plough; at Belleisle, Co. Fermanagh, he reports 'Much corn, etc. by poor people, put in with spades, which they call loys, because they have no horses, and one acre of oats dug, is worth one and a half ploughed; some do it on this account, though they have horses.'

Arthur Young saw Ireland from horseback or through the windows of a post-chaise. Were he touring today in a motor-car, he would be amazed at the tall hedges along the roadside which obscured his view, he would wonder where the masses of people had disappeared to, he would remark on the improvement in the standard of housing, he would notice some trees, but much of the rest would still look familiar to his eyes.

THE POTATO AND THE POPULATION PEAK, AD 1785–1850

It is not easy to pinpoint the cause, or combination of causes, that drastically accelerated, around 1785, the rate of population-increase in Ireland. We can picture that in 1741 the population was about three million, in 1785 it was about four million, while in 1841 – shortly before the Famine – when a census was taken the figure was 8,200,000.

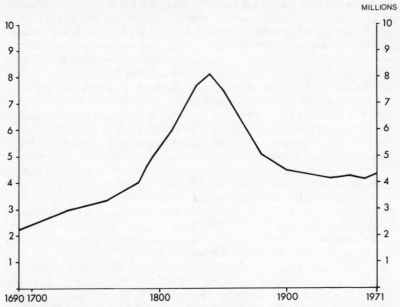

A graph to illustrate population growth and decline in Ireland, AD 1690 to 1971. (After Connell and Gilmor).

The death-rate was falling. As the 1840s approached medicine was improving, vaccination was adopted, and a chain of hospitals and dispensaries was spreading through the country. Food was improving in quality and also in quantity – there was no major famine (apart from the Great Famine) after 1740, and the improved transport system made the movement of food within the country more easy. The birth-rate was rising; more young people in the population meant more alliances, and the better diet may have raised the fertility rate.

In other European countries the populations were also rising, but not as fast as in Ireland; the potato was being eaten in other countries, but not to the same extent as in Ireland, and it is difficult to resist the conclusion that the

PLATE 31 *Above*, Tonelagee, Co. Wicklow. Blanket-bog is being eroded away, at an altitude of 530m. *Below*, Lough Mask, Co. Mayo. Stumps and trunks of pine, perhaps about 4000 years old, have been exposed by peat-cutting. Such 'bog-deal' was formerly valued both for fuel and for building.

PLATE 32 *Above,*
nr. Dingle, Co. Kerry.
When large rocks have
been pushed aside, and
the soil re-distributed,
and fertiliser spread,
great areas of new
grassland will arise. In
the process much
evidence of earlier
human activity will
disappear. *Right,*
Derrygreenagh,
Co. Westmeath. This
large raised-bog was
drained by the cuts
seen running left and
right. The surface is
scarified to produce a
layer of loose,
quickly-drying plant
debris. The debris is
swept up into ridges,
sometimes protected by
polythene sheeting.
Such a ridge is being
loaded for removal to
the power-station.

potato, not only by its dietary influence, but also by its social influence, was the chief cause of the fantastic – and disastrous – rate of population growth in Ireland.

The potato is one of the great food crops of the world, and alone of them finds conditions in Ireland entirely to its liking. The potato favours water-retaining soils, and these are not in short supply in Ireland, particularly in the west and south. Conditions for wheat are minimal, and those for barley little better; oats and rye are more at home. The summer temperatures are rarely high enough for the sugar-beet to produce its full potential of sugar, but they are more than enough for starch production by the potato, whose homelands are the Andean uplands of South America. Though 75% of the tuber is water, the food value of an acre of potatoes is greater than that of an acre of any grain crop. The potato yields starch, amino-acids and Vitamin C, and the consumption of 6·5 lbs per day provides an adequate diet. In Ireland an acre can be expected to yield about 9 tons, enough to feed 6 adult men for one year, and more than adequate to support a relatively large family. It is thought that the consumption per head may have reached 8 lbs a day.

For most of us forcible feeding in prison would seem preferable to thrusting half a stone of potatoes down our throats day in day out throughout the year. And for many this was all there was for months on end. We have only to read Arthur Young's litany as he perambulated the country; at Castletownroche 'They live the year through upon potatoes, and for half the year have nothing but water with them'; at Johnstown 'Their food is potatoes for at least eleven months of the year, and one month of oat, barley or bere bread.'

For those with courage, there could be money in potatoes. W. S. Trench tells us how in 1846 he took 160 acres of rough mountain pasture worth one shilling an acre. He scattered lime over it and then ploughed it into ridges five feet wide; the potatoes were sown, guano was added as manure, and the ridges were further built up by hand. 'The potato grew to perfection in this rude description of tillage.' He expected to get a crop of potatoes worth £3000 'at the very moderate price of 3d per stone', and be left with the land with its value raised twentyfold to one pound an acre, and ready to grow a good crop of corn or grass. But 1846 was the year of the blight, and he lost all.

In Ireland, as in other rural countries before farming was mechanized, the social pyramid was the land-owners, the tenant-farmers and the landless labourers. We have seen the land-owners in their elegant mansions, set in a tree-studded demesne, which was now surrounded by a wall, built as a relief-measure by the local labourers. The tenant-farmers lived in a modest way; Lewis tells us 'Farmhouses though varying in size are all built on the same plan, with an open chimney at one end, and at the other a small room separated by a partition, and serving both as a bed-chamber and as a store-room. Few farm yards are attached to the houses, and these are very small and confined; the corn being frequently stacked on circular stages supported by upright capstones; barns are never used for any other purpose than thrashing, and are consequently built very small; the common farmer indeed is often unprovided with either stage or barn, and thrashes his grain in the open air'. (Pl. 29)

We can liken the social pyramid to a stratified bee-hive, in which the three layers ought to be in appropriate proportions. Unfortunately after 1785 the boards containing the base of the bee-hive burst outwards, and the labourers began to expand beyond the confines of the hive. The bee builds flimsy cells of wax, the labourers built their rickety cabins wherever they could find a sufficiency of square feet free from obstruction, and if possible one wall already provided – against a field-bank, in a ditch, against a rock-face. On the hillsides (far above the present level of cultivation) there were still patches of ground on slopes where lazy-beds could be laid out, and a cabin set up. With luck there would be blanket-bog not too far away, and a more easy supply of fuel to compensate for the harder struggle on higher ground. On rougher ground, stones could be cleared away. (Pls. 25, 29)

In the east, sub-division of land at first sufficed to produce the necessary acre per family. In 1830 the Royal Dublin Society was offering premiums for schemes to divide up land so that there would be allotted 'to the greatest number of cottages a quantity of land not less than one acre, Irish', and also 'for the best account of actual experience of the quantity of land required to support a labourer's family with vegetables and potatoes, and to enable him to keep a pig and a cow all the year'. Those at a level higher up in the hive saw no reason to object to such fragmentation; the farmer by splitting some of his fields, and letting the land at £5 or more per acre automatically received cash to make the payment of his own rent secure, and the landlord was delighted to get prompt payment. Lest any suggestion should arise that the labourer should acquire even a shadow of title to the land he rented, he often got it on *conacre*, or possession for eleven months only, which made its reversion clear beyond doubt.

But where to get the money to pay the rent? There can have been no sale for surplus potatoes; in Ireland potatoes are always a rags to riches crop. If the harvest was a light one, hunger might loom before the next harvest came round, and the pressure to eat the seed-stock might be impossible to resist. If the crop was a bumper one, there was no market for the surplus. Home spinning could bring in some cash, and if the dwelling was substantial a loom could be set up. A bonham could be purchased, and reared on family scraps for later sale as bacon. Sometimes the £5 rent would bring in addition to the acre of land the right to graze a cow for the year, and milk and butter would make a welcome supplement to the potato diet. Only at planting-time and at harvest was any serious labour required by the crop, and the able-bodied members of the family were able to migrate in search of paid work. But the more the population increased, the more candidates there were for the jobs, and the farmer had no difficulty in moving his wage-rate down.

A family, once some of the children had reached the age of seven or eight, was probably an asset rather than a liability. Capital outlay was almost nil. There were no agricultural implements needed, beyond a spade for everyone big enough to use one. No farm buildings, because the potatoes could lie quite happily in a clamp in the field. A roof over the cabin, fuel for the fire, and straw to lie in were essential. Clothes were patched beyond all recognition, and handed down from one to another. Boots and shoes were for adults only,

A drawing of Irish labourer with spade in one hand and shoes in the other, *c.* AD 1850.

and then only on special occasions. If necessary, the potatoes could be roasted in the ashes of the fire, or boiled in a *fulacht fian*, and eaten from the hand without benefit of pot, plate, knife or fork. It was subsistence-existence, in the fullest sense of the word.

The larger children could assist in the spade work. The others could gather herbs to flavour the potatoes, tend the cow and the pig, forage for manure – because the potato is a greedy crop – and, most important of all, scour the countryside for fuel, leaving no bush, bog or marsh unattacked. Nineteenth-century writers take up the tale where Arthur Young left off; in Co. Dublin 'the hedges are demolished without mercy, and, in many places they gather the dung from about the fields, and even burn straw'.

Both the raised-bogs and the blanket-bogs were being heavily cut for fuel, and even the swamps and marshes were being robbed of their muds. The mud was dug or dredged up, spread on the surrounding lands, tramped underfoot to a uniform consistency, moulded into lumps, dried and burned. West Cork today shows many small ponds; if we look at them closely we can see the still-jagged peat-cuttings that form their margins; before the Famine they were closed marshes; their open-water was created by peat-cutting, just as on a much larger scale the Norfolk Broads are the product of medieval peat-cutting.

It is hard to realize today just how serious the struggle for fuel was. Even in Arthur Young's time hedges and fences were being stolen for firing. How much worse it must have been when the population was approaching its maximum. The countryside must have presented an extraordinary appearance. There were the walled demesnes with their trees, like oases in a desert. The boughs of the trees hung down over the walls, but inside the walls there were man-traps to deter timber-poachers. There were the farmers' houses surrounded by shelter-belts of trees, and the farmer would have a blunderbuss to protect them. And then there was nothing, not a tree, not a bush, to break the view of the bare landscape dotted over with cabins and endless potato-patches. (Pl. 30)

Everything was done with the spade, and every region had its own variety of spade. At one time a spade factory in Cork used to produce at least seventy-five different forms of spade-blade. As we have seen, to use the spade rather than the plough is by no means a sign of inferior husbandry. The user of the spade gives to his work the detail of the gardener, rather than the broader stroke of the plough, and yields will usually be higher from the spade-plot than the ploughed field. If excess of labour has allowed wage-rates to drop below a certain level, it will be cheaper for the farmer to use teams of men with spades, rather than the plough, with its attendant cost of keeping the draught animals.

And hand in hand with the spade went the cultivation-ridge or 'lazy-bed', and we have seen that this method of cultivation is of high antiquity in Ireland. Though lazy-beds today are largely confined in distribution to the poorer west and in crop to the potato, they were formerly in use throughout the whole country, and a wide range of crops was raised on them. The width of the bed, and the height to which it was built up, varied both with the nature of the soil and the requirements of the crop to be grown. The plough was sometimes used in the first laying out of the bed, but after that the spade took over, and the shape of the bed might be adjusted to the needs of the crop at various stages of its growth. After the bed had been in use for some time it was divided down its centre; and what had been the ridge-crest became the new furrow. (Pl. 27)

As I have said before, the general connotations of the word 'lazy' are quite inappropriate here, because the careful management of the cultivation-ridge is a sophisticated method of coaxing the best out of a soil that is often wet and unpromising to begin with. The water content can be improved by suitable proportions of ridge and furrow, and the fertility can be raised by manuring, and a low-grade soil can often be brought to a reasonable level of productivity.

In the west the spade and the lazy-bed ruled all, and cultivation depended on teams of men with spades, rather than teams of oxen or horses with ploughs. We can picture groups of men each armed with a spade turning out of their clachan to the arable common-field each morning, ten to the acre if lazy-beds were to be set up, forty to the acre if potatoes were to be planted. There was no special factor controlling the shape or size of the field, and a number of people would either own separate blocks within the field, or much more sensibly rights on a certain number of lazy-beds in the field. Here we see a version of the common-field system that had flourished on the better land of eastern Ireland when the mouldboard-plough appeared, and may go back to still earlier time. Cultivation in common withered away in the 'planted' east of the country, but may well have survived in the native west, and blossomed out again into the *rundale* system when eighteenth-century population pressures developed (see figure f on p. 201).

In rundale there was the common arable field, and nearby the clachan, a cluster of modest houses with outbuildings and small enclosures. Around the perimeter was the outfield, used for pasture and periodic cultivation, and perhaps farther away the meadows, the mountain-grazing and the bogs, all of which were shared in common. (Pls. 25, 28)

With a balanced community such a system was viable, and could stand limited expansion. More potatoes could come into the arable field, and the productivity of the outfield could be raised. But once population-growth exceeded a certain rate, the system had to collapse. Holdings and rights fragmented under succession in severalty. As the potato expanded to take up the whole of the arable field, it left no aftergrass to feed stock and to receive its dung in return. If stock numbers were reduced the total amount of manure available for the arable field fell. Ultimately if all were not to be reduced below the subsistence level, there had to be movement, either to higher levels up the hill-slopes, to the east where potato-patches could still be rented to the further detriment of the existing fields, or out of the country altogether, to England or America.

The population of an overfull bee-hive can be relieved in two ways. Swarms can carry large numbers away in search of new feeding-grounds, or disease can decimate the colony. Long before the Famine the swarms of emigrants had begun to leave Ireland, and by 1830 the rate of population-growth was beginning to slacken off. But this was not enough, and when in 1845 potato blight finally caught up with the potato in Ireland, disaster was inevitable. During the Famine years (1845–51) about 800,000 people died, and twice as many emigrated. The heart was knocked out of Ireland, and the population continued to fall without interruption until 1930, when it was only 4,000,000, and Ireland was one of the emptiest countries in Europe (p. 204).

THE AFTERMATH OF THE FAMINE, AD 1850–1903

If we were to look back to 1850 BC, we would see a well-wooded Ireland, and in clearings we would see a Bronze Age population enjoying a standard of life equivalent to that of anywhere in western Europe. If instead, we look back to AD 1850 we see a ruined landscape, almost destitute of any woody growth, and with the fertility of much of its soils grossly depleted by endless repetitions of potato crops. Those of its people in whom any element of *élan vital* had survived had only one goal – to seek a higher standard of living elsewhere. And it is on the foundations of that ruined landscape that much of what we see around us today has been built.

One thing was clear; the land had to be rebuilt into larger units, which might have some hope of economic survival. Some holdings fell back into the landlord's hands when the former tenants emigrated, and he rapidly repossessed himself of others by means of eviction if the tenants fell into arrears with their rents. For the landlord himself was now facing ruin. Relief measures, both indoor and outdoor, had been organized for famine victims, and these were charged on the local rates; not only had the landlord to pay his own dues, but if his tenants failed to pay, and their valuation was less than £4 – there were vast numbers of such tiny holdings – then he had to pay their dues as well; for him it was only good sense to buy the family emigrant tickets to America, and demolish their cabin, lest another occupant should revive his liability for rates. Programmes of tree-planting were abruptly terminated. Many estates collapsed under the strain, and in 1849 legislation made it possible for estates encumbered by debts to pass into new hands. But whereas many of the older landlords had lingering strains of paternalism towards their tenants, the newcomers had not, and for many small land-holders it was out of the frying-pan into the fire.

After 1850 things improved rapidly. Increasing population and increasing prosperity in England meant good prices for Ireland's farm produce; the tenant farmers prospered on their larger farms; continued emigration of younger men meant that the services of those that remained were in demand and wages rose; at the top the landlord was happy. A railway boom was opening up the country; before the Famine there were 65 miles of rail; twenty years later there were 2,000 miles. Imported manufactured goods and food-stuffs could reach all parts of the country, with the result that shops thrived while local industries decayed.

But the essential dichotomy between the more favoured and more accessible east, and the poorer and more distant west persisted. And paradoxically it was the east that provided the bulk of the emigrants; in the west a still dispirited population lacked the initiative to go further than seasonal work in Britain, and the population obstinately remained at a level that was too high for the local resources.

The self-perpetuating flame of Irish resistance to British domination that had been encouraged to flare up by the Act of Union in 1801, had almost flickered out during the distresses of the Famine, but it gradually warmed to life again, and England was forced to adopt, through the person of Mr

Gladstone, a policy that has been aptly described as 'a nauseous mixture of slaps and sops', the slaps being the coercion of political unrest, and the sops being the bringing about, as a first step, of co-partnership between the landlord and tenant, and, as a second, of transfer of ownership from landlord to tenant. The Land Act of 1870 was the first important sop; if a tenant surrendered his farm he was entitled to be compensated for any improvements he had made; if he was put out, for any reason other than non-payment of rent, he was entitled to compensation for disturbance; if he wished to purchase his holding, he could borrow money from the state.

The all-too-brief good times ended abruptly in the middle seventies, when bad weather brought crop failures on a massive scale. Prices for what modest home produce there was did not rise, because the new generation of large cargo steamers was carrying in cheaper produce from overseas. Rents could not be paid, evictions started up again, and political agitations accompanied them. A further dose of coercion was accompanied by Mr Gladstone's second Land Act, that of 1881, with its famous 'three F's' – fair rents, fixity of tenure and free sale. A few years later it was supplemented by an act by which the state would advance the whole of the purchase price of a farm, and be repaid by annuities, and about 25,000 farms soon changed hands.

From 1850 on the process of realigning field boundaries, enclosing new fields and planting their boundaries with trees and bushes had gone steadily on, but landlords were no longer able to afford new plantations of trees on the scale that had obtained before the Famine; planting was balanced by cutting to finance it, and the acreage under plantations remained the same. The Act of 1881, which brought nearer the transfer from landlord to tenant, had disastrous effects on the attitude of the landlord to his estate; he could no longer see it as something to be husbanded so that it could be passed on in tail-male in perpetuity, and he decided to turn his estate into cash while the going was good. As always, timber was turned to as a source of cash, and many landlords sold their stands of timber to travelling sawmillers, who came over from England and moved across the country from estate to estate, leaving devastation again in their wake. As a footnote we may add that the woods that survived this cutting enjoyed only a brief respite before they vanished in World War I, and when that was over 200,000 acres of woodland had disappeared, and less than half of one per cent of Ireland was covered by forest.

The grim cycle came round again in the late eighties. Poor yields at home, cheap imported foreign goods, rent arrears, evictions, violence, coercion, and more Land Acts. Tenant protection was further extended, and more money was made available for farm purchase.

Economic conditions improved again in the nineties, and from this time on the more favoured east was economically viable, and was beginning to develop the appearance that we know today. Some trees had survived on some estates, the trees that had been planted in the field-banks were growing to maturity, and while the total number of trees was still minute, the view across the landscape did contain some trees, and the ghastly dreariness of immediately post-Famine times was fading away, though numerous house ruins and shrunken clachans were still evidence of the vanished population.

The west remained on the precarious edge of subsistence, and special attention was given to its improvement. In 1889 a system of light railway lines was threaded along the west coast in defiance of all economic principles. In 1891 a Congested Districts Board was set up to help those western regions where the density of the population manifestly outstripped the local resources. The Board built roads, bridges and harbours, and much of the modern tourist traffic enjoys the benefits of its activities. It stimulated fishing, gave agricultural advice, and encouraged cottage industries. Added income was vital, and this came from the cottage industries and seasonal earnings in Britain, now made easier of access by the new roads and railways. But as Louis Cullen points out, even before the Board had been set up, emigration rates from the west and the age of marriage had both started to rise which were positive moves, portending better than the palliative remedies of the Board. New cash sent home in remittances from emigrants may well have exceeded new cash generated by the Board, and the modernization made possible by the new money probably tended to promote more emigration in search of still higher standards rather than to stem it.

Foreign food products were now flooding into the English markets, and it was no longer sufficient for Ireland to produce in quantity, she must produce in quality also. In 1894 Horace Plunkett founded the Irish Agricultural Organization Society to promote joint purchases and sales, and to bring the dairy industry to a level where it could meet competition from Denmark and New Zealand. He followed this up in 1899 by securing the creation of a government Department of Agriculture and Technical Instruction to raise the general standards of farming in Ireland.

1903 marks a turning point in the history of the Irish landscape. In that year the new department established its first forestry centre, and assumed responsibility for the management of its first block of woodland. Here we have the first step at national level to restore to Ireland a substantial area of woodland – and the first step drastically to alter the appearance of the Irish landscape. It was also the year of the culminating Land Act – the Wyndham Act – which, when there had been added to it the power of compulsory purchase, made the completion of Gladstone's ambitions possible. Entire estates, not just piecemeal holdings, could now be offered for sale, and very generous financial terms made easy purchase possible. When the possibilities of the Act had worked their way through the system, Ireland was indeed a land of small farmer proprietors.

6

Modern Ireland,

AD *1903 to 1973*

THE SOIL, THE WOODLANDS AND THE WETLANDS

WHEN the transfer of land was complete, all vestiges of early Ireland and of feudal Ireland had disappeared. In their stead authority was represented by institutions of government, both at national and at local level, and the land was held by farmer proprietors who clung with a vice-like grip to their small units of inefficiently worked fields. Even today half the Irish farms are of 30 acres (12 hectares) or less. But at least at the national level the landscape could now be viewed and managed on a country-wide basis, rather than operate as a patchwork of estates, worked at various levels of interest and efficiency.

It was realized that the soil was a matter for nation-wide concern, and soil investigation units were added to the Geological Survey. The absolute deficiency of timber had to be rectified, and a state forestry programme was initiated. Because of the virtual absence of coal, the winning of peat on an industrial scale had already attracted attention by the middle of the nineteenth century, and one hundred years later this operation was placed on a national basis.

The soil of a country is its most important single resource. Unlike other resources such as oil or metallic ores, the soil is – or should be – inexhaustible, and no nation can afford to ignore its management. In Ireland, because the humid climate encourages soil deterioration, such management is a matter for special concern.

In coastal districts since at least the twelfth century man has been drawing shelly sand and seaweed from the shore, and spreading it on his fields to improve both the fertility and the drainage of the soils. It was only this practice that made farming possible along much of the western and southern fringe. Here the soils had first degenerated to peaty podzols, and then become smothered by blanket-bog. As population pressures grew in the late eighteenth century much of the peat was cut for fuel, to reveal the poorest of soils. But if the soil was stripped down to the iron pan, and the latter was broken up with crowbars, it was again possible for water to move downwards. Sea sand and seaweed were added to the soil, which was then replaced as a surface layer; over the years the otherwise idle hours of winter were spent in drawing and spreading more material, until in some places as much as 1 m had been deposited. Sometimes the sand was first used as bedding for cattle, where it absorbed large quantities of dung and urine. In the Aran Islands such soils were built up on bare rock. In this way a first-class soil replaced a very poor one. (Pl. 27)

Today the practice has been largely abandoned, but the improved properties of the man-made soils remain; the prosperous onion-growing that is carried on in the vicinity of Castlegregory in Kerry is entirely based on the soils that were laboriously built up by past generations. Could today's mammoth earth-moving machinery be harnessed to a wide-scale programme of soil improvement based on the same principles? Such machinery is utilized on the podzols of the uplands when these are being prepared for large-scale tree-planting; a huge caterpillar tractor draws a great vertical knife – an outsized plough-share – through the soil, and this smashes the pan like the bow of an ice-breaking ship. Here again history repeats itself; just as on the coast, this was formerly done with a crowbar, and many a small potato-patch high up on a hillside was only made fit for cultivation by the back-breaking process of 'crowing'. (Pl. 25)

The preparation of the ground for upland afforestation often presents difficulties. If the area is uniformly covered by blanket-bog, one type of machine will be appropriate; if the area is one of mineral soil, a different approach will be adopted. But in many upland areas the peat – for reasons which nobody understands – is being stripped away by erosion, and a complicated mosaic presents itself. In one place deep channels are beginning to dissect a still continuous peat cover, in a second strips of mineral soil are separated by islands or 'haggs' of peat, while in a third, mineral soil is dominant, its surface broken only by a few isolated mounds of surviving peat. It is not easy to find a machine sufficiently versatile to cope with the broken ground. Various reasons have been put forward to explain the erosion, which presumably stems from a breaking of the continuous vegetation-cover. A climatic change, overgrazing by sheep, burning of the surface-vegetation to encourage young growth – all have been suggested. (Pl. 31)

It seems unlikely that peat would continue to form after the bog surface had been broken. We have seen that around AD 1700 pine was reintroduced, and exotic trees were brought in for planting purposes. We can trace the pollens of these trees in the superficial layers of some upland blanket-bogs, and so these bogs must have continued to grow after AD 1700. It is thus possible that the erosion only started relatively recently; it certainly is proceeding actively today, and if it had been going on for a very long time, presumably very much more peat would have disappeared, and left the summits in a barer state than we find them today.

Many Irish drumlins are composed of a till, which though basically fertile, is so rich in clay that soil-water movement is almost nil, and the soils remain wet even when they are lying on the sloping flank of a drumlin. The western county of Leitrim, which is almost smothered by drumlins, pinpoints the problem. One-quarter of the county lies below bog, and one-half carries gley soils, chiefly surface-water gleys on the drumlins. Such soils cannot compete agriculturally in the modern world, but are very suitable for forestry. Some conifers from the Pacific coast of North America – such as Sitka Spruce

(*Picea sitchensis*) – find conditions in Ireland very similar to those of their homeland, and grow extremely well.

The debate on what to do with the wet soils of western Ireland has now been in progress for more than a century. Most authorities agree that of the twenty million acres of land in Ireland about six million, say one-third of the whole, are unfit for profitable agriculture; the bulk of this unprofitable land lies in the west. In 1845 Griffith in his Valuation Report said that half the unprofitable land should be planted. In 1883 Gladstone invited a Danish forester, Howitz, to report on the possibilities of reafforestation in Ireland; his report echoed that of Griffith – five million acres were more fitted for forestry than anything else, and three million of these acres lay along the western seaboard.

The matter still remains unresolved. From modest beginnings, and despite the set-backs of two world wars, the annual rate of planting has been pushed up to 30,000 acres per annum, though the final target is not yet decided on. Much of the planting hitherto has been on the uplands above the recognized limit for cultivation, or on blanket-bog, but sooner or later the main question must be answered – Are the low-lying poorly-drained soils of western Ireland to be taken boldly out of marginal agricultural production, and transferred instead to timber production, where the yield can be expected to be generous?

As the twentieth century opened, history was tending to repeat itself on the more fertile soils of the east and south. Another agricultural revolution was taking place, this time consequent on the introduction of the so-called 'artificial' fertilizers, which made it possible directly to replace calcium, potassium, nitrogen and phosphorus in the soil. External and internal wars then distorted this gradual development. The First World War, and especially the two years after it, were the most hectic period of agricultural prosperity in Ireland's history, surpassing even the best years of the Napoleonic wars. Food and timber were in unlimited demand. The soil's reserves of fertility were heavily drawn on, while timber stocks were butchered. With the aid of artificial manures the first could be relatively quickly replaced, but it was a matter of many years before the scars the second left on the landscape could be healed over. The difficulties of the post-war crash were intensified by military activities at home, first against British forces and later on an inter-necine level, but the first Dublin government was strongly in favour of agriculture, and prices in general were kept low to encourage agricultural exports. The aftermath of the Great Depression of 1929 was intensified in Ireland by an 'Economic War' with Britain, which pushed agricultural prices down still further. But if agriculture came under fire, the protective tariffs, which were part of the campaign, provided the screen in whose shelter the major industrialization of the south of Ireland was born.

The Second World War again created demand for agricultural products, but on this second round government control of prices and other matters was more rigorous, and the bonanza of 1914–18 was not repeated. Once again production was increased at the expense of reserve-fertility, and once again there was wholesale felling of park trees, hedgerow trees, woodlands and plantations, creating a new generation of landscape scars. The end of hostilities left the land of Ireland in such poor shape that intervention at government level was necessary. Generous grants for field improvement both by the cutting of drains and by the removal of tree stumps and large boulders were made available, but through the enthusiasm of contractors and other interested parties, grandiose schemes were often embarked on which expended money on a scale far beyond the benefit that might be expected. To restore the calcium that had been leached from the soil, ground limestone was made available at subsidized prices; this innovation brought about the final demise of one characteristic feature of the Irish landscape, the lime-kiln, where small quantities of limestone had been burned with peat or coal, at least since the eighteenth century. To restore the other nutrients an ambitious and expensive scheme was launched, whereby by undertaking to pay an annuity over a period of years, in the same way as the land purchase annuity was being paid, a farmer could have the necessary amount of fertilizer applied to his fields.

Great areas of blanket-bog were planted, or marked down as areas for future afforestation. In north Mayo, where the blanket-bog is remarkably extensive and continuous, the generation of electricity in peat-fired power-stations was begun. The First World War had created an intensive demand for native fuel, and considerable experimentation sought to generate electricity efficiently from peat. In 1946 bog development was nationalized, and by 1970 135,000 acres of bog, nearly all raised-bog, were yielding over four million tons of peat per annum. Elimination of unnecessary handling has been the goal, and more than three-quarters of the total is won by tearing up the surface with a harrow, allowing the debris to dry, and then sweeping it into a ridge along the bog, from which a light railway carries it to the power-station. The dry ridges are protected by enormous lengths of polythene sheeting, and seen from a distance the shimmering ridges create the illusion of a vast and unexpected lake. If the windmill has disappeared from the Irish countryside, the steaming cooling-towers of the bog-side power-stations have added a new feature. At the outset of the programme it was decided that the exhausted boglands would be turned into farmlands or forests, and this stage is just beginning to be reached. Whatever the economics of the transformation may be, it is certainly a dramatic sight to cross a high ridge of still uncut peat, and come upon a herd of Friesian cows grazing on the grassland that has clothed the cutaway trough. (Pl. 32)

Like the peat bogs, the water resources have also been harnessed to generate electricity. But here alas the topography of the country creates dilemmas. The rain that falls on the mountainous rim of the country either falls quickly to the sea by numerous small streams, or debouches on to the central low-lying area, where it waterlogs the soil, if indeed it does not cause flooding. The hydroelectric engineer wishes to retain the water in the soil, so as to maintain a steady flow in the river for the benefit of his turbines, the farmer wants to get the water off his land and out into the sea as quickly as possible. The Shannon is the country's greatest source of hydroelectric power; the farmer is constantly calling for a major drainage scheme, even though much of the land liable to flooding is of poor quality. We have seen that in early Littletonian time part of the Shannon basin was occupied by large lakes, and it would not be impossible to restore these to some extent, and greatly increase the storage capacity of the hydroelectric system. Unfortunately this is a zone where politics and economics overlap. It was proposed to develop the River Boyne for hydroelectric purposes, and expensive preliminary works were undertaken; then the decision was reversed, and it was agreed to undertake a major drainage scheme, though even the simplest of cost-benefit-analyses could show that the money expended on drainage would never be recouped by increased agricultural output. But the sight of a great excavator crawling up and down a river bed, even if it is ruining the landscape by degrading the river to the status of a half-filled canal, destroying its fish, and piling up raw spoil-banks along its margins, is a much greater winner of local rural votes than the idea of a distant power-station bringing benefit to faceless city-dwellers. The concept of an unspoiled wetland as a local, national and even international resource is one which it is equally difficult to sell to the rural voter.

THE PEOPLE AND THE LAND

Inexorably we return to the contrast between the more favoured east and the less favoured west. The east has the lower rainfall, the better-drained soil, and from a coast with a chain of thriving ports, looks across a narrow stretch of sea to a highly industrialized and densely populated neighbour. The west is wetter, has poorer soils, and under-utilized ports which stare out into an empty ocean. And yet if one is prepared to tolerate a subsistence existence, one can exist in the west on an under-capitalized, extensive farming system.

Such was, until the end of World War II, the farming system of the entire country, which had changed little since the beginning of the century. But just as post-war industry has had – in order to survive – to concentrate on competitive exports, agriculture has had to follow, and this means injection of capital to make intensive working possible. Such expensive development may be justifiable in the east, but becomes completely uneconomic in the west.

What is to happen in the west? Those who are not prepared to accept a level of existence sub-standard to that available elsewhere leave, either by moving to the more prosperous east, or by emigrating. While it is not fair to contrast Mayo with no town with more than 10,000 inhabitants with Dublin with its city now past the half-million mark, during the period 1901–71 the population of County Mayo halved, falling from 200,000 to 100,000, while that of Dublin County and City almost doubled, rising from 450,000 to 850,000. When we remember that Mayo with its 100,000 has six times the area of Dublin with its 850,000, we can see how thinly populated it has become.

This movement is a reflection of farm size. In the west some 40% of farms are less than 30 acres in size, and it is here that it is hardest to maintain a living standard. After the war the number of men working in agriculture fell by one-quarter, but the loss was not evenly distributed; farms of less than 30 acres lost half their labour, while the drop in those over 100 acres was about 10%. A large, intensive farm can afford labour, a small, unspecialized one cannot. Is the population of the west to continue to fall until the reciprocal growth in farm size brings the incomes of those who do stay to a tolerable level? Is afforestation to extend over those areas of land where soil conditions make even such a modest target impossible?

If so, there will be drastic repercussions on the landscape. The image dear to the city man, and to the still more important tourist, is one of happy peasants living in thatched cottages, from which they sally forth now and again to dig in patchwork fields, or fish from rocks. Are those who like the image prepared to pay to preserve their illusion, and employ the surviving inhabitants as landscape gardeners, to keep the countryside reasonably free of weeds and bushes, with a few property cows standing around here and there, and picturesque but uneconomic sheep wandering on the hillsides?

Short of direct subsidy, what can be done to make the standard of life in the west approximate more closely to that in the east? Rural electrification has been carried out. Starting in 1945, when it was estimated that 400,000 rural homes were without electricity, a thirty-year programme has been completed, during which electric supplies were made available to over 380,000 homes. At first it was decided that only areas where the cost of installation would not be utterly uneconomic should be supplied, but in 1971 all areas were brought into the scheme. But even electricity, and its accompanying television set, could not arrest the exit, and in some cases the engineers carrying the supply up the valley had to step to the side of the road to make way for the lorries laden with the furniture of those who were moving down and away from the valley. Much the same can be said of many arterial drainage schemes; by the time the water had been carried away in the newly cut drains, many of the inhabitants for whom the scheme was designed had been drained away also. If the same amount of money had been spent on rural water and sewage schemes, the proportion of population remaining might have been higher.

Self-help, in the drawing together of enough money to make possible the acquisition of a motor-car, has probably been a much more potent force in improving the quality of rural life. One of the most striking changes in the post-war landscape scene has been the proliferation of the rural motor-car. Before the war, in a remote country town such as Dingle, there would have been on Sunday morning perhaps five motor-cars outside the Protestant church; there would have been the same number, together with a miscellaneous collection of carts, traps and bicycles, outside the Catholic church. Today there are the same number of cars outside the Protestant church, but the streets of the town in the vicinity of the Catholic church are completely blocked by cars, not only by those parked on both sides of the road, but by those abandoned in the middle of the road by late-comers hastening to their devotions. The number of private cars for which road taxation had been paid has trebled in the last fifteen years in the Republic, and now stands at half a million – to which figure must be added the many cars for which taxation has not been paid. There has been a similar rise in Northern Ireland. Almost no inhabited rural dwelling is inaccessible by car, and a very high proportion of rural dwellers are car-owners. By its power dramatically to reduce, if not to

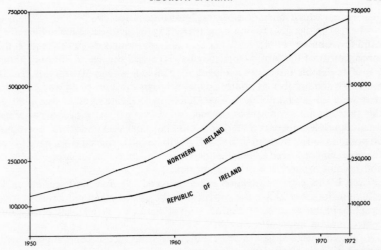

A graph to illustrate increase in the number of private motor-cars in Ireland, 1950 to 1972.

abolish altogether, the feeling of rural isolation, the motor-car is perhaps the most important influence to sustain the population in remoter areas. One can only pray that by the time this half-million cars come to the end of their mechanical lives – and like their owners cars are long-lived in Ireland – a shortage of raw materials will give them some value for recycling, and that they will not be tossed in their hundreds of thousands – to follow the thousands that have already been so tossed – down mountain-sides, into bog-cuttings, on to the seashore, to the complete ruin of the countryside.

If self-help provided the motor-car, the state has provided the school bus. Rural children are no longer retained in isolation in a small local school with a restricted number of settled teachers, but have access to new friends in larger schools with an ebb and flow of teaching staff. Will these wider contacts tempt them to move still farther away, or will they return to their local community with a more real awareness both of its limitations and of its opportunities?

The gas cylinder has also been important by weakening another element of drudgery, the back-breaking winning of peat for domestic use. The Aran Islands are completely without any local sources of fuel, and in days gone by one of the most picturesque island scenes was the arrival of the sail-borne cargoes of peat from the bogs of Connemara. Today the pier at Kilronan is so cluttered up with yellow cylinders that the tourist can barely find space to step ashore.

But for many the visits of the school bus, the possession of a motor-car, a gas stove and a television set, will not be sufficient to keep them in the under-privileged west, where, as Hugh Brody has recently put it, to remain on the land is tantamount to accepting a limited, restricted, inadequate life in a milieu which offers neither real advantage nor compensatory dignity.

The real challenge is to break the present age-structure and make the milieu valid for younger people. Sixty per cent of Irish farmers do not relinquish the management of the farm before they have reached the age of 70; only about 1% of the viable farms are managed by people less than 30 years of age. In the 1950s the number of young people between the ages of 14 and 18 years who were on the family farm was 17,500; in 1973 the number was 4300. If this state of affairs cannot be changed, emigration will move people out of the west, and unless there is a marked industrial expansion elsewhere, it will not be possible to retain them in Ireland. It will be bitter indeed if we have to see the government forced to assume the role of the nineteenth-century landlord, and become a purchaser of emigrant tickets.

Even if this extreme position is not reached, we may well see inevitable economic forces establish the pattern that the Cromwellian reorganizers tried to set up in the seventeenth century – an affluent east, a relatively prosperous centre, and an impoverished west.

In the east we will have a coastal industrial rim focused on the ports, with behind it a belt of intensive factory-type crop-farming making high demands on capital. Larger units and larger machines will necessitate still larger fields, and we may expect to see many of the hedgerows and their trees disappear, just as they are disappearing in England. The naked look, so familiar to Arthur Young, will return. From north to south down the centre of the country there will be a broad belt of grass, where cattle will be kings, just as they always have been in Ireland. The relatively good land will repay good management, and stocking rates will be high. Secondary industries, based on milk, meat and hides, will add to the general prosperity. The industries will be concentrated in a limited number of centres, to give added amenities to the local population, and make it possible to give adequate treatment to sewage and factory effluents.

Farther west the human population will fall off sharply. The poorer land cannot repay good management. Where husbandry is possible, farm sizes will increase, but stocking-rates will remain low, limited by the poor drainage and poor structure of the soils. The green grassland of the farms will be broken up by great wedges of darker green, where coniferous plantations will occupy the difficult soils. Village-dwelling forestry workers will far outnumber the scattered farm families. It would be nice if the plantations could contain hardwoods, but these plantations are being reared as a crop, and the conifers will be ripe in half the time the hardwoods would take to come to maturity. Just as the east has developed a coastal rim, so the west will have its prosperous edging, but of hotels and guest-houses, not of factories. The crowded city-dwellers of eastern Ireland, of Britain and of western Europe, will produce a constant stream of off-beat holiday-makers, who want solitude and scenery rather than sun and sand, and find rain and wind a pleasant antidote to over-heated offices.

7

1973 – Epilogue or Prologue?

WHY should 1973 be singled out as a year that in time to come might be looked back to as a year of decisive change for the Irish landscape? For two reasons – first because it was the year in which Ireland's long anticipated marriage to the European Economic Community was finally consummated, and second because it was the year in which the oil-producing countries of the middle east came to the realization that in unity lay strength.

Much of what was forecast in the previous chapter was based on two postulates, first that membership of the Common Market would give added opportunities to Irish industry and agriculture, and second that cheap energy, principally of electricity, would make it all the easier to avail of such opportunities. With unlimited access to the cheapest of fuels, Ireland's total consumption of oil trebled in the decade 1960–70, to the point where it was producing half the energy requirements of the country. Sixty per cent of all electricity generated in 1972 was produced from oil. There is no easier way of producing electricity than by burning cheap oil in power-stations with high chimney stacks from which the waste fumes will be carried off to distant lands. But if the price of oil rises threefold overnight, and shows every sign of going still higher, then alternate sources of energy will suddenly excite interest, and pressures on landscape will arise on all sides. The largest and easiest Irish bogs have already been ransacked, and their rehabilitation continues to present problems; there are still more bogs but their exploitation will be more expensive, their life as a source of energy will be short, and their rehabilitation will be difficult. More coal may yet be discovered, but like all Irish coal it will be expensive to work. A nuclear power-station would have very high initial capital costs, and lurking suspicions as to its operating safety and its ultimate effects still remain.

We are gradually ceasing to regard water as something to be first polluted, and then hustled into the sea as rapidly as possible, carrying its pollution with it. There may be areas in the west where flooding for hydroelectric purposes would pay a calculable dividend, whereas draining fifth-class land to make it into fourth-class land for non-existent farmers clearly does not make sense. The first pumped-storage scheme has had teething trouble, and until it has been more fully assessed, further development in that field will be slow. The winds, the tides and the waves that carry out continual assaults on Ireland have energy in plenty, but how to harness their energy, and how to store it when secured, still eludes us, just as solar energy remains outside our grasp. Ireland's volcanoes died away too long ago for us to have much hope of sources of geothermal power.

221

Oil costs have only an indirect effect on agriculture, but they can have a double effect on industrial expansion. Ireland almost completely lacks a heavy chemical industry, and such has often been suggested as a goal for further development. But chemical industry, such as the synthetic fibre factories of the north of Ireland, require oil twice, first as a raw material for their product, and second as a source of the energy necessary to bring forth their product.

In many ways we should be grateful to the Arab states if they force upon us a recognition of the need to conserve the fossil fuels of our planet. The gas cylinders may vanish from the pier at Kilronan. There can be few more extreme forms of folly than to use some oil to turn more oil into an artificial fibre that has, outside the limits of an affluent society, little advantage over natural fibres that have been known to man for thousands of years. Wool and flax have meant a lot to Ireland in the past; they may yet return to her in the future. Ireland has now about half a million acres under trees, all of which are building up cellulose and wood out of sunshine, water and carbon dioxide; until recently it seemed not impossible that chemical industry by manu-facturing synthetic cellulose and plastic out of oil would make much wood redundant, and put Ireland's plantations in jeopardy; but ill winds do some-times blow good, and the future of Ireland's plantations would seem to be reassured.

After the climax of the wedding come the heady joys of the honeymoon – and then the anticlimax. Among the wedding lures of the Community were the prospects of higher agricultural prices, and of a regional fund which would make EEC monies available for the development of under-capitalized areas, such as the west of Ireland. As the space-rocket takes off it appears to defy the laws of gravity, and to suggest that infinity will be its destination; as the price of cattle rose with equal speed the Irish farmer thought that the rise would defy the laws of economics, and continue upward for ever; so he held on to his cattle, the rise collapsed, and he was left trying to feed two cows on one blade of grass.

The farmer alone was not to blame; the central authorities should have foreseen the inevitable development, the Department of Agriculture should have been more forthcoming with advice, and the bankers less forthcoming with credit. But the experience was a salutory one, in that it showed that Ireland, its lands and its industries, had to learn to pick their way through the complications of the Community.

The Community had been launched in more expansionary days when the liabilities of regional funds could be lightly thought of. But by 1973 a colder wind was blowing, and when Ireland came to seek it the fund had become just as elusive as – and rather smaller than – the pot of gold at the rainbow's end. But if the regional fund fails, there will be other grants. Since blanket-bog started to form, and more recently since the population fell in the nineteenth century, the Irish uplands have been under-used, carrying light herds of sheep, for whom the heather was occasionally burned to stimulate younger growth for grazing. Now Community grants for hill land improvement are bringing heavy machinery to the uplands, dramatically altering the vegetation, and doubtless destroying many unrecorded sites of earlier human activity. When fertilized and reseeded, the upland landscape will be profoundly altered, and perhaps enriched. (Pl. 32)

But if climaxes can intoxicate, anticlimaxes can also go too far, and there is no doubt that the future of Ireland and her landscape lies in the Community. Whatever may be the strains in rationalizing the current far too complicated controls on agricultural products and prices, Ireland north and south can only gain by getting freer access to the large demand for agricultural produce that exists in the great industrial complexes of western Europe, which have hitherto been supplied by relatively small-scale and inefficient producers. Industry is turning to these centres both as export markets and as sources of capital. Tourists from these crowded lands are seeking the empty spaces of Ireland. Contact with her European partners will bring a broadening of horizon to Ireland, crammed for too long against her English neighbour in a love-hate relationship.

Possibilities for further large-scale change confront the Irish landscape, influenced as it will inevitably be by membership of the Community, and by the rationing of fossil energy, as well as by other factors yet unknown. But both the landscape and the people who make it will meet these changes with the resilience that has carried them in co-partnership through five millennia, and will carry them further still.

Bibliography

THIS bibliography does not attempt to be comprehensive, but endeavours to suggest sources for further reading. Emphasis is concentrated on recent publications as far as possible, and many of these themselves contain detailed bibliographies of the sphere of interest in question. References to articles in *Proceedings, Journals*, etc., give only the year of publication and the volume number; they do not give page references.

GENERAL

BÖCHER, T. W., SCHOU, A., and VOLSØE, H., 1967–72. *Danmarks Natur* (12 vols.). Politiken.

COMMON, R. (Ed.), 1964. *Northern Ireland from the Air.* Queen's University.

EVANS, JOHN G., 1975. *The Environment of Early Man in the British Isles.* Paul Elek.

FREEMAN, T. W., 1960. *Ireland* (2nd edition). Methuen.

GILLMOR, D., 1971. *A Systematic Geography of Ireland.* Gill and Macmillan.

ORME, A. R., 1970. *The World's Landscapes – Ireland.* Longmans.

PRAEGER. R. Ll., 1937. *The Way that I Went.* Hodges, Figgis: Methuen.

STEERS, J. A. (Ed.), 1964. *Field Studies in the British Isles* (papers on Irish topics, pp. 422–515). Nelson.

STEPHENS, N., and GLASSCOCK, R. E. (Eds.), 1970. *Irish Geographical Studies.* Queen's University.

1. THE ROCK SKELETON

CHARLESWORTH, J. K., 1963. *The Historical Geology of Ireland.* Oliver & Boyd.

CHARLESWORTH, J. K., 1966. *The Geology of Ireland; an Introduction.* Oliver & Boyd.

GEORGE, T. N., 1974. Prologue to a geomorphology of Britain. *Inst. Brit. Geog., Special Publication* 7.

NAYLOR, D., and MOUNTENEY, N., 1975. *Geology of the North-West European Continental Shelf: I The West British Shelf.* Graham Trotman Dudley.

WHITTOW, J. B., 1974. *Geology and Scenery in Ireland.* Penguin.

2. ALTERNATING HEAT AND COLD

BRYANT, R. H., 1974. A Late-Midlandian Section at Finglas River, near Waterville, Kerry. *Proc. R. Irish Acad.*, B, 74.

COLHOUN, E. A., DICKSON, J. H., McCABE, A. M., and SHOTTON, F. W., 1972. A Middle Midlandian freshwater series at Derryvree, Maguiresbridge, County Fermanagh, Northern Ireland. *Proc. Roy. Soc.*, B, 180.

COLHOUN, E. A., and MITCHELL, G. F., 1971. Interglacial marine formation and late glacial freshwater formation in Shortalstown townland, Co. Wexford. *Proc. R. Irish Acad.*, B, 71.

DICKSON, CAMILLA A., DICKSON, J. H., and MITCHELL, G. F., 1970. The Late-Weichselian flora of the Isle of Man. *Phil. Trans. R. Soc. Lond.*, B, 258.

FARRINGTON, A., and JESSEN, K., 1938. The Bogs at Ballybetagh, near Dublin, with remarks on Late-glacial conditions in Ireland. *Proc. R. Irish Acad.*, B, 44.

JESSEN, K., ANDERSEN, S. T., and FARRINGTON, A., 1959. The interglacial deposit near Gort, Co. Galway, Ireland. *Proc. R. Irish Acad.*, B, 60.

LEWIS, C. A., 1974. The Glaciations of the Dingle Peninsula, County Kerry. *Sci. Proc. R. Dubl. Soc.*, A, 5.

MITCHELL, G. F., 1970. The Quaternary deposits between Fenit and Spa on the north shore of Tralee Bay, Co. Kerry. *Proc. R. Irish Acad.*, B, 70.

MITCHELL, G. F., 1972. The Pleistocene history of the Irish Sea: second approximation. *Sci. Proc. R. Dubl. Soc.*, A, 4.

MITCHELL, G. F., COLHOUN, E. A., STEPHENS, N., and SYNGE, F. M., 1973. Ireland, in Mitchell *et al.* A correlation of Quaternary deposits in the British Isles. *Geol. Soc. Lond., Special Report No. 4.*

SINGH, G., 1970. Late-glacial Vegetational History of Lecale, Co. Down. *Proc. R. Irish Acad.*, B, 69.

SPARKS, B. W., and WEST, R. G., 1972. *The Ice Age in Britain.* Methuen.

STEPHENS, N., 1970. The West Country and Southern Ireland, in *The Glaciations of Wales and adjoining regions.* Lewis, C. A. (Ed.). Longmans.

WATTS, W. A., 1963. Late-glacial pollen-zones in western Ireland. *Ir. Geog.*, 4.

WATTS, W. A., 1967. Interglacial deposits in Kildromin townland, near Herbertstown, Co. Limerick. *Proc. R. Ir. Acad.*, B, 65.

WEST, R. G., 1968. *Pleistocene Geology and Biology.* Longmans.

3. IRELAND BEFORE MAN

BARRY, T. A., 1969. Origins and Distribution of Peat-Types in the Bogs of Ireland. *Irish Forestry*, 26.

GODWIN, Sir HARRY, 1975. *History of the British Flora.* (2nd edn). Cambridge University Press.

HAMMOND, R. F., 1968. Studies in the Development of a Raised Bog in Central Ireland. *Proc. 3rd Int. Peat Congr., Quebec.*

IVERSEN, J., 1973. The Development of Denmark's Nature since the Last Glacial. *Geological Survey of Denmark, V Series*, No. 7-C.

JESSEN, K., 1949. Studies in Late Quaternary deposits and flora-history of Ireland. *Proc. R. Irish Acad.*, B, 52.

MITCHELL, G. F., 1965. Littleton Bog, Tipperary: An Irish Vegetational Record. *Geol. Soc. Amer., Special Paper* 84.

MITCHELL, G. F., 1970. Some chronological implications of the Irish Mesolithic. *Ulster J. Arch.*, 33.

MOORE, J. J., 1962. Die regionale Verteilung der Moore Irlands. *Proc. 8th Int. Cong. Soc. Univ. Moor Res., Bremen.*

MOORE, P. D., and BELLAMY, D. J., 1974. *Peatlands.* Elek Science.

O'ROURKE, F. J., 1970. *The Fauna of Ireland.* Mercier Press.

PENNINGTON, W. 1974. *The History of British Vegetation* (2nd edn). English Universities Press.

PRAEGER, R. Ll., 1934. *The Botanist in Ireland.* Hodges, Figgis.

PRAEGER, R. Ll., 1950. *The Natural History of Ireland.* Collins.

ROHAN, P. K., 1975. *The Climate of Ireland.* Stationery Office.

TANSLEY, A. G., 1939. *The British Islands and their Vegetation.* Cambridge University Press.

WEBB, D. A., 1943. *An Irish Flora.* Tempest.

WOODMAN, P., 1974. 12. Mount Sandel Mesolithic Settlement, in *Excavations 1973,* T. G. Delaney (Ed.). Ulster Museum.

4. THE FIRST FARMERS

CASE, H. J., DIMBLEBY, G. W., MITCHELL, G. F., MORRISON, M. E. S., and PROUDFOOT, V. B., 1969. Land Use in Goodland Townland, Co. Antrim from Neolithic times until today. *J. R. Soc. Antiq. Irel.,* 99.

COLES, J. M., HIBBERT, F. A., and ORME, B. J., 1973. Prehistoric roads and tracks in Somerset: 3. *Proc. Prehist. Soc.,* 39.

EOGAN, G., 1964. The Later Bronze Age in Ireland in the light of recent research. *Proc. Prehist. Soc.,* 30.

EVANS, J. G. (Ed.), 1975. The effect of man on the landscape of the Highland Zone. *Council Brit. Arch, Res. Rep.* 11.

HERITY, M., 1974. *Irish Passage Graves.* Irish University Press.

KAVANAGH, RHODA M., 1973. The Encrusted Urn in Ireland. *Proc. R. Irish Acad.,* C, 73.

MADDEN, AEDEEN C., 1969. The Beaker Wedge Tomb at Moytirra, Co. Sligo. *J. R. Soc. Antiq. Irel.,* 99.

MITCHELL, G. F., 1965. Littleton Bog, Tipperary: an Irish agricultural record. *J. R. Soc. Antiq. Irel.,* 95.

MITCHELL, G. F., and STEPHENS, N., 1974. Is there evidence for a Holocene sea-level other than that of to-day on the coasts of Ireland? *Coll. Int. du C.N.R.S.* No. 219.

Ó RÍORDÁIN, S. P., 1953. *Antiquities of the Irish Countryside* (3rd edn). Methuen.

PIGGOTT, S., 1965. *Ancient Europe.* Edinburgh University Press.

RAFTERY, J., 1972. Iron Age and Irish Sea: Problems for Research. *Council Brit. Arch., Res. Rep.* 9.

RENFREW, C. (Ed.), 1974. *British Prehistory; a New Outline.* Duckworth.

THOMAS, W. L., Jr. (Ed.), 1956. *Man's Role in Changing the Face of the Earth.* University of Chicago Press.

DE VALERA, R., 1960. The Court Cairns of Ireland. *Proc. R. Irish Acad.,* C, 60.

5. THE RISE AND FALL OF POPULATION

BATESON, J. D., Roman Material from Ireland: a Re-consideration. *Proc. R. Irish Acad.,* C, 73.

BUCHANAN, R. H., 1973. Field Systems of Ireland, in *Studies of Field Systems in the British Isles,* edited by Baker, A. R. H., and Butlin, R. A. Cambridge University Press.

CONNELL, K. H., 1950. *The Population of Ireland, 1750–1845.* Clarendon Press.

CULLEN, L. M., 1968. *Life in Ireland.* Batsford.

DOLLEY, M., 1972. *Anglo-Norman Ireland.* Gill & Macmillan.

EDWARDS, RUTH DUDLEY, 1971. *An Atlas of Irish History* (maps by J. Bromage). Methuen.

EVANS, E. E., 1957. *Irish Folk Ways*. Routledge & Kegan Paul.

HENCKEN, H., 1950. Lagore Crannog. *Proc. R. Irish Acad.*, C. 53.

LUCAS, A. T., 1974. Irish Ploughing Practices, 3. *Tools and Tillage*, 2.

LYDON, J., 1973. *Ireland in the later Middle Ages*. Gill & Macmillan.

LYONS, F. S. L., 1971. *Ireland since the Famine*. Charles Scribner's Sons.

McCRACKEN, Eileen, 1971. *The Irish Woods since Tudor Times*. David & Charles.

MACCURTAIN, MARGARET, 1972. *Tudor and Stuart Ireland*. Gill & Macmillan.

NORMAN, E. R., and ST. JOSEPH, J. K., 1969. *The early development of Irish society*. Cambridge University Press.

O'KELLY, M. J., 1970. Problems of Irish Ring Forts, in *The Irish Sea Province in Archaeology and History*. Cardiff (Cambridge Arch. Assoc.).

O'MEARA, J. J. (Translator), 1951. *Giraldus Cambrensis: The Topography of Ireland*. Dundealgan Press.

Ó RÍORDÁIN, S. P., 1969. *Tara; the monuments on the hill*. Dundealgan Press.

RYAN, M., 1973. Native Pottery in Early Historic Ireland. *Proc. R. Irish Acad.*, C, 73.

YOUNG, A., 1780. *Tour in Ireland* (edited by Hutton, A. W., 1892). George Bell.

6. MODERN IRELAND

FITZPATRICK, H. M., 1965. *The Forests of Ireland*. Society of Irish Foresters.

FLATRÈS, P., 1957. *Géographie rurale de quatre contrées Celtiques, Irlande, Galles, Cornwall & Man*. Librairie Plihon.

GARDINER, M. J. (Project Leader), 1973. County Leitrim Resource Survey, I, Land Use Potential. *an Foras Talúntais, Soil Survey Bulletin* 29.

MURPHY, J. A., 1975. *Ireland in the Twentieth Century*. Gill & Macmillan.

Index

Numbers in **bold** type indicate that a relevant figure appears on that page.

Pinus (Pine) 26, 29, 31, 43, 45, 47, 54, 98-9, 105, 108, 122, 135, 138, 141-3, 150, 167, 177-8, 214, Pl. 31
Pisa 180, 199
Planation-surfaces 29, 31
Plantago lanceolata (Ribwort Plantain) 114-15, 134-5, 154, 159, 164, 166, 174
Plantations
Connaught 198
Leix-Offaly 193-4
Munster 194-5
Ulster 174, 196-8, **197**
Williamite 198-9
Pleistocene **16**, 32, **33**, 34, 37, 39-42, **43**, 53, 56, 59, 66, 74-5
Correlation-table **43**, 57
Plough 117, 142, 180, 193, 203, 208
Ard- 141-3, 158, 163-5, 172, Pl. 20
Coulter- 135, 165-6, Pl. 20
Mouldboard- 135, 171-4, 209, Pl. 20
Plough-furrow, 142, 158, 172, Pl. 24
-marks 141-2
Ploughing, Cross- 172
Plunkett, Sir Horace 212
Pollen-assemblage-zone (PAZ) 41
Pollen-counts, Absolute 41
Adjusted 114
Relative 41, 164
Pollen-diagrams (in order of age)
Neogene/Pleistocene transition **33**
Gortian Warm Stage **44**, 45-6
Warm Stage (Shortalstown) **55**
Woodgrange Interstadial **71**, 70-3
Nahanagan Stadial **71**, 72-3
Littletonian Warm Stage, Early **97**, 98-9, 105-6
Neolithic land-clearance (Fallahogy) **115**
Littletonian Warm Stage, Late (Red Bog) **136-7**, 134-8, 154, 157, 159-60, 173
Changes in land-use (Goodland) **173**, 173-4
Expansion of heath (Lagore) **164**, 165
Pollen-rain 41
Pollen-zones (former) **96**
Polygonum 157, 180, 189, 191
Polytrichum alpinum 47
Pondweed 108
Populus (Poplar) 122, 157, 167, 177
Population 199, 202-3, **204**, 205-13, 217-18, 220
Porcellanite 120
Postglacial, *see* Littletonian 35, 39
Potamogeton 108
Potato 199, 203, 204-10, 214
-blight 205, 209
Potentilla palustris 108
Pottery 115, **120**, 125-6, **145**, 146, 148, **149**, 155, 160 174
Poverty of Irish Flora and Fauna 95-6
Praeger, R. Ll. 86, 132
Pre-Cambrian 15, **16**, 18
Preglacial Beach **46**, 47
Pre-Gortian Cold Stage **43**, 45, 54
Primrose (*Primula vulgaris*) 88
Prunus 122, 167, 177
spinosa 174, 177-9
Pteridium aquilinum 115, 135, 154, 159, 164, 166, 174, 177, 192
Purple Moor-grass 144

Quartz 18-19
Quartzite 18, 65, Pl. 1
Quaternary **16**
Quercus 27, 40, 45, 54-5, 98-9, 100, 105-6, 115, 122, 141, 150-1, 157, 159, 166-7, 175, 177-9, **190**, 192, **194**, 196
Quern *see* Grinding-stone

Rabbit 184, 189, 193
Radiocarbon dating 42, 57, 77, 98, 134
Raftery, B. 154
Raftery J. 160
Railways 210, 212
Rain-days **87**, 185
Rainfall 88
Raised beach, *see* Beach
Raised-bogs 28, 144, 208, 216, Pl. 15
Development of 106-13, **107**, **109**, 138-42, 158-9
Sections of **109**
Rangifer tarandus 59, 66, 72, **76**
Raspberry 157, 177, 192
Rath 160, 167-71, 174, 185, Pls. 21, 22
Rathgall, Wicklow 154-5
Ráth na Ríogh, Tara, Meath 161, Pl. 21
Rath of the Synods, Tara, Meath 161, Pl. 21
Rathinaun, Sligo 157, 159-60
Ratoath, Meath **71**, 73
Recurrence-surface 111
Red Bog, Louth 134-8, **136-7**, 158-9
Redwood 26, 29
Reed 108
Refugia 53-4, 65, 79
Reid Moir, J. 66
Reindeer **76**
Reptiles 22-3, 25, 96
Rhododendron (Rhododendron) 29, 45, 47-9, 54
Rhynchospora alba 110, 144
Ring-barking (girdling) 117
Ring-fort, *see* Rath
Ringneill Quay, Down 123, 131-3
River
Bann 98, 100, 103
Barrow 29, 31
Blackwater 31
Boyne 130, 176
Lee 31
Mattock 130
Nore 31
Shannon 81
Slaney 31
Vilaine, Brittany 29
River-courses 24-5, 29-31
River gravels 91
Roads 171, 190, 196, 199, 212
Roches moutonnées 56, Pl. 9
Rock-engravings 146
Rocksalt 22
Roddansport, Down 133
Romans 160-2, 166, 171
Rosa (Rose) 177
Roscommon, Co. 81
Rosslare, Wexford 18
Rostellan, Cork 182
Roundstone, Galway 72, 144, Pl. 19
Rowan 177-8
Royal Dublin Society 200, 202, 206

238   *Index*

Royal Irish Academy 86
Royal Society 199
Rubia tinctorum 178
Rubus 157, 177, 192
Rumex 70, 72-3, 114-15, 166, 173
Rush 139-40, 192, Pls. 22, 23
Rye 180, 191, 193, 205

St. David's Head, Wales 61
St. Erth, Cornwall 31
St. George's Channel 27
  Land 19, **20**
St. Patrick 178
Salix 29, 45, 72-3, 98, 108, 157, 174, 177-8,
  194
  herbacea 65, 72
Saltee Islands, Wexford 83
Sambucus nigra 122, 177-8
Sandstone 17, 19-21, 83-4
Sandwort, Fringed 65
Sandy Cove, Kinsale, Cork, Pl. 10
Sarothamnus scoparius 177-8
Satellite tombs 126, **129**, Pl. 16
Saturation-deficit **87**, 88
Sauer, C. 117
Saxifraga oppositifolia 65
Scariff Bridge, Meath 151
Schist 18
Schoenoplectus lacustris 108
Schoenus nigricans 144
School-bus 219
Sciadopitys 29
Scilly Islands, Cornwall 50, 127, 182
Scrabo Hill, Down 22
Scree 18, 63, 65, Pl. 1
Scrub 122-3, 135, 162, 167, 174, Pls. 21, 23,
  26
Scythe 180, 189
Sea-levels (in order of age)
  Neogene 29, 31
  Pleistocene 40
  Gortian 44, 46-7
  Munsterian 50-1
  Ipswichian 53, 56
  Midlandian 62-3, **68**, 69-70, 77, **96**
  Littletonian **68**, 84-5, **96**, 131-4, 182
Seal, Grey 123
Secale 180, 191, 193, 205
Sedge 72-3, 108
Sequoia 26, 29
Severn Valley, England 125
Shale 17-18, 21, 83-4, 89
Shannon Estuary 83
Share, Plough- 158, 165-6, **167**, 214
Sheep 116, 123, 147, 157, 162, 174, 176,
  179, 181, 184, 193, 198, 222
Sheep-walk 163, 198
Shepherd with dog Pl. 20
Ship-building, Timbers for **194**, 195
Shore-platform, Wave-cut **46**, 47, 50, Pl. 10
Shortalstown, Wexford **55**, **60**, 71, 74
Shrule, Mayo Pl. 21
Siberia, nr. Yakutsk Pl. 5
Sieveking, G. 66
Silica 23
Silicates 26
ApSimon, A. 114
Singh, G. 68
Skibbereen, Cork 188

Slate 18, 83
Slaves 169, 176, 178
Slide-cars 193
Slieve Bloom Mountains 81
Slieve Gallion, Tyrone 144, 154
Slieve Gullion, Armagh 83
Slieve League, Donegal 65
Smith, A.-G. 108, 114, 140
Sods 128, 131, 167
Soil 213
  A-horizon 89-90, 92
  Acidity 29, 165
  B-horizon 89-90, 92, **139**, 188
  Base status, Primary 89
  C-horizon 89
  Clay-rich 21, 84, 89, **91**
  Degradation of 40
  Development of 89, 106
  Enriching-process 89
  Fertility, Loss of 115-17, 131, 143, 162-5
  Fertility, Regaining of 115
  Fossil 92
  Fresh 40, 75
  Humus 28, 89-90, 115
  Iron-pan 92, **139**, 213-14
  Leaching-process 89
  Organic activity 89
  Parent-material, Calcareous 90-1
  Parent material, Non-calcareous 92
  Parent material, Weakly calcareous 90,
    92
  Podzolization 90, 92, 139, 143
  Poorly-drained 90, **91**, 215
  Profile 90
  Profile, Double **139**
  Sandy 19
  Texture 89
  Topography 92
  Water-logging 142-3, 185
  Well-drained 90
Soil-types
  Acid brown earth 92, 185
  Brown earth 90, 185
  Brown forest 90
  Brown podzolic 90, **139**, 185-6, 188, 194
  Gley 90, 185, 214
  Gley, Groundwater 90
  Gley, Peaty 90, 178, 185
  Gley, Surfacewater 90, 214
  Grey-brown podzolic, 92, 163, 165, 185-8
  Man-made (Plaggen) 213-14, Pls. 25, 27
  Peat **112**, 185, 213
  Podzol 92, 214
  Podzol, Peaty 92, 138, **139**, 140, 150, 178,
    185, 213
Soils in Ireland
  In Anglo-Norman time 185-8, **186**
  With high clay content **91**
  Modern, Map of **187**
  Neolithic 143
  With double profile **139**, 140
  Tropical, Fossil 26-8, Pl. 2
  Wet, Afforestation of 215
Solanum tuberosum 199, 203, 204-10, 214
Solifluction 36, 47, 56, 63, 77, 89
Solution-pipes **24**, 27
Somerset Levels, England 138
Sorbus 122, 177
  aucuparia 177-8

Index

Index 239

Souterrain **129**, 169, 171, 174-6, Pl. 16
South Street, Avebury, England 141-3
Spade **142**, 172, 203, 206, **207**, 208-9
Spergula arvensis 176
Sphagnum-moss 29, 108, 144
   cuspidatum **110**
   fuscum 109, **110**
   imbricatum **110**, Pls. 15, 19
   pulchrum Pl. 15
Sphagnum-peat **107**, **109**, **110**, 111, 113, 134, 138
Spiddal, Galway 133
Spindle 177
Spinning and Weaving 198, 200, 203
Spruce 43, 45, 49, 215
Stadial, Nahanagan **58**, 70, 72, 77-9, 93, 97
Staffordshire, England 61
Stage, Cold 35-9
Stages, Cold
   Anglian **43**
   Devensian **43**
   Midlandian **43**, 57-79, **60**
   Munsterian **43**, 48-53, **49**
   Pre-Gortian **43**, 45
   Wolstonian 43
Stage, Warm 39-42
Stages, Warm
   Eemian 53-4
   Flandrian **43**
   Gortian **43**, 44-9, **48**, 53-5
   Hoxnian **43**, 44
   Ipswichian **43**, 53-5
   Littletonian 35, **43**, 45, 49, 80 onwards
   Shortalstown 55
Star Carr, England 98-9
Stelfox, A. W. 73, 162
Stone implements **101**, **145**, **149**
Stone-stripes 36
Stores in churches 175
Strangford Lough, Down 132-3
Straw 167, 192
Strawberry-tree 93, 177
Striated boulders 32, 47
Sub-glacial chute 38, 61
Succession in primogeniture 169, 194
   in severalty 170, 172, 209
Sugar-beet 205
Sun-dew 110
Sunshine 88
Superficial soil-mantle 27-8
Surveys, Topographical 193-4
Sus 116, 118, 123, 147, 157, 162, 174, 176, 178-9, 181, 189, **190**, 193, 203
Sutton, Dublin 131-2
Swamp-cypress 26, 29
Sweet Gum 29
Sycamore 100
Synge, F. M. 62, 77

Tabula rasa 65
Tara, Hill of, Meath, 148, 161 Pls. 16, 21
Taxodium 26, 29
Taxus 45, 47, 99, 157, 167, 174-5, 177-8
Tectonic movements 18, 21, 23, 25-6, 30, 134
Temperature
   Accumulated day-degrees **87**
   Changes AD 900-1900 **184**
   Gradient 53

Ipswichian 53
Littletonian **58**, **85**, **96**
Midlandian **58**
Modern 85-6
Temple, The, Down Pl. 6
Tenantry 200, 202
Termonfeckin, Louth 85
Tertiary **16**, 31, **33**
Thistle 176
Three-Rock Mountain, Dublin 56, 83, Pl. 9
Tilia 27, 40
   cordata 100
Till 37, 214
   Containing marine clay 49, 90
Timber 178, **194**, **195**, 196
Time-scale, Geological **16**
Tin 146
Tollund Man, Denmark 180
Tonelagee, Wicklow Pl. 31
Toome Bay, Londonderry 103-4
Tors 56, 83, Pl. 9
Tourism 212, 220, 223
Tower-house 190
Townleyhall, Louth 126
Towns
   Anglo-Norman 190
   Plantation **197**
   Viking 175
Trees
   Absence of 202-3, 208, 210, Pl. 30
   Buried below peat **107**, **109**, 111, 113, 140-4, 154, 177, Pl. 31
   Early values for 177-8
   Exotic 138, 199, 202, 214
   Felling of 211, 215
   Planting of 202, 210, 212-16, 218, Pl. 30
Trench, W. S. 205
Trichophorum cespitosum 111
Triticum 157, 180, 184, 191, 193, 205
Tsuga 29, 31
Tudor Ireland 122, 135, 192-8
   Woodland exploitation 122, 135
Tundra 32, 46, 57, 59, 65, 70, 75, 79, 95
Turoe Stone, Galway 160
Tuskar Rock, Wexford 83
Twentieth century 215-23
Two-Rock Mountain, Dublin 83
Tynagh, Tipperary 27-8

Ulex 177-8
Ulmus 40, 45, 55, 98-9, 105, 114-15, 117, 134-5, 150, 154-5, 159-60, 166-7, 174, 177-8
Umbrella Pine 29
Underground water 27
Uplands 92, 138, 178, 206, 214-15, 222-3
   Reclamation of 214, 222, Pl. 32
Ursus arctos 59, 102, 123
Urtica 114-15
Utricularia 106

Vaccinium myrtillus 192
de Valéra, R. 125, 140, 148
Vegetables 181, 191, 199
Vegetational Development (in order of age)
   in Warm Stage **39**, 40-2
   in Gortian Warm Stage 45-9
   in Shortalstown Warm Stage 54-6
   in Littletonian Warm Stage 93 onwards

Vicia faba 180
Vikings 175-6
Village, 'Deserted' 190, Pls. 23, 28
Viscum 86
Volcanic rocks 17, 18, **24**, 25-6, 30, 83
Vulpes vulpes 102, 118

Warner, R. 161
Water-cress 193
Waterford 127
Water-lily, White 108
    Yellow 104, 108
Waterville, Kerry 79
Watts, W. A. 44, 134
Weathering, Chemical 56
    Tropical 27, 83, Pl. 2
Weeds 173, 178
Wetlands 93, 106-13, **107, 109**, 138, 178, 217
Wexford 34, 83
Wheat 157, 180, 184, 191, 193, 205
Whitebeam 122, 177
Wicklow Mountains 18, 30, 83, 130, 188
Wicklow town 69
van Wijngaarden-Bakker, Louise 147
Williams, W. 73
Willow 29, 45, 72-3, 98, 108, 157, 174, 177-8, 194
    Least (*S. herbacea*) 65, 72
Water-willow 55-6
Wind 87-8, 183, 221

Wine 184
Woad 180
Wolf 59, 76, 102, 118, 123, 178, 200
Wolstonian Cold Stage **43**
Wood-peat 108, **109**
Woodford, Galway Pl. 15
Woodgrange, Down 68, 70, **71**, 73
Woodgrange Interstadial **58**, 67-77
Woodland 75, 79, 90, 94-5, 192, 194, 211, 222
    Clearance 114, 117
    Phases **39**, 40-1
    Gortian phases 44-9
    Littletonian phases **96, 97**, 98-101, 105-6, 134-8
    Shortalstown phases 54-6
    Woodgrange phase 73
    Secondary 122-3, 141, 166-8, 174, 194
Woodman, P. 98, 100
Wood-sorrel 88, 193
Wool 183, 198, 200, 222
World War I 215
    II 215, 217
Wrench-fault **17**, 18, Pl. 2
Wright, W. B. 46, 86

Yew 45, 47, 99, 157, 167, 174-5, 177-8
Young, A. 202-5, 208

Zagwijn, W. H. 33
van Zeist, W. 138